TRU

Also by Nigel Blundell

'World's Greatest' series
Marvels and Mysteries of the Unexplained
Strange But True
Incredible Destiny
Fall of the House of Windsor

True Tales of the Macabre

Nigel Blundell

HEADLINE

First published in 1994
by HEADLINE BOOK PUBLISHING

10 9 8 7 6 5 4 3 2 1

ISBN 0 7472 4339 5

Typeset by Keyboard Services, Luton

Printed and bound in Great Britain by
Cox & Wyman Ltd, Reading, Berks

HEADLINE BOOK PUBLISHING
A division of Hodder Headline PLC
338 Euston Road
London NW1 3BH

Foreword

Tales of murder, mystery and mayhem have fascinated mankind, in fiction and fact, far more than any other subjects in history. Books galore have been written about them. And the most successful have one common, compelling factor . . . It is an element of the *macabre* – the key that turns a mere mystery or murder story into a classic of its kind.

But what is the macabre? Why does it fascinate us so? Indeed, what does it actually mean?

The *Oxford Dictionary of Quotations* does not list the word. It is as if no one has ever quoted it. The *Macmillan Treasury of Relevant Quotations* also omits it. Does that mean it is just not *relevant*? Of course not.

The answer must surely be gleaned from a dictionary. Open your handy, desktop Oxford dictionaries and you will find: '[mə′ka:br] *a*. gruesome, grim'. Collins' dictionaries confuse further, describing macabre as: '[mak-**kahb**-ra] *adj*. strange and horrible, gruesome, ghastly'. The Penguin *Thesaurus* is more generous. It places its meaning alongside: 'horrifying, terrible, hair-raising, blood-curdling, ghastly, grisly, creepy, weird, eerie'.

So is 'macabre' any of these – or all of these?

The truth is that macabre is an intangible quality. It is more than a feeling; it is a sense.

For instance, the bald facts of a story may be grim or gruesome, as some of the dictionaries quoted above suggest. But does that make them macabre? No, it requires an extra dimension of horror.

All of the stories in this book are steeped in the macabre. *True Tales of the Macabre* is a *unique* collection of weird, sometimes wonderful, often awesome, always eerie deeds. In uncovering many grisly truths, it reveals the darker side of man's psyche and knowledge.

Contents

Voodoo Crazy
A machete slices through the air as a screaming
boy is forced to bow his head over a steaming
cauldron. Bone, hair, blood and brains tumble
into the satanic brew. A scene from the Middle
Ages? No, this was voodoo America in 1989 ...

The Dingo Baby
It was grisly, gory, painfully bizarre, and quite
beyond belief to a judge and jury. But it was *not*
murder. What happened to the baby snatched by a
dingo in Outback Australia is still a macabre but
fascinating mystery.

Herman Mudgett
He built himself a mansion in the heart of Chicago
and lured scores of innocent girls to it. It became
known as the 'Torture Castle' when police discovered in its labyrinth the grisly dungeons where
Mudgett put paid to as many as 150 victims.

Pol Pot
He was the evil despot who destroyed an entire
nation for a fanatical ideal. He tried to take his
country back to the Middle Ages – and if that
involved the most inhumane cruelties, so be it.
Millions paid the ultimate price.

The Waco Siege
They were told to be ready for death. They lined
up their children first – and prepared them for the
fiery hell that was their fate. Their 'Messiah' David
Koresh claimed they would find God. They found
only infamy.

The Arm In The Shark

It was a fine morning for fishing in the foam-flecked waters off Sydney, Australia. Bert Hobson had been up since the early hours, checking the lines he had baited with mackerel about a mile off the city's eastern seaside suburbs. Mackerel was his favourite lure for his favourite quarry – shark.

Sharks abounded off the coastline – mainly Tigers and Whites, although fisherman Hobson had only ever caught one White before, and that after a titanic four-hour struggle in which the beast fought with every ounce of its strength, nearly turning over his small boat. Hobson spent a leisurely morning in the boat, bobbing about in the April swell. Eventually, satisfied that all was in order, he left his lines and returned to shore.

The next day he followed the same pattern. Again, he set out from Coogee Beach to check and change the baited lincs. But this day was to be more eventful. Off the shore of nearby Gunnamatta Bay, near Cronulla, he saw that a small shark was in the process of being devoured by a larger one. This predator was in the throes of a 'feeding frenzy', the crazed state which sharks fall into after smelling blood. Hobson watched with awe as it thrashed about wildly, its jaws ready to snap fiercely at anything that moved. By the time he drew his vessel cautiously near, the shark, a three-metre Tiger, was well and truly caught on his lines. The Tiger, a superb specimen, was exhausted as Hobson turned the boat for shore with his prize in tow.

On previous, similar occasions, reporters from the local newspaper would have turned up and taken a photograph of such a prize catch. Hobson, a well-known local character, would have made a particularly good picture, standing next to his shark as it hung on the pier-head scales. But this time he had other plans. This shark was not going to be killed.

Hobson's brother Charles ran an aquarium at Coogee and had requested a decent-sized shark to thrill and frighten the customers. Bert was only too happy to oblige. He transported the killer of the deep to the aquarium, where it lived up to its fearsome reputation. Captive sharks have a macabre fascination for a city of surf lovers and the big Tiger attracted crowds daily. Visitors who gaped at it through glass panels in its huge pool felt they had got their money's worth.

At first, all went well with 'Sharky', as he was nick-named, but after the first four days it rejected food and its manoeuvres became more and more sluggish. Then, at about 4 p.m. on 25 April 1935 – the seventh day of its captivity and, as it happened, Australia's Anzac Day – the shark was seized with a violent attack of indigestion. Sharky went into convulsions . . . and threw up the macabre key to a murder mystery.

Bert Hobson was among the crowd watching as his prize catch surged around in the water, disgorging the contents of its stomach. It regurgitated all sorts of half-digested debris, including rats, birds and parts of the smaller shark it had eaten. Then the morbid fascination of the onlookers turned to horror as the beast vomited out a human arm.

Bert's shouts brought his brother Charles, who phoned Randwick police station to report the gruesome find. As many of the day trippers headed for home, sickened by the grisly sight, Charles warily fished out the arm while he waited for the police to arrive.

Detective Frank Head and Constable John Mannion reached the Coogee Aquarium at 4.45 p.m. and examined the shark's contents. They soon realized that they were looking at the left arm of a man. Tattooed on the forearm were two boxers, slugging it out in blue-inked outlines, their shorts in red. And attached to the wrist was a length of rope tied lightly with two half-hitches.

Police took the grisly specimen for forensic examination. Initially they were content to believe that the arm must have been that of a stray swimmer, perhaps someone who was heading for shore with a small boat in tow, which could account for the rope that was attached to the severed limb. Sharks infested the waters, and it was an all-too-common occurrence along the New South Wales coastline for intrepid swimmers to end their dip as a snack for a shark.

But after several days police were forced to change their mind; no one had been reported missing, and a police pathologist announced that the arm had not been ripped from the body by the jagged teeth of a Tiger shark but had been neatly severed with a sharp clasp knife.

Fingerprints were taken, plus a palm print. Constable John Lindsay, of the fingerprint section at Sydney police HQ, found the task a difficult one. He had to peel some skin from the hands to make the impressions, but even so they were mostly blurred. Surprisingly the thumb and ring fingers produced reasonable prints that matched up with those of a man on police files – one James Smith, aged thirty-three, who ran a seedy billiard room called the Rozelle Sports Club and who was on their records for having been arrested for illegal bookmaking in 1932. Smith had been missing from his home since 8 April 1935.

Meanwhile, Smith's brother Edward, a rope-maker, read of the forensic detective work and called at the police station. After being shown drawings of the tattoo, he said he had no doubt that the arm was that of his brother Jim.

The next stop was a visit to the Gladesville home of the victim's unknowing widow, Gladys. Edward Smith went along, too. So did the dead man's mother-in-law, Mrs Joanna Molloy. Between them, all they could tell detectives was that James Smith had appeared unworried and in the best of health when they had last seen him. He had planned to go away on a fishing expedition – 'to drive acquaintance Greg Vaughan and a party at five pounds a week' – while Gladys visited relatives. The widow said that her husband had escorted her to the tram stop at about 9 p.m. on 7 April and had bid her farewell. When she asked him why he had not yet gone on his trip, he told her that his friends had not sent the money for his fare. Edward Smith said his brother had at one stage invited him to join the fishing trip. He had not wanted to go, however, and had told his brother: 'I'm not keen on going fishing with strangers.'

The dead man's mother-in-law, Joanna Molloy, took up the story. She said he had indeed left home on 8 April. That morning she had heard him in conversation with a small boy at his garden gate. Smith then came indoors and told her he would be going fishing after all. 'He told me they had sent the money for his fare,' said Mrs Molloy, 'and I wasn't to worry. He left here about half-past nine that morning.

He said he was to meet a man of independent means from another state.' Mrs Molloy had told him: 'You be careful, Jimmy.' He had replied: 'I'll be careful, Mum.'

None of the family was particularly concerned when James Smith failed to return from the fishing excursion. Apparently, long absences from the marital home were a trademark of his. But there was another reason for their lack of concern: a message to Gladys Smith five days after her husband had left home, seemingly proving that he was still alive.

On Saturday, 13 April, a neighbour passed on a telephone message that Gladys's husband would not be home until the following Monday but that she was not to worry. Gladys told her eighteen-year-old son Raymond about the strange message, and he relayed it to Edward Smith in a pub the same day. Edward recalled telling the boy, 'That's funny. He knows where to find me but he never let me know. Something must have happened.'

Another week elapsed, however, before Gladys Smith began to worry about her missing husband. On 20 April, she telephoned one of his fishing haunts, the Hotel Cecil, at Cronulla, and was told he had been 'seen about the place' a few days earlier. It was not until 24 April that Gladys did what many said any normal wife would have done days before – she telephoned Greg Vaughan and asked him where her husband was. Vaughan replied that he didn't know what she was talking about. He told her, 'I don't know what you mean. He did come here before he went to Cronulla; he said he was taking a boat out or something. But he wasn't going fishing with me.'

That telephone conversation between Greg Vaughan and Gladys Smith took place just one day before Smith's arm was disgorged by the shark in Coogee Aquarium.

Gladys was next to see what was left of her husband when she was taken to the morgue to identify the tattooed limb as that of her husband.

With few real clues from James Smith's family, the police began tracing the dead man's friends and accomplices. Eventually, their enquiries centred on John Brady, a man who knew Smith well and who was used to living on the wrong side of the law. He was wanted by Tasmanian police for questioning on forgery charges and was also known to have been involved in various nefarious plots with Smith.

Brady was eventually found on 17 May, living with his wife in a squalid rented flat in North Sydney. He admitted that he had stayed in a small cottage with the dead man at Gunnamatta Bay, near Cronulla – the bay where the shark, with its human meal, was caught. But he categorically denied having had anything whatsoever to do with the killing. Police divers, boats and aircraft scoured the sea and coastline, hoping the deep would yield more clues to Smith's macabre demise, but they found absolutely nothing.

Three months after the murder, police charged Brady, believing that he and Smith had plotted a new crime together at the cottage, had fallen out, and that Brady had killed his accomplice and then dumped his body at sea, possibly in several pieces. They theorized that the dead man's arm was trailing in the water when it was swallowed by the smaller Tiger shark – eventually to be eaten by the large Tiger which ended up on display to the public in Charles Hobson's aquarium.

The police reckoned that James Smith and John Brady had been plotting an insurance fraud on a yacht that had disappeared. Regarding the vessel's former owner as a key witness, they went to interview him. But they were too slow. The day before an inquest was to be heard into Smith's death, the yacht-owner was murdered. He was found shot dead in his car which was parked in a most dramatic setting – under the approaches of the Sydney Harbour Bridge.

The inquest went ahead. Following identification of the victim, expert witnesses were called to testify that, although the arm had the marks of shark's teeth on it, the limb was actually severed not by a shark but by a knife. One of these witnesses was Dr Victor Coppleson, a shark expert who had published an authoritative book on shark attacks. Coppleson had been called in to help with the case by his friend Dr Aubrey Palmer, the Government Medical Officer, whose comments on the case were later comprehensively reported in the book *The Shark Arm Case* by Vince Kelly. Together, Coppleson and Palmer had inspected the arm the day after it had been delivered to the city morgue.

Their evidence was again crucial in the subsequent trial of John Brady. Every word, every grisly exhibit, every gruesome detail, was lapped up by the national press for the edification of the reading public. Australia held its breath.

Dr Palmer was called to the stand to be questioned by the police prosecutor, Sergeant William Toole. This is the record of their exchange.

DR PALMER: I made a preliminary examination [of the arm] with Dr Coppleson. A piece of rope was attached to it. It was tight on the wrist, with an ordinary clove hitch. The arm had been disarticulated at the shoulder joint, a more or less circular incision.

SGT TOOLE: From your examination of the skin of the arm did you form any opinion whether a sharp instrument had been used to remove it?

DR PALMER: Yes. A fairly sharp instrument, I think.

SGT TOOLE: And the cartilage covering the bone?

DR PALMER: The cartilage covering the head of the bone had several scratches. A number of scratches and one small cut. The cartilage was soft in one place, too.

SGT TOOLE: Were there any other wounds on the arm?

DR PALMER: Above the elbow in front there was a transverse wound five inches long. That is the wound showing above the elbow. For a good part it was fairly clean cut and in other parts more ragged. I think the raggedness was due to changes taking place after death.

SGT TOOLE: Was the arm in a good state of preservation?

DR PALMER: Comparatively a fair state of preservation. It had some smell of decomposition. The cut on the shoulder was fairly clean. At the first examination Dr Coppleson was with me. Constable Raines signed for and took the limb and the limb was later returned to me.

SGT TOOLE: Later, did you submit the bulk of the soft tissues of the arm to the Government Analyst?

DR PALMER: Yes, the report from the Government Analyst showed no chemical preservation had been used to preserve the arm. And I thought also that it was unlikely that the person to whom the arm had belonged had died from poison, or at any rate from more common poisons.

SGT TOOLE: From your dissection of the arm did you arrive at any conclusion as to how the arm had been removed?

DR PALMER: I took it that the arm had been removed from the body by a fairly sharp instrument.

SGT TOOLE: Would you say it was done by a surgeon?

DR PALMER: It was obviously not done by a surgeon. There were no flaps left. It was obviously not done by a surgeon in an operation.

SGT TOOLE: Did you form any opinion as to whether the arm came from a living person or a dead body?

DR PALMER: I would not be absolutely certain that it came from a dead body, owing to the changes that took place. The difficulty of deciding is largely due to the changes that took place after death, partly owing to decomposition and partly possibly owing to digestion. But I could not conceive that the person from whom the arm was taken was alive, or still alive at any rate.

SGT TOOLE: Did you notice if there was any blood in the tissues?

DR PALMER: There was no blood effused, thrown out, in the tissues at the cut edges, but there was a little blood in the different vessels and through the limbs, in the nature of clots.

SGT TOOLE: Did you form any opinion as to how long the arm had been removed from the body?

DR PALMER: Not exactly; no more than a few weeks at any rate. An arm keeps better when severed

9

from the body. It might be some weeks. But it is impossible to tell exactly.

SGT TOOLE: Would it be possible for a man to remove his arm himself in the manner in which you found it?

DR PALMER: I think it extremely unlikely that a man could remove it himself. It is not a thing he could do with one sweep, although it is remarkable what terrible wounds some people, lunatics, do inflict on themselves.

SGT TOOLE: Have you had any experience in connection with the digestion of sharks?

DR PALMER: Not personally but through the courtesy of Dr Dakin, Professor of Zoology at Sydney University, I have learned a little.

SGT TOOLE: From that did you arrive at any opinion as to a shark's digestion?

DR PALMER: Yes. It is a cold-blooded animal and the digestion is slow, more especially in cold water. Sometimes they starve for some time and then when they have a feed it takes some time to digest, from days to weeks.

SGT TOOLE: If the arm had been swallowed by a small shark and the small shark swallowed by a large shark, would that have any effect on the arm?

DR PALMER: No doubt the digestion would be slower. There would be a certain amount of shark digested first, although there might be some digestive juices left in the swallowed shark. But I should think that there would not be much digestion by the swallowed shark, so the swallowed shark would have to be digested first. But in any case, there would not be anything unusual about an arm

10

remaining in a shark for a week without being digested.

A gruesome exhibit was then produced in court. Dr Palmer was asked about the visit to the city morgue by the dead man's wife, Gladys Smith. He said he had showed the widow two pieces of tattooed skin. Sgt Toole, who had been present at the morgue at the time of this distressing visit, asked him if he had brought the pieces of skin with him to court.

'I have them,' Dr Palmer replied, 'but I do not usually produce dead bodies, or parts of dead bodies, unless the court asks me to do so.'

The court did indeed ask, and Dr Palmer reluctantly produced his two pieces of skin, which were duly tendered to the judge and were marked for exhibit.

A discussion followed about the theories of a German professor, Dr Ernest Weinhart, which appeared in the textbook *Zeitschrift Für Biologie*. Brady's barrister, Mr Clive Evatt, asked Dr Palmer: 'Relying on this thesis of the German doctor, I suppose you agree that it is conceivable that if as much of the human arm as existed in this case, if it were torn or cut off the trunk, that the individual could survive? If met in train accidents, machinery and factory?'

To the detriment of the prosecution's case, Dr Palmer had to agree, saying that the evidence he relied on principally was 'the state of the arm, that it came off after death'. Again, Dr Palmer had to agree with the defence: that a severed limb did not prove its owner dead.

MR EVATT: There are two conclusions that I put to you: that there is no evidence available as to how the man died, that is, assuming he is dead, and secondly,

11

that the individual from whom the arm came could still be alive today?

DR PALMER: I would not deny the possibility, but I could hardly conceive that he would be.

Next into the witness box was Dr Coppleson, who told the court that he had identified the arm, which he believed had been severed at the shoulder joint by a sharp knife.

SGT TOOLE: Did you form an opinion as to whether it had been removed by a surgeon or otherwise?

DR COPPLESON: I formed the opinion that it had not been removed by a surgeon. In the first place, there were no flaps actually cut.

SGT TOOLE: Did you form any opinion as to whether it had been removed from a living being or a dead body?

DR COPPLESON: My examination was mainly from the surgical aspect and I formed the opinion from such evidence as there was. My chief point was not so much as to whether it was removed before or after death. Such evidence as there was appeared to show it was removed after death.

(For Brady) MR EVATT: Your chief interest was to ascertain whether the arm was bitten off by a shark?

DR COPPLESON: I don't know. Dr Palmer rang me and told me that he had an arm down there and would like me to come down.

MR EVATT: Dr Palmer regarded you as having experience in shark bites at St Vincent's Hospital?

DR COPPLESON: Not necessarily at St Vincent's. He knows I am interested in shark bites. I have seen shark bites at the morgue with Dr Palmer.

MR EVATT: You consider it was not a shark bite, neither that on the shoulder or on the arm?

DR COPPLESON: There was evidence that this arm had been bitten in parts by a shark. There was evidence of shark's teeth marks on the forearm. On the back of the arm there were small marks which appeared to have been made by a shark's teeth. There were a number of small triangular marks.

MR EVATT (showing Dr Coppleson a photograph): What about this mark?

DR COPPLESON: I cannot remember that exactly, I would not say whether it was or was not. The wound over the elbow, there is some doubt whether that was caused by a knife or by a shark's bite.

MR EVATT: You agree that it is impossible to say definitely whether the arm came from a dead or living person?

DR COPPLESON: That is so.

MR EVATT: You agree generally with the conclusions that I put to Dr Palmer – that the arm itself in no way revealed how death eventuated, assuming that the person is now dead from whom the arm came, either before or after death?

DR COPPLESON: If it came from a dead body, there is no evidence how that person died.

MR EVATT: Suppose it had been cut off by a machine?

DR COPPLESON: That is different. A machine tears the arm off, pulls it off.

MR EVATT: And in other cases it is cut off?

DR COPPLESON: I can't say that I have heard of a person living after that. But in a tearing injury it is

> possible that a person might live. In a tearing, the arteries react differently.
>
> MR EVATT: I am putting it as a theory.
>
> DR COPPLESON: With immediate attention, a person could survive, provided the arteries and vessels are tied.
>
> MR EVATT: Have you ever known an arm to be torn off by a shark in that manner?
>
> DR COPPLESON: Yes, in the Sydney Hospital. A boy there had his arm taken off at the shoulder. The boy died.

Both Doctors Coppleson and Palmer clearly believed that the arm had been cut with a knife, cleanly severed from an already-dead torso. Yet the police case collapsed as Brady's counsel threw down his trump card: that a case of murder can barely be proven on the evidence, not of a corpse, but of a limb. Brady's trial lasted only two days. The judge halted the hearing and directed the jury to acquit the accused.

John Brady continued his career of crime, spending no fewer than twenty years of his life behind bars. He died of a heart attack at the age of seventy-one in a prison repatriation hospital. And with him died hopes of answering the many questions that still surrounded the Arm In The Shark case.

However, Sydney's tough police force have always believed that the case was solvable. They claim that James Smith went to stay with John Brady at Cronulla while the two men planned their next fraud. It is assumed that the pair fell out – possibly over the distribution of the loot – and that Brady murdered his accomplice. Having hacked up the body, Brady placed the remains in a metal trunk. Every limb fitted inside but for the left arm, which he roped to the outside of the trunk. He then took his boat out into Gunnamatta Bay and dumped the dreadful evidence of his crime into the sea.

A small shark would have been tempted by the smell of blood. It would have circled the trunk cautiously, coming ever closer until it felt brave enough to attack the trunk, severing the rope with its razor-sharp teeth. The arm would have floated free – and the shark would have gulped it down whole.

What was the shark's next meal? Perhaps a mackerel from one of the lines of fisherman Bert Hobson. And that was when the unlucky shark became a meal itself, gobbled up by the three-metre Tiger that was to be Coogee Aquarium's most famous inhabitant.

Rev. Jim Jones

In the beginning, the Rev. Jim Jones and his followers spoke about God, peace, equality and goodness. Just before the carnage that signalled the annihilation of them all, they could only mutter about conspiracies, Armageddon and the righteousness of their earthly leader. God was never mentioned.

Thousands bowed down to Jim Jones, preacher, prophet, socialist and healer. The poor, sick and wayward clung to his every word, convinced by his promises of a better life. In reality, he was a sadistic ogre who tortured children, and a sex maniac who seduced both women and men in a bid to satisfy his rampant urges.

When the end came, after a bloody shooting match, he chose to take his disciples to the grave by feeding them a soft drink laced with cyanide. The only woman who objected to being part of the mass suicide was shouted down by the rest of the fanatical following.

Jim Warren Jones was born on 13 May 1931 in Lynn, Indiana, a small farming community near the Ohio border. Later in life he proudly proclaimed Cherokee Indian ancestry through his factory-hand mother Lynetta, which perhaps accounted for his dark complexion and ebony features. Yet his father – a veteran of World War I and stricken with lung disease because of it – was a member of the race hate sect, the Ku Klux Klan. The sight of his Dad in white, hooded robes preaching loathing towards black people scarred the youngster.

An only child, young Jim escaped the harshness of his poor, bigoted background by sinking himself into the Bible, spreading himself between the six churches in his small-town home. Jim was kind, but was known to have a fiery temper and masterful use of abuse.

In 1949 at the age of eighteen, he took a job as a hospital porter in nearby Richmond to finance the religious studies course he was doing at Indiana University. In the same year he married nurse Marceline Baldwin, four years his senior. Before his twentieth birthday he was a pastor in Indianapolis at Sommerset Southside church, despite the fact he had not yet been ordained a minister. He championed the down-trodden and the underdog, typically black people or the white working classes at the time.

This made him few friends in the ministry, which was in the home town of the Ku Klux Klan. He found dead cats thrown into the church and other animal corpses stuffed into the toilets. If he was taken aback by the ferocity of hatred towards him, he also learned well from the lessons it taught him. When he came under attack, his congregation closed ranks around him and even those who had been doubtful about his leadership were united behind him. But when the conservative leaders of the church opposed him, he quit and moved on to new pastures. It was a pattern he followed throughout his life. Jones always cut and run, rather than battle it out.

At one stage he even ended up selling pet monkeys, imported from South America or Asia, door to door – which served not only to raise cash but also spread the word. By 1956 he finally had enough money to open his own church, entitled the People's Temple, in a former synagogue in a run-down area of Indianapolis. By now, Jones had adopted seven children of mixed ethnic backgrounds and clearly believed wholeheartedly in his message of integration. His sincerity was a magnet which attracted scores of faithful followers.

But around this time, he began to change. Worryingly, he formed an interrogation committee, a police force of loyal church members who would quiz doubters and critics in the congregation. His sermons were also getting longer and more rambling, lasting for up to four hours on a Sunday. The People's Temple became more aggressive and demanding of its members.

Jones studied the techniques used by other preachers of the day, most notably Father Divine, a black showman orator from Philadelphia, who indulged not only in faith-healing, but also enjoyed an enviably comfortable lifestyle, surrounded as he was with unquestioning, all-giving supporters.

A campaign of hate was apparently launched against Jones by anonymous right-wingers who objected to his multiracial approach. In hindsight, it is clear that this systematic urban warfare was probably welcomed by Jones himself. In any event, he became something of a hero to his public and the press and won himself a $7,000-a-year job on the Indianapolis Human Rights Commission.

In 1960, Jones claimed to have had a vision of nuclear holocaust and he took a trip to Brazil, listed in an American magazine as one of the safest places in the world in times of Cold War conflict. Jones was unimpressed with Brazil, but intrigued by British Guiana, a colony which later became Guyana.

He returned to Indianapolis with renewed vigour, pronounced that the holocaust was 'on hold' and ventured into faith-healing. His sessions to cure the sick were frenzied affairs: Jones would walk through the audience, passing his hands over the sick and being rewarded as they jumped up, cured of their ills. Of course, there were 'plants' in the audience, followers in disguise who were never poorly in the first place so had no problem with leaping for joy at their supposed cure. But it was Jones' claim that he could cure cancer that proved to be the real bone of contention for the authorities.

It's now known that his wife Marceline carried a rotting chicken's liver with her to these meetings. She would retire to the toilets with the person being cured of cancer and emerge parading the foul-smelling 'tumour' in a piece of tissue paper. Jones also claimed to have raised forty people from the dead. Those who joined the church would never die, he proclaimed.

Clearly, the boast sparked an influx of new members who were old or sick. By now, however, newspapers and the State Board of Psychology were beginning to examine his activities. When in 1960 their investigations started getting uncomfortably close to the shabby truth, Jones dramatically decided to move his headquarters to Ukiah, in California's Redwood Valley, also identified as a nuclear-safe zone. An estimated 150 people from his flock joined him.

The haven some 125 miles north of San Francisco was ripe for Jones' brand of humanitarian mission, and he set about infiltrating the local community with the same zeal he had for sermonizing. While he courted the local politicians and press, his members ingratiated themselves into every branch of society. They would busy themselves baking for sales, working long unpaid hours for charity, taking in problem children from the city, staffing a church-run pet shelter. Jones himself contributed to a fund for the widows of police officers and later gave enormous cash awards to local newspapers in a successful bid to mollify them.

Once again, orchestrated terror was waged against the church, outraging the local citizens who were impressed with the work its members had done in their district. Membership boomed still further when Jim Jones organized forays into San Francisco. He held prayer meetings injected with music, singing and dancing followed by faith-healing with uniformly spectacular success.

People signed up in droves. Jones' message of loving and giving captured their hearts and souls. Once they had signed up, he then persuaded the recruits to hand over money, first 5 per cent of their salary, then 10 per cent and then much more. Devoted church members ended up giving all their cash to Jim Jones' church and received an allowance of only peanuts in exchange. This meant that those who became disillusioned and wanted to leave the People's Temple had nowhere to run and no money to run with.

The church, meanwhile, was steeped in dollars – more than enough to finance a temple in downtown San Francisco and, later, Los Angeles. With disquiet about Jones' methods being voiced in Ukiah, he shifted his operation to San Francisco in the late 1960s. But even in this cosmopolitan city, it seemed the race hate bigots were out to get him. In August 1973, a mystery blaze destroyed the People's Temple building. As luck would have it, Jones had a premonition and that night took all the regular followers who would otherwise have perished in the flames on a trip.

Jones himself was a changed man now. He wore sunglasses day and night, was obsessively vain about his dyed black hair, wore new clothes when his followers were compelled to wear tatty second-hand ones, insisted on being called 'Father', and surrounded himself with armed body-guards. He frequently abandoned the usual second-hand bus which had been a hallmark of his movement in favour of luxury jet flights around the country.

His own bus, No. 7, had been customized to include all mod cons, including bullet-proofing on the outside. But the change in him was not sufficiently sinister to set alarm bells ringing among San Francisco's leaders. They put him on the Housing Committee and in charge of dispensing free hot meals daily to the city's down-and-outs. Little did they know that Jones' own hard-up followers were standing in line in order to eat.

The techniques he used on his followers – an eerie mixture of flattery and terror – succeeded in brainwashing most of them. They remained apparently unaware of his hypocrisy, happy to be humbled while he basked in glory. Those that did escape the tentacles of his organization were pursued relentlessly with a campaign of hate and revenge. Some even died in mysterious circumstances, possibly victims of the vengeful Jones.

In 1976, a political worker organizing a reception for Rosalynn Carter, wife of president-in-waiting Jimmy, feared a low attendance and turned to Jim Jones for help. He bussed in dozens of church members and won for himself the right to make a speech. While the 'rented crowd' remained discreet and polite through most of the proceedings, they gave their leader a tumultuous reception.

The next day, rally organizers were flooded with letters,

all praising the Rev. Jim Jones. The embarrassed official who had invited him to attend explained afterwards, 'We never get mail so we notice even one letter, but a hundred? And they had to be mailed before the rally even started in order to arrive the next day.'

Storms of letters became another Jones trademark. There was a school of letter-writers at the church that was dedicated to spreading the reputation of their leader by targeting newspapers, venues and civic dignitaries with letters bursting with praise for Jones, written in different inks, in varying styles on a selection of different types of paper. Again, it seems few questions were asked about the disturbing single-mindedness displayed by Jones' followers.

But there was a small voice of opposition struggling to be heard. It came from the ex-church members who had left the organization in fear and disgust. Their stories seemed too fantastic to be true. They told how sex had become an obsession with Jones. Not only did it feature at length in his sermons but was a driving force in his private life too.

He broke up relationships by urging celibacy on the men, whom he branded as homosexuals, while seducing their wives or girlfriends. Women were summoned to him by telephone calls from a secretary. He also had affairs with young men in his flock and crowed endlessly about his conquests. His wife, it seems, was upset about his raunchy behaviour but was pacified with gifts.

Even more appalling were the tales of physical beatings and torture, especially those carried out on small children. They were punished with a 'blue-eyed demon', either a cattle prod or heart defibrillator, which sent an electric charge through their helpless little bodies. Their screams would ring around the meeting from which they had been led. But they always returned, repeating the words 'Thank you, Father' over and over again.

Youngsters were also brutally clubbed with a paddle board. Adults, meanwhile, were put into boxing matches against taller, stronger opponents so that they would receive a good hiding. Sometimes there were several weighty boxers fighting one transgressor. It was at weekly meetings that those believed to have slighted their leader were hauled out in front of the assembly and humiliated. After each painful punishment they bowed down in front of Jones and uttered 'Thank you, Father' into a microphone.

Jones was by now caught up in a paranoia that infected his entire church. He could easily believe that any number of his followers were plotting against him. In turn, they were convinced that dire consequences would befall them if they left the church, as he threatened.

Although the authorities were apparently beguiled by him, Jones trusted neither the press nor local politicians with his future. As early as 1973, he turned his attention to Guyana, the promised land for him and his followers. He chose an isolated spot covering some 27,000 acres of steamy jungle and unsavoury swampland on the Caribbean coast. An advance party had fended off poisonous snakes, a plague of rats, hosts of mosquitoes and light-fingered locals to put up a pavilion and dormitories in time for the exodus called for by Jones in November 1977.

Astonishingly, hundreds of people did join Jones in Guyana – facing, to the say the least, an uncertain future. Many departed at a moment's notice, leaving scant details for their concerned relatives. Once in Guyana, their passports were confiscated and they were subjected to harsh conditions, working from dawn until nightfall under the watchful eye of armed guards. Their diet consisted of little more than rice and onions. The lush paradise they had been promised never materialized, while the violence and the abuse they had witnessed in the United States went on.

Now children in trouble were led in trepidation through the jungle by Jones, only to be pounced on and dunked in the sinister gloom of an underground well. Adults were put in tiny underground boxes containing barely enough air to breathe for given periods, sometimes lasting as long as a week.

There were also the psychologically devastating White Nights: rehearsals for full-scale suicide among the sect members. After followers slurped a drink they were told by Jones they were going to die within the hour. But when that hour passed he admitted it was nothing more than a spoof. Everyone would survive after all. One inhabitant explained: 'The physical pain of exhaustion was so great that this event was not traumatic for me.'

Rumours were now abounding in the US about what exactly was going on in the pompously named 'Jonestown'. One anxious grandfather, a former press photographer, got in touch with an old friend, Leo Ryan, the determined Democrat politician with a reputation for getting his hands dirty. He had been in a solitary confinement cell in a tough prison and worked as a teacher under cover in a ghetto school. With a typically bull-nosed approach, Ryan insisted on flying out to Jonestown to see for himself what was going on.

Accompanied by newspaper and TV reporters, he flew to Guyana's capital Georgetown on 14 November 1978 and, after much delay, they penetrated Jonestown. When they expressed concern at the military hardware being brandished by the guards, Jones told them they were at risk from bandits. He went on to host a show enthusiastically supported by his followers.

Afterwards, Ryan announced that anyone who wanted to return to the US could accompany him the following day without fear of reprisals. Ryan stayed the night at Jonestown while the press were told to camp at a nearby town. It was there that they heard tales of terror similar to, or even worse than, those they had heard from former church members back in the United States. Only this time the witnesses were Guyanese policemen.

One of the TV men, Don Harris, discovered a note in his pocket saying, 'Please, please get us out of here before Jones kills us.' Several other individuals had also approached the group, pleading for an escape. By the time they returned to Jonestown the following day, about twenty people had bravely come forward asking for a pass-out. As the party gathered, it became clear that another plane would be needed to ferry everybody to safety. Ryan agreed once more to stay at Jonestown to allow the others to escape.

Suddenly, there was a scuffle and a cheer. A fanatical Jones supporter had produced a knife and lunged at the Congressman, slashing himself in the process. The journalists hauled the shaken politician on to a truck and sped off on the rough ride to rendezvous with the plane. But they were not prepared for what followed.

A tractor bearing four armed men trundled on to the concrete runway and a volley of gunfire cut through the group. Ryan died, his face blown off. NBC cameraman Bob Brown was killed when a shot was fired inches from his head. Don Harris was murdered the same grisly way. Another reporter and a fleeing Jones follower lay dead too.

One small plane managed to escape the bloody scene

despite a Jonestown lieutenant firing wildly at the pilot. The rest of the survivors, some severely injured, had to wait in terror until the following day when the Guyanese army mounted a rescue.

In contrast to the chaos at the airstrip, there was an orderly scene at Jonestown, where men, women and children were queuing to receive a poisoned drink of Kool Aid laced with potent cyanide. Babies too small to drink from a cup had the fatal brew squirted into their mouths by syringe. Armed guards watched as the population drank itself to death in less than ten minutes, hearing the final cries of its demented leader. 'I warned you this would happen,' thundered Jones. 'We were too good for this world. Now come with me and I will take you to a better place.'

Over 900 people died, including Jones, who was killed with a single bullet to the head. The handful of survivors either took flight or were too sick to leave their beds at the time of the mass suicide.

Back home in the USA, family, friends and the 100 or so remaining church followers were stunned. The pictures of piles of bodies stunned the nation. How could this have happened? Why did this man get away with so much for so long? And when an arsenal of high-powered weapons was discovered in Guyana, they wondered just what his future plans really would have been. The nation was in trauma.

Without anyone really realizing it, the 'lamb of God' had turned into a mad dog.

The Black Panther

It started like a classic slice of Hollywood horror. A dark country house, a pretty teenage heiress sleeping naked in bed, the eerie creak of a floorboard ... Yet not even the movie world's most perverted imagination could have conjured up the terror and cruelty which lay ahead for seventeen-year-old Lesley Whittle. She was about to fall into the clutches of the Black Panther. And she would never see her family again.

The Whittle kidnap – for so it was first described in the newspapers – was to go down as one of the most spine-chilling episodes in the history of British crime. The Panther had prepared the grimmest of dungeons in which to hold his victim. It lay 62 feet below the grasslands of Bathpool Park, in Kidsgrove, Staffordshire, a beauty spot loved by children and courting couples – a place where old folk could enjoy a little peace on a summer's day.

Unknown to all of them, the Panther – alias ex-soldier Donald Neilson – was often at work beneath them, exploring a labyrinth of drainage tunnels until he knew every dead end and every route by heart. In this lair, he would keep Lesley tethered naked to an inspection platform, a wire noose tight around her neck, for seventy-two tortuous hours. Then he would tip her off the platform, leaving her to die of fright on his makeshift gallows.

Donald Neilson had been a loner since his school days when classmates would taunt him about his real surname – Nappey – a memory that haunted him for ever. It rankled so much that by 1965 he had changed his name by deed poll. Those lonely early years tainted Neilson's character for life. His attempts at business – joiner, jobbing builder, taxi cab boss – all failed.

Neilson's two greatest assets were an eye for detail and a sense of discipline, traits he had honed while serving in the British Army. Both were to serve him well when planning Lesley's kidnapping. In newspapers he had read how Lesley's father, George, had died after building up a lucrative coach business and had left £300,000 in his will. As Neilson was later to tell police, 'I estimated £50,000 would be sufficient for me to finish with crime and would not be too great a loss.'

He reckoned that Lesley's mother Dorothy and 31-year-old brother Ronald would quickly bow to his demands. So it was that at 4 a.m. on 14 January 1975, the hooded Panther broke into Lesley's home in Highley, Shropshire, through the connecting door of a garage. His first words as he woke her were spoken in a bizarre pidgin English aimed at disguising his voice. 'Don't make any noise. I want money.'

Terrified, she got out of bed, slipped on a dressing-gown and slippers, and was forced from the house at the point of his shotgun. Neilson then taped sticking plaster over her mouth, eyes and wrists and dumped her in his car. He then dashed back to the house to leave his ransom demand. The family found it that morning – printed on three strips of 'Dymo' tape stuck on a drawing-room vase. The message gave instructions for a white suitcase packed with £50,000 in used notes to be taken to Kidderminster's Swann shopping centre. The carrier was to wait for a call at a public telephone box between 6 p.m. and 1 a.m. that evening. The penalty for failure was spelt out: 'If police or tricks – DEATH.'

From now on 39-year-old Neilson would deploy his most powerful weapon: sheer, devil-bred cunning. He had learned it in the army while fighting in Kenya against the feared Mau Mau terrorists. He had sharpened his instincts for danger in Aden and Cyprus. He had learned how to plan an operation, and knew the value of stealth and reconnaissance. Most of all, he had seen how a lone attacker could defeat overwhelming opposing forces with discipline and forethought. Now that cunning was to pit him against 500 detectives.

Neilson drove Lesley to Bathpool Park, keeping her on the back seat under a foam mattress. At one point during her struggles he sternly lectured her: 'If you do not behave I will put you in the boot. If you are good you can stay here.'

At Bathpool Park he dragged her, still naked except for the dressing-gown, to a centre shaft. Then through the 1 ft 10½ in opening she went down. Down a 62-foot dripping, slippery ladder, along 300 feet of tunnels – jumping a 5 foot gap and a waterfall at Neilson's command – and, finally, on to the 5 ft by 2 ft 6 in platform. There he made her take off her dressing-gown, by now soaked from water that dripped constantly from the tunnel roofs, and dry herself.

Neilson later claimed that she had remained calm, though the fear she must have endured standing naked before a hooded man in the bowels of the earth is hard to imagine.

She then crept into a sleeping bag, placed on a thin,

sponge mattress, with a bottle of brandy – one of Neilson's few acts of humanity. He had spare clothes for her but he cruelly denied her the chance to wear them. From now on, the dark, dank tunnels would occasionally echo to the sounds of Lesley's small voice sobbing as she made taped ransom demands. She would read by torch from the notebook Neilson held in front of her, messages that would later be used to torment her family.

Back at Highley, Ronald Whittle was comforting his mother. He'd made the decision to contact the police and had already started raising cash from the family firm and re-mortgaging both his and Mrs Whittle's house. Yet the initial reaction from some policemen was sceptical. Surely, Lesley had just stayed out late with a boyfriend. Teenage girls were always pulling stunts like that.

Detective Chief Superintendent Robert Booth wasn't so sure. He instructed Ronald to wait by the Kidderminster phone with the secretly marked cash, while Booth himself stayed with Mrs Whittle. But the plan was abandoned when TV news leaked details of the kidnapping. Neilson called all night, but Ronald wasn't in place to answer.

Detectives were certain that a new ransom call would be made the following night, 15 January. And Neilson had fully intended to try. Instead, as Lesley huddled in her deep, lonely prison he was out spilling blood. The Panther had parked a stolen car near a telephone kiosk at Dudley zoo. But as he loitered, steeling himself for the call to Highley, night worker Gerald Smith grew suspicious and asked him what he was up to. Neilson replied by pulling a gun and squeezing off six rounds into Smith's back. They were terrible wounds but it would be fourteen months before he gave up the fight to live. As he lay in hospital, Smith managed to give detectives a clear description of his attacker. Forensic scientists quickly confirmed that the gun and bullets were the same as those used in two unsolved sub-post office murders in the Midlands. Those killings had been the work of a fiend known to operate hooded and dressed all in black. The few witnesses who had seen him spoke of his speed and stealth. For the first time, the Whittle detectives began to form the suspicion that their man could be the most wanted killer in Britain: the Black Panther.

The days of 15 and 16 January passed without contact between the Whittles and Neilson. But on the 17th, Neilson rang the Whittle coach company and spoke to manager Len Rudd. Rudd clearly heard a tape of Lesley's pitiful voice played over the phone, in which she gave instructions for a new meet in a Kidsgrove phone box. Ronald prepared to follow orders.

That night Scotland Yard detectives had been summoned to help Booth's team, and they took control of a plan to trap the Panther. Undercover Yard men were to shadow Ronald's every move. The kiosk message had told him to drive to Bathpool Park, flash his headlights and run towards a torch beam with the money. But on that cold, frosty night he didn't make the rendezvous until 3.30 a.m.

Neilson had been in place much earlier, spying through binoculars from a drainage cover leading into the tunnels. He had seen a car arrive from the direction he expected and had watched the driver kill the lights. There was no response to his torch flashes but, as he later explaincd to police: 'It could have been a courting couple who I had seen on other nights coming to Bathpool as late as 4.15 a.m.'

Another car entered the park and again the driver failed to respond. Neilson was now getting edgy. His mind spun with thoughts of a double-cross. A further forty-five minutes passed and a helicopter zoomed directly above him. 'It seemed from this obvious there was a police trap in operation,' he said later. 'I was not panicked.'

He went back to the shaft, and climbed down it for what was to be the last time. He believed he had been cheated and Lesley was to pay the penalty. Neilson told police:

I saw the light from the other side as the girl had on her torch. As I came down out of the short tunnel onto the platform the girl moved to her right to allow me onto the platform beside her. As I stood on the platform she went over the side and was suspended from the wire I had placed there earlier to prevent her leaving the tunnel. I moved to the side of the platform that she had gone over. Her head was below the level of the platform. I saw her face. Her eyes seemed to be half closed and stopped moving. I froze ... and then panicked.

Medical evidence later proved that Lesley literally died of fright. Her heart stopped beating before she was strangled.

By the time Ronald Whittle's car rolled into Bathpool Park, Neilson had fled. It was not until 7 March – eight weeks later – that Lesley's horribly decayed remains were found by police.

A local headmaster had watched the coverage of the kidnapping unfold on TV. As soon as he heard mention of Dymo tape he remembered how one of his pupils had found some similar tape in Bathpool Park. It had been punched with the order: 'Drop suitcase into hole.' Police moved in to search that part of the park and quickly noticed that a shaft cover had been moved. An officer was sent down to discover, by torchlight, the most macabre sight he was ever likely to witness.

Now the biggest manhunt ever seen in Britain began in earnest, with 28,000 statements, 32,000 taped telephone calls and 60,000 interviews. Neilson's discarded shoes, found by Lesley's corpse, were identified as part of a 30,000 production batch – and all but forty-two pairs were tracked down. Detectives even sifted through 500,000 driving licence applications by hand to find writing which matched that found in a stolen car used by the Panther.

It was all in vain. But where dogged police work failed, Lady Luck was to triumph. Later that year, on 11 December, two Nottinghamshire Constables stopped a man outside a Mansfield sub-post office. He immediately pulled a shotgun out of his holdall and forced them to drive him off in their patrol car. Six miles later, using a combination of eye signals and instinct born out of fear, courageous PCs Stuart Mackenzie and Anthony White overpowered their abductor. He squeezed off one shot during the struggle which missed the officers by inches.

Later, at Mansfield police station, a search revealed the grim tools of his evil trade – cartridges, two knives, a bottle of ammonia and a garrotte. The officer in charge, Detective Superintendent John McNaught, had good reason to suspect that he had got his hands on Britain's most wanted man. Yet in the cells, handcuffed and naked except for a blanket, Neilson still refused to accept that the game was up. He told McNaught: 'I would never shoot a policeman. I'm no Black Panther. When Black Panther works, he shoots to kill. If you say I am Black Panther they lock me up and throw away the key.'

It was a prediction that was chillingly close to the mark. At Oxford Crown Court the following year Donald Neilson was convicted of four murders and sentenced to four life-terms, plus sixty-one years for kidnapping. The jury took just five hours and five minutes to convict. Mr Justice Mars-Jones told the Panther:

> In your case life must mean life. If you are ever released from prison it should only be on account of great age and infirmity ... The enormity of these crimes, in my opinion, puts you in a class above almost all convicted murderers in recent years. Your activities must have struck terror into the hearts of sub-postmasters, their wives and families all over the country. You were never without a loaded shotgun or weapon and you never hesitated to shoot to kill whenever you thought you were in danger of arrest ... You showed no mercy whatsoever.

Neilson, dressed in a smart, dark suit and white shirt, bowed his head as Mars-Jones spoke of Lesley's killing. The judge explained that he had the power to suggest a specific number of years which the Panther should serve. But he went on: 'Such is the gravity and the danger to the public when you are at large, no minimum period of years would be suitable.'

Gasps went round the courtroom as the sentence was handed down. One woman in the public gallery cried, 'Good, good, good'. Another called out, 'Thank God'. There was even a crowd waiting outside the court to congratulate the judge. They greeted him with loud applause as he emerged and several shouted out, 'Well done, sir.'

Earlier, some experts had argued that although Neilson was a psychopath, his condition was not easy to define. His obsessions, they claimed, were rooted in early childhood, when he had received insufficient love. In a plea for mitigation one doctor even claimed: 'Violence is not a normal part of his behaviour and conduct.' Such sentiments cut no ice with an aghast public.

But it was only after Neilson went down from the dock for the last time that the full extent of his macabre personality was finally laid bare. If the jury needed any more convincing about the character of the man they had convicted, they got all they needed in a newspaper report three days later.

Neilson's only daughter, Kathryn, told how he had forced her to take part in bizarre war games. It started innocently enough. When she was eight, Neilson bought her an Action Man figure for Christmas, even though she had asked for a Sindy doll. A year later, it was a giant papier-mâché model of a battlefield, complete with plastic tanks and soldiers lined up for an assault on a bridge. Neilson invented the rules and little Kathryn would be forced to spend up to five hours at a time throwing dice to see whether her soldiers, 'the Americans', would kill off Neilson's army, 'the Germans'. She went along with her father's wishes because his black moods terrified her. But as she entered her teens the role-playing games began. She would be forced to accompany her father 'on patrol' through Pudsey Woods, near Bradford, on Sunday after-noons. Each would carry small branches as make-believe rifles. Neilson would order her to lay down covering fire, dive into foxholes and crawl through ferns to deliver an attack on a derelict shed he pretended was a pillbox.

Now the army fantasy games were becoming more and more extreme. Neilson bought an ex-army Champ and took his family out for rides in the country. These were no ordinary trips, for Neilson would be in full combat uniform and forced Kathryn and her mother Irene to dress the same way. Once he decided to produce some war photographs using as a setting an abandoned Jeep. Smoking rags were stuffed inside the Jeep while Irene was forced to pose sprawled across the driver's seat as though she'd been blown up. All the time an excited Neilson danced around the wreck, clicking off his sick pictures.

Even family holidays turned out to be more like army manoeuvres. He would take Irene and Kathryn camping to woods only a quarter of a mile from home. A blackboard would be set up with his operations maps and the family would receive briefings on each day's march. Neilson would inspect pots and pans after Kathryn washed them and scream at her like some insane sergeant major if he found a speck of food. At night Kathryn would lie shivering in her sleeping bag, conscious that her father was sleeping with a machete at his side.

She told one newspaper: 'The whole week was spent under a kind of military discipline. I had to jump to it when given an order . . . If things hadn't turned out so tragically you could have joked about My Dad's Army. I hated every minute.'

There were only a few occasions when Neilson would relent and treat his family to a short break in Blackpool. And it was on one such rare outing that Kathryn received a present which would later fill her with dread. Speaking in 1976, she revealed: 'It was on a trip there only two years ago that I spotted an ornament I liked in a shop window. My father asked if I would like to have it. "Oh, yes," I said. It cost him about £2. Today I know the ghastly significance of that six-inch ornament which he bought so readily. It was a black panther.'

Ghosts That Kill

The traffic speeding through London's fashionable Berkeley Square makes it difficult these days to hear the sound of the nightingale immortalized in the hit wartime song. During daylight hours the square is as busy as any in a bustling capital. And after dark it is thronged with Rolls Royces, millionaire gamblers and elegant diners. This is the heart of London's Mayfair. This is the playground of the rich. Surely not the haunt of ghosts and ghouls? Yet Berkeley Square once held the most feared address in Britain. It was the home of the deadliest spectral killer of all time.

There are ghosts the world over, from heathlands to highways, haunting people, places, the sea, the skies and the atmosphere. There are benevolent ones and there are malevolent ones. But few are credited with the evil which the murderous ghost of 50 Berkeley Square exerted in its hauntings of this now infamous address. The spectre which walked this residence in one of London's smartest areas carried out murders, drove people to madness and defied the attempts of latter-day 'ghostbusters' to exorcise its spirit from the spacious rooms. It has not been seen on the premises for some years now. Its infamy, however, lives on . . .

* * *

In Victorian times, such was the ghoulish fascination exerted by No. 50 Berkeley Square that it became a tourist attraction. It was the most famous haunting in all of London. And the fact that the square had been the home of so many rich and famous merely added to the excitement. Lit by elegant gas lamps and guarded by ornate iron railings, Berkeley Square was the home of statesmen and noblemen such as Horace Walpole, William Pitt and Earl Grey. The great colonial hero Clive of India had ended his own life in a house two doors away from the haunted house. And No. 50 itself was the home of Prime Minister George Canning until his sudden death in 1827.

However, the peculiarly macabre nature of the Ghost Of Berkeley Square only came to be realized in the 1840s when the house was empty and shuttered for long periods. Weird noises were reported to emanate from the building. Servants' bells rang for no reason in the deserted basement. Neighbours heard the sound of furniture being moved across the carpetless floors. Heavy boxes were heard being moved from room to room. The ghost of No. 50, said one neighbour, was 'shapeless and slimy and emitted gruesome slopping noises' as it walked up and down the stairs. 'Too horrible to describe' was how a contemporary newspaper reported on the apparition within.

Some time after the death of Prime Minister Canning, the old house was bought by a Miss Curzon who died there at the age of ninety in 1859. The building was then leased by a Mr Myers; and it is from this stage that much of the legend surrounding No. 50 stems.

The story of Mr Myers was not told until 1880, and even then was published anonymously. Mr Myers, it seems, was an eccentric who could have come straight out of a Charles

Dickens novel. A cross between Scrooge in *A Christmas Carol* and Miss Havisham in *Great Expectations*, he was known and tolerated in the neighbourhood as a bit of a character. In 1873, he was taken to court by the local authority for not paying his property taxes. Failing to appear in court to answer the summons, the kindly magistrate said that he would deal leniently with the old man because his failure to pay 'arose from eccentricity'. The magistrate added that 'the house in question is known as the "haunted house" and has occasioned a good deal of speculation among the neighbours'.

What had caused Mr Myers' eccentricity? According to the anonymous writer of 1880, Myers had rented and furnished No. 50 in preparation for his new bride but she had rejected him at the last moment. 'This disappointment is said to have broken his heart and turned his brain,' said the Victorian scribe. 'He became morose and solitary, and would never allow a woman to come near him.'

The miserable Myers hid himself away in the topmost room of the house – the same room from which the poor victim of a lecherous guardian had leapt to her death. He would sleep throughout the day, only opening his door to allow his butler to pass in a tray of victuals. At night, however, he would light a candle and creep around the house that was to have rung with the laughter of a family.

'And thus,' said the writer, 'upon the melancholy wanderings of this poor lunatic, was founded that story of the ghost . . . those whom so many persons insist on calling "mad doctors" could tell of hundreds of cases of minds diseased and conduct similar to that of poor Myers. His sister was, it was said, his only relative, and she was too old or great an invalid to interfere.'

What happened to poor, jilted Myers we do not know.

Perhaps he too died in the house of misery and torment. What we do know, however, is that the next owner was a man named Benson, a fellow who somewhat revelled in the reputation of his London pile. Rumours about the house were spreading around Victorian London like wildfire when a gentleman by the name of Sir Robert Warboys met Benson and rashly accepted a challenge to spend a night in his haunted rooms. Sir Robert did his homework first. He discovered that the house had already been responsible for three deaths, and that it had reduced a parlour maid to such a state of gibbering insanity that she spent the rest of her days in a lunatic asylum, unable to talk coherently about anything except for the dark, ethereal shape that had driven her to madness.

Benson was reluctant to allow Warboys to go ahead with the bet unless he was armed. Reluctantly, he agreed to take a shotgun with him. On the night of the challenge, the house, which usually stood empty, was once again in service. Benson arranged for a hearty dinner, and told Warboys that he would spend the night with friends stationed below the bedroom – 'just in case'. Warboys was provided with a cord attached to a bell and was instructed to ring as soon as there was any danger. 'My dear fellow,' he scoffed to Benson, 'I am here to disprove the bunkum of a ghost, so your little alarm will be of no use. I bid you goodnight.'

Forty-five minutes later he was dead.

The sentinels below had been woken at midnight by the jangle of the alarm. They bolted up the stairs, but before they got to Warboys' room, they heard a shot ring out. They burst open the door . . . and found him dead on the bed, his features contorted into a look of sheer terror, the flesh drawn back over his teeth in a ghastly death mask, his eyes bulging with terror of the last thing he had seen alive. The gunshot had evidently been a futile attempt to destroy the thing he disbelieved in.

After this, the house was locked up and shuttered and, despite being in Mayfair and offered for rent, it remained a place which no one wanted to live in. People came to gape and to gawp, much to the distress of snooty residents.

Musty newspaper files were rifled through in the search for a historical basis for the hauntings. They certainly turned one up at No. 53. In his book *Our Haunted Kingdom*, Andrew Green relates how 'during the seventeenth century a middle-aged gentleman lived here with his attractive daughter. After a few years she eloped, but in devotion to her father she promised to return after her marriage. Her father continued to wait for her arrival patiently, and more anxiously until he died, more of a broken heart than old age, for his daughter never returned to her former home.'

Since then, on moonlit nights, the sad figure of the man wearing a white satin coat and wig, with lace ruffles at his neck and wrists, has been seen at No. 53, staring forlornly out of one of the windows overlooking the square. 'He seemed so sad,' said a neighbour, 'with such a hopeless expression.'

Another haunting inside No. 50 itself was recounted in the *Grey Ghost Book* by Jessie A. Middleton. She said the house was haunted by a Scottish girl who had died of fright after being tortured in the topmost attic room. The frail little girl returned there from time to time and appeared wearing a kilt, weeping and wringing her hands. Jessie A. Middleton was coy about putting a name to the child or the family who had lived there. She left a clue in another of her ghost investigations, however, when she referred to a girl

43

by the name of Adeline who was brought to live at No. 50 by her uncle. The lecherous guardian kept her as a sex slave until finally, to avoid being raped for the umpteenth time, she leaped to her death from the top floor window.

Number 50 Berkeley Square kept its secret over the years. It also became a challenge to the brave or the foolhardy. Perhaps inspired by Sir Robert Warboys' attempts to beat the murderous ghost, another aristocrat, Lord Lyttelton, in 1878 resolved once and for all to unmask the house's mysterious occupant. He persuaded the new owner (Benson had sold out after the death of Warboys) to let him spend a night in the room where the man had died of fright.

He took two guns: one loaded with regular shot, the other with silver sixpenny pieces which, according to folklore, were charms that would ward off evil spirits. The idea was to discharge both at any vision which manifested itself during his time there.

During the night he managed to sleep fitfully. But then he saw a blurred, spectral vision coming towards him. He had time only to fire the weapon loaded with the coins. It seemed to do the trick: the vision vanished.

A year later the peer, who confessed to having been deeply disturbed by his night in the haunted house, wrote about his experiences in *Notes and Queries*, published in 1879. He recorded his opinion that the house was 'supernaturally fatal to mind and body'.

He went on to trace some of the history of the place, revealing that as well as the maid, a girl who had stayed in the house once had been driven mad, while another man who had slept in the haunted bedroom died during the night. Another maid found whimpering in terror was also a victim; she died in hospital the morning after a nocturnal visit from the ghost. But he was not able to discover why the spectre was so evil, nor whether it was perhaps the ghost of someone who had been wronged in the house, returning to wreak his ghostly revenge for all eternity.

The account obviously fed on the Victorians' love of melodrama. But despite the excitable language, the tale had enough of a ring of truth to build a legend around No. 50. To quote:

The house in Berkeley Square contains at least one room in which the atmosphere is supernaturally fatal to mind and body. A girl saw, heard, and felt such horror in it that she went mad, and never recovered sanity enough to tell how or why. A gentleman, a disbeliever in ghosts, dared to sleep in it, and was found a corpse in the middle of the floor, after frantically ringing for help in vain. Rumour suggests other cases of the same kind, all ending in death, madness, or both as the result of sleeping, or trying to sleep, in that room. The very party walls of the house, when touched, are found saturated with electric horror. It is uninhabited, save by an elderly man and woman who act as caretakers; but even these have no access to the room. That is kept locked, the key being in the hands of a mysterious and seemingly nameless person, who comes to the house every six months, locks up the elderly couple in the basement, and then unlocks the room and occupies himself in it for hours.

In his excellent book *Ghosts Of London*, Jack Hallam gave a less hysterical view of the old house. He turned up the papers of psychic researcher Charles Harper who, in 1907, revealed: 'The secret of the house was that it belonged to a Mr Du Pre, of Wilton Park, who shut his lunatic brother in one of the attics. The captive was so violent that he could only be fed through a hole. His groans and cries could be distinctly heard in the neighbouring houses.'

Peter Underwood, who, as president of The Ghost Club, claimed to have heard more first-hand ghost stories than any man alive, reported in his *Gazetteer of British Ghosts* that the Berkeley Square house was indeed haunted. He told how a Colonel A. Kearsey had called on an aunt in the square and was asked to wait in a room where a fire was blazing. He sat down in one corner, having nodded a greeting to the only other occupant of the room, an attractive lady.

He tried not to stare at the woman, however, because she was obviously distressed. But as he watched out of the corner of his eye, he noted with puzzlement that she was weeping quietly into a handkerchief. He also noted that she had on a long dress and a broad-brimmed hat. Eventually, he stood up and moved towards her to offer his help. But before he had a chance to reach her, she rose from her chair and, without even glancing at him, walked to the window. Colonel Kearsey watched in horror as she passed straight through the folds of the thick curtains and vanished out of sight. Opening the curtains himself, he found a locked window and a sheer drop on to the railings below.

Colonel Kearsey inquired of his aunt as to who the disappearing lady might have been. She told him that her children had often heard an unseen person sobbing in that room, but they had never discovered the identity of the ghost. Kearsey decided to do some detective work. He traced the previous tenant of the house, who told him that a woman who had once lived there had a very unhappy marriage. She would sit weeping hour after hour while her husband was absent, and eventually left him for another man.

In later years, No. 50 Berkeley Square gained a more respectable claim to fame. For more than thirty years it was occupied by a famed firm of antique booksellers, Maggs Brothers. During World War II, members of staff would sleep in the haunted top-floor room while on fire-watching duty. Afterwards, it became the firm's accounts department.

One of the partners said: 'None of us have ever seen, heard or felt anything in the slightest way unusual. Tourists still come in and ask us about the ghost. We can tell them nothing.' And yet the legend persists, all of a century since the ghost of Berkeley Square claimed its last victims . . .

The final deathly appearance of the ghost came in 1887 when two sailors on shore leave found themselves in London without a bed for the night. Edward Blunden and Robert Martin were crewmen of HMS *Penelope*, a frigate docked in Portsmouth. On Christmas Eve they wandered into the city as the gas lamps were being lit. Down on their luck and out of cash, they traipsed the streets until they found themselves outside the gracious exterior of 50 Berkeley Square The 'To Let' notices were enough to convince them the property was empty, and they prised open a window to take advantage of the free lodging on that cold winter's night.

They wandered through the empty house, finally stopping in the second-floor bedroom where the ghost had claimed the life of Sir Robert Warboys. Martin was soon asleep, but Blunden was nervous; he was aware of something moving in the house, even though they had taken care to cover up traces of the way they had come in, in case a passing policeman got curious. Blunden heard scratching footsteps outside the door, slowly, slowly coming towards the room . . .

He woke Martin in time for the pair of them to witness a dark, ghostly shape, its form unrecognizable, entering the room. Blunden made a frightened bid to grab a heavy object from the mantelpiece. The ghost seems to have anticipated his movement and gone after him, enabling Martin to dive for the door. He ran, panic-stricken, into the cold night air and found a policeman on the beat. He returned with the bemused constable, blurting out his strange story.

When they got back to the haunted house they found Blunden dead on the basement steps, his eyes fixed in abject terror, his neck broken. He was the last recorded victim of the demon of No. 50 Berkeley Square.

Spontaneous Human Combustion

The inquisitive landlady studied the telegram intently. Few telegrams were delivered to the quiet apartment block on Florida's sleepy Gulf of Mexico coast. This one was clearly marked: 'Mrs Mary Reeser, Allamanda Apartments, 1200 Cherry Street, St Petersburg'. But there was no clue as to its contents. The landlady, Mrs Pansy Carpenter, lived in the same block and often passed the time of day with Mrs Reeser, a plump widow of sixty-seven. She was sure that, given the chance, the old lady would tell her about the urgent message this missive contained.

Eventually, Mrs Carpenter could bear the suspense no longer and walked up the stairs to the hallway outside Mrs Reeser's modest but pleasant three-roomed apartment. The door was fractionally open and she knocked persistently, each time more loudly. There was not a sound from within. Then she tried the doorknob – and recoiled, screaming in pain. It was burning hot.

Pansy Carpenter summoned two painters who were working nearby. Much agitated, she asked them to accompany her into the apartment. As they opened the door, the landlady and the workmen reeled back under a blast of furnace-hot air. They expected a ball of flame to surge from the open doorway and they all instinctively ducked and scurried for cover. But there were no flames. There was no smoke. Only the incredible heat. Even when they summoned up the courage to peer over the threshold, there was no sign of the conflagration they had expected.

Inside, in spite of the intense heat, there was no fire. All they could see was a feeble flame flickering on one wall. It was the flimsy partition wall that separated the sitting room from the apartment's small kitchen. Cautiously walking over to it, they easily extinguished the flame, then peered round the partition into the kitchen.

What did they expect to see? One of the workmen guessed he'd find Mrs Reeser's frying pan ablaze. The landlady thought she might find her friend asleep in an armchair she kept in the kitchen. But all she saw of the armchair were a few springs. Even less remained of the widow. She was unrecognizable.

The heat had shrunk her skull to half its normal size – to about the circumference of a baseball. Part of her liver, attached to a section of her backbone, was still recognizable. Apart from that there were only her teeth, a few charred bones . . . and an untouched left foot, wholly intact, but burned off at the ankle. On the foot was a single satin carpet slipper.

Pansy Carpenter looked at the scene in terror. Then, her curiosity abated, she fled. But police and firemen who later arrived were able to take a more measured view of the horror.

They discovered that plastic utensils in the kitchen had been melted and a mirror had been shattered by the heat. Two candles about twelve feet from the body had also melted. There was soot on the walls and ceiling above, although there was no smoke damage below the level of four feet. A greasy substance saturated part of the carpet and Mrs Reeser's slipper; it turned out to be human fat.

The only other sign that there had been a fire were scorch marks on the floor. A small area of carpet around the chair was charred. Linen on the bed was quite unaffected. And a newspaper lying near the body was entirely unscorched, its date clearly visible. The day was Monday, 2 July 1951.

At an inquest held into Mrs Reeser's death, the experts admitted that they were utterly baffled. The blaze which had consumed her body had been more intense than the 2,500°F needed to dispose of the corpses in the city's crematorium. In addition, the smell of such a cremation would normally have spread through the entire building. Yet the fire had not extended by more than inches from the old woman's body.

The coroner asked for witnesses to go into considerable detail in order to build up a picture of Mary Reeser's lifestyle and events during the hours before her death. Mrs Reeser, it appeared, was not a happy woman . . .

Mary Hardy Reeser had been brought up in the small town of Columbia, Pennsylvania, where she was something of a socialite. Her husband was the community's leading doctor and she was thrilled when their son Richard took up the same profession. Dr Richard Reeser graduated from Cornell Medical School and was posted to Florida during World War II. After the war he stayed in the state and set up practice in St Petersburg. When Richard's father died in 1947, his mother moved to Florida to be near him.

Mrs Reeser could not come to terms with her lower station in life. Her apartment was modest compared with the grand home she had enjoyed in Columbia. She took little exercise yet ate hearty meals, her petite 5ft 7in frame

51

balllooning to more than 170 1b (12 stone).

Her life revolved around her son, his wife Ernestine and their children. Dr Reeser would visit his mother daily at around 11 a.m. and the two would sit drinking coffee. If she went into town, it would usually be to carry out errands for her son.

On the last day of her life, Sunday, 1 July, Mrs Reeser was invited to her son's house for the afternoon. The sixty-seven-year-old widow was depressed. She complained about the Florida heat and resumed an old theme: that she wanted to move back to her home town of Columbia. Her son and daughter-in-law tried in vain to cheer her up. Later, they accepted her offer to babysit for their youngest child but returned home after only an hour because they were worried about Mrs Reeser's state of mind. When they re-entered the house, they found her weeping.

Dr Richard Reeser told his mother that he would shortly drive her home. But when he returned from taking a shower he discovered that the old lady had vanished. His wife immediately got into her car and drove off looking for her. By the time she caught up with her, however, Mary Reeser had walked all the way to her apartment. Again there were tears. Ernestine left her mother-in-law at 5 p.m.

Mrs Reeser's son remained anxious about his mother, and at about 8 p.m. he drove over to the apartment to check on her. He found her sitting in her nightdress smoking a cigarette and listening to the radio. She had not eaten and said she was not intending to cook herself supper as she had just taken two Seconal sleeping tablets – and was planning to take another two before going to bed. Dr Reeser kissed his mother goodnight and departed, watched by Pansy Carpenter, the apartment block's owner, who also lived on the premises.

Later that evening, Mrs Carpenter, herself a widow, decided to look in on the old lady and found her still seated in her overstuffed easy chair, wearing her rayon nightgown and black satin bedroom slippers and smoking yet another cigarette. Mrs Reeser was still upset and the landlady thought there must have been a family quarrel. Although it was by now about 9 p.m. the night was hot and humid, and Mrs Carpenter offered to go to a nearby store to buy them both some ice-cream. When she returned, however, she found the lights out and the radio silent. The kindly landlady never saw old Mrs Reeser again.

Pansy Carpenter awoke at 5 a.m. on Monday, 2 July. She thought she had heard a dull thud and opened the door of her apartment. Nothing seemed amiss but she thought she could smell smoke. Mrs Carpenter went down to her garage and turned off a water heater, then went back to bed. At 6.30 a.m. a newspaper delivery boy dropped the morning paper outside her door. He later said that he neither saw nor smelled anything peculiar.

It was Mary Reeser's daily habit to rise at 6 a.m., eat a hearty breakfast and listen to the radio. On this particular Monday, Mrs Carpenter thought it odd that she was so silent. Her curiosity aroused, the landlady still made no inquiry of her neighbour until telegraph boy Richard Bruce arrived at 8 a.m. with a Western Union telegram for Mrs Mary Reeser. The landlady signed for it, finished reading her paper, then took both to the apartment of her neighbour. She put her hand to the door handle – and screamed.

The two painters who had been working nearby were first on the scene, closely followed by the telegram delivery boy. It was some time later that fire-fighters arrived at the apartment block. A police team followed.

A report was later compiled by the police investigators, and a copy was obtained many years later by the well-known British investigator into the paranormal, Jenny Randles. In 1992, she and co-author Peter Hough wrote a definitive study *Spontaneous Human Combustion*, in which they quote from this revealing police report:

The entire apartment ceiling was blackened by smoke. Drapes in the dining area were blackened around the top but were not scorched. Screen window in the dining area was clogged with soot. Folding doors between the dining area and the kitchen were also blackened but not scorched. Face plates on light switches in the apartment were not damaged at all. Folding doors from living area to dressing room were scorched around the top. The heater in the living room appeared in good shape and was turned off. The bathroom was heavily smoked although there was no damage to light fixtures. Two plastic bathing caps hanging behind the bathroom door were not damaged. There was a heavy burning in the partition between the living area and the kitchen, although papers on the table-top water heater which was against the wall were not scorched.

The kitchen equipment, consisting of a refrigerator, three-burner stove and table-top water heater, are in good shape and show no sign of an electric short. None of the furniture left in the apartment shows any fire damage. The sheets on the one day-bed which have been made up are not scorched and have their original life. Two candles which were on a table in the dining area were melted. A plastic curtain in the dressing room was in no way damaged by fire.

Not present in the house, but which was reported as having been present at the time of the fire, was an over-stuffed easy chair, end table and lamp. The chair was destroyed by the fire with the exception of the springs. The end table was destroyed with the exception of two small pieces of the legs. The legs are the bottom portion of the table and are hardly scorched. The lamp was of a wooden standard which was burned off. The lamp shade was destroyed, but the bulb would still burn and the hard rubber switch was not damaged.

The police report refers to an electric clock 'which had stopped at 4.20 a.m.' yet which worked perfectly when it was plugged into another electric socket. The report went on to talk about the lack of gasoline or chemicals in the apartment to explain the fierce blaze: 'The absence of any traces of volatile inflammable fluids does not preclude the possibility that such fluids were used in destroying the body of the deceased. Because of their nature, gasoline, ether and similar inflammable fluids are consumed ordinarily in the early stages of a fire. Where there has been almost complete combustion, as in this case, it would be most unlikely to find such fluids even though they had been present at the beginning of the fire.'

The FBI were also called in to produce a simple solution for the mysterious death of Mrs Reeser. They said they had already discounted the notion that deaths such as this could be caused by spontaneous human combustion or other 'preternatural causes'. However, the FBI report on the Reeser case said its investigators were satisfied that 'almost complete combustion' of a human being in these circumstances was perfectly possible. It continued: 'The absence of any scorching or damage to furniture in the room can only be explained by the fact that heat liberated by the burning body had a tendency to rise and formed a layer of hot air which never came in contact with the furnishings on a lower level. This situation would have occurred particularly if the fire had smouldered rather than burned fiercely.'

A neat solution! Both the FBI and the local police department were anxious to deposit their files on Mrs Mary Hardy Reeser in the 'Case Solved' archives.

Other experts had been looking at the St Petersburg case, however. Mrs Reeser's hideous death throes had also been investigated by forensic scientist Dr Wilton M. Krogman, who was one of the first to highlight the true and macabre nature of her dramatic demise.

Dr Krogman, a renowned forensic anthropologist from the University of Pennsylvania School of Medicine, had worked on several fire investigations involving burned corpses. He reported that it would have taken a heat of about 3,000°F (1,650 ° C) to melt bone in the way that Mrs Reeser's body had been affected – and such a fire should have burned the whole apartment.

He said he had watched a body burn in a crematorium for more than eight hours at 2,000°F and still leave bones that were recognizable. He added: 'Only at 3,000 degrees-plus have I seen bone fuse or melt. These are very great heats. They would scar, char or otherwise mark everything within a considerable radius.'

The inquest heard such evidence with horror and with bafflement. Despite the 'rational' evidence of the police and FBI, the coroner could find no cause of the blaze. There was no sign of any chemical or other outside agent that could have caused the body to burn so fiercely and so completely. The suggestion that Mrs Reeser had fallen asleep while smoking and had set fire to her clothing was laughed out of court.

The debate, of course, continued and any number of fresh theories were put forward. It was postulated that the body had been burned elsewhere and that her unknown killer had restored the corpse to her apartment to make her death look like an accident. It was suggested that she had poured petrol over herself and set light to it. Someone even had the brainwave that a flame-thrower had been used to murder her. None of these propositions fitted the facts.

Forensic analyst John F. Fischer launched an in-depth investigation and came up with the logical theory that Mrs Reeser, drowsy after taking her sleeping pills, had nodded off. She had dropped her cigarette which had ignited her clothing. Coming out of her sleep, she had not been swift enough to save herself. As the fire had taken hold of her clothing, her body fat had melted and helped fuel the inferno.

However, in the knowledge of the heat required to break down a body, Fischer's theory failed to satisfy other experts. As Dr Krogman later wrote:

I cannot conceive of such complete cremation without more burning of the apartment itself. In fact the apartment and everything in it should have been consumed. Never have I seen a human skull shrunk by intense heat. The opposite has always been true; the skulls have been abnormally swollen or have virtually exploded into hundreds of pieces. I regard it as the most amazing thing I have ever seen. As I review it, the short hairs on my neck bristle with vague fear. Were I living in the Middle Ages, I would mutter something about black magic.

Thus, confronted with this 'modern' phenomenon, the experts admitted defeat. Yet the key to the horrific fate of Mrs Mary Reeser lies in the reference by Dr Krogman to the Middle Ages. For our ancestors quite regularly spoke and wrote about this dreadful curse, this consumption by fire ... this Spontaneous Human Combustion.

For one of the first reported cases of spontaneous human combustion, the historian must go back to the year 1613 when two mysterious deaths occurred in the peaceful English town of Christchurch. On the night of 26 June, neighbours in the Holnehurst area were awoken by screams coming from the home of carpenter John Hitchen and his family. The carpenter's mother-in-law, Agnes Russell, had raised the alarm after finding her daughter groaning in agony in the bed that she shared with her husband and their young child.

Mrs Hitchen had been badly burned down one side where she had been lying beside her husband. He was dead. So was their child, also badly burned. The carpenter's body was dragged into the street where, although outwardly there was no sign of fire, his corpse continued to smoulder for three days until it was reduced to ashes.

Further reports of spontaneous human combustion were scant. But in 1673 the remains of a poor Parisian were discovered on a straw bed in a tenement block. He was an alcoholic and, as he slumbered in a drunken state, his body was reduced to a pile of ash. Only a few finger bones remained to indicate the living being he had once been – although the straw bed was entirely intact.

The death of the 62-year-old Countess Cornelia Baudi, near Verona, is another of the earliest, substantiated reports of spontaneous human combustion. We rely on the evidence of a priest in Verona who, on 4 April 1731, wrote a reasonably detailed account of the lady's demise.

After finishing supper, the countess had been put to bed by her maid. The noblewoman engaged her servant in conversation for more than an hour but then fell into a deep sleep. In the morning, the maid returned to wake her. Before even reaching her chamber, she smelled a foul aroma. On entering the room she found the air thick with soot, covering every surface. The rest of the bedchamber and bed were undamaged. The sheets were turned back, as if the countess had just arisen from her bed.

This was the contemporary report of the ghastly scene:

The floor of the chamber was thick-smear'd with a gluish moisture, not easily got off ... and from the lower part of the window trickl'd down a greasy, loathsome, yellowish liquor with an unusual stink. Four feet from the bed was a heap of ashes, two legs untouch'd, stockings on, between which lay the head, the brains, half of the back-part of the skull and the whole chin burn'd to ashes, among which were found three fingers blacken'd. All the rest was ashes which had this quality, that they left in the hand a greasy and stinking moisture ...

A document dated 1789 bears the report of an Italian surgeon named Battaglio on the death of a priest in the town of Filetto. The priest, named Bertholi, was on a visit to his brother-in-law and was alone in his room reading a prayer book. Fearful screams were heard from the room and Bertholi was found on the floor engulfed by a pale, blue flame. The flame receded as the witnesses approached, and they were able to examine the dying man. They found that his outer clothes had burned away leaving intact the sackcloth which he wore next to his skin. The skin itself, however, was burned to shreds.

Although spontaneous human combustion had been known about for centuries, it was not until the nineteenth century that doctors began to study the phenomenon and to treat it seriously. A strange, public fascination for this area of the unknown began to grow. Charles Dickens even referred to a case of spontaneous human combustion in his novel *Bleak House*, which he wrote between 1832 and 1833. The grisly death which his character Krook suffers in the book is believed to have been based upon the previously documented case of Countess Baudi.

Doctors in the censorious Victorian age tended to believe that victims were guilty of being drinkers or otherwise high-living libertines. It was a theory that suited the religious fervour of the age. But it also provided a spurious medical explanation for the phenomenon. A typical victim was thought generally to be intoxicated at the time of death. It helped support the theory if he or she was also a smoker, probably elderly and in all likelihood a person of heavy weight and therefore sedentary habits. A fat, lazy, drink-sodden body was thought to be highly inflammable!

Divine retribution was a popular theme in Victorian days. Such an explanation was readily accepted by the readers of the lurid volume, Trotter's *Essay On Drunkenness*, published in 1804. It quotes a case from the previous century, as related by a Monsieur Merille, a surgeon in Caen, Normandy.

On 3 June 1782, Merille was asked by 'the king officers' in the city to report on the death of Mademoiselle Thaurs, a lady believed to have been in her sixties and with a liking for strong drink. That very day she had been observed to have drunk three bottles of wine and a bottle of brandy. Merille examined the body and reported to his superiors:

The body lay with the crown of the head resting against one of the hand-irons 18 inches from the fire. The remainder of the body was placed obliquely before the chimney, the whole being nothing but a mass of ashes. Even the most solid bones had lost their form and consistence. The right foot was found entire and scorched at its upper junction; the left was more burnt. The day was cold but there was nothing in the grate except two or three bits of wood about an inch in diameter, burnt in the middle. None of the furniture in the apartment was damaged. The chair on which she was sitting was found at the distance of 12 inches from her and absolutely untouched.

Another case investigated by a physician occurred in 1841. The death of a forty-year-old woman was researched by Dr F. S. Reynolds, whose report was carried at length in the *British Medical Journal*. The woman, it seems, had fallen near her hearth and was found still burning. By the time the fire was extinguished, the bones of her leg were carbonized, yet her stockings were entirely undamaged.

The nineteenth century was a fascinating age of discovery, and readers avidly lapped up tales of adventure, mystery and suspense. They readily accepted that spontaneous human combustion, although a conundrum of science, was nevertheless a fact of life. The twentieth century, however, ushered in a period of 'realism', and scientists became highly sceptical about the phenomenon.

Cases of it were rarely studied, and even when they were, they were seldom well documented.

The so-called 'human candle' theory was often employed to explain away reported instances of human combustion – usually when a victim had fallen on to a hearth below an open chimney. But it could not be used to explain the case of Mrs Gladys Cochrane who was found burned beyond recognition at her home in Falkirk, Scotland, in 1904. Her body was discovered still seated in a chair surrounded by cushions and pillows, none of which had been touched by fire.

A year later, on 5 February 1905, the journal *Lloyds Weekly News* reported that a woman had fallen asleep facing her fire. She awoke to find herself in flames and later died. The oddity was that, although she was found facing the hearth, the blaze had consumed her back and had left the front of her body intact. The coroner confessed himself totally baffled.

Not all coroners are so open-minded. One of that profession, the coroner for Whitley Bay in Northumberland, heard the case of Wilhelmina Dewar, who burst into flames at midnight on 22 March 1908. The elderly spinster was discovered by her sister Margaret, who called on neighbours for help. When they arrived, however, they found Wilhelmina dead in her bed. There was no fire anywhere else in the house, yet her body was severely charred.

At an inquest, witnesses related this story and were effectively labelled liars by the coroner. When Margaret, a retired schoolteacher, testified that her sister's bedclothes had been untouched by fire even though it had consumed the body, the coroner told her to change her evidence. She refused. The coroner then adjourned the hearing for six days until poor Margaret, browbeaten by officialdom, returned to court to recant. She now said that she had found her sister ablaze in another part of the house and had carried her to the bedroom where she had expired. However, other witnesses pointed out the ludicrous nature of this evidence – given that there was no sign of fire in any other part of the house.

In 1919, a well-known English author of the day, J. Temple Thurston, died at his country home in Kent. He was found in his armchair, the lower half of his body horribly burned. The verdict of an inquest was that he had died from heart failure. But this official solution went nowhere near explaining how the writer came to be burned over half his corpse when the rest of his body was untouched, how the rest of his room was entirely untouched by the fire or smoke – and how Mr Temple Thurston had blazed away under his clothes without even singeing them.

There are many other examples of spontaneous human combustion in England. One extremely well-documented case is that of Mrs Madge Knight, whose screams were heard in the early hours of the morning of 19 November 1943. She had been sleeping alone in the spare bedroom of her home in Aldingbourne, Sussex, when she awoke in terror at 3.30 a.m. and screamed out that she felt as if she was burning. Her husband and sister leapt from their beds and were soon at her side comforting her. They found that she was naked under the bedclothes and as she writhed in agony beneath the covers they saw with horror that she had terrible burn marks across her back. Most of her skin had been removed from her back, yet there was no smell of burning and there was not a single scorch mark on the bed linen.

Madge Knight was given morphine to block out the pain,

and thereafter was questioned many times before she went into a coma three weeks later. She died from blood poisoning at Chichester Hospital on 6 December.

Her doctor had already handed the case on to a Harley Street specialist but neither came up with any satisfactory explanation as to Mrs Knight's death. The specialist told a coroner that, because there had been no signs of a blaze on the bed or anywhere else in the room, he suspected she had been burnt by some corrosive liquid. However, no such liquid and no container which could have held it were found in the house.

Another case in the 1950s involved an unusually young victim, a pretty nineteen-year-old secretary named Maybelle Andrews. Maybelle was dancing with her boyfriend at a club in London's red-light district of Soho when flames suddenly shot from her chest and back. Horrifyingly, the flames resisted all attempts by other dancers to beat them out. Within minutes they had consumed her.

In a statement, her distraught boyfriend, William Clifford, said: 'The flames seemed to come from within her body.' An inquest came up with no solution to the mystery of her death. Its verdict was: 'Death by misadventure, caused by a fire of unknown origin.'

Two other well-authenticated cases of recent years occurred in the United States. The deaths were far apart geographically but had amazing similarities.

Billy Peterson was sitting in his parked car in Detroit when flames apparently burst from his body. Rescuers found the heat inside the car so intense that the dashboard had melted. Billy Peterson's corpse was removed from the vehicle, his torso utterly charred, yet his clothes had not even been singed, even though a plastic statue on the dashboard had melted.

Almost as baffling was the discovery of five charred bodies in a burned-out car near Pikeville, Kentucky, in 1960. The coroner reported: 'They were sitting there as though they had just gotten into the car. With all that heat, there should have been some sort of struggle to escape. But there hadn't been.'

The following year an article appeared in the journal *Fate*, written by the Reverend Winogene Savage. According to the clergyman, a friend's brother awoke one morning to the sound of his wife screaming. He found her lying on the living-room floor, her entire body engulfed in flame. As her prostrate form blackened, the distraught husband saw a strange fireball above her. He rushed out to summon help and returned, along with neighbours carrying several buckets of water. The fire was extinguished but not in time to save his wife. The neighbours then realized that although the woman and all her clothes had been burned beyond recognition, the carpet on which she lay was untouched. Neither was there any other sign of fire within the room.

In recent years, many medical experts have attempted to explain away the phenomenon of spontaneous human combustion – but have almost always come up with hypotheses that fail to account for all the known facts of most of the best documented cases. One of the most quoted was (and still is) Dr D. J. Gee, emeritus professor of forensic medicine at Leeds University, who delivered a paper entitled *A Case Of Spontaneous Combustion*, which was well publicized in the early 1980s, and whose findings were the subject of a BBC television investigation.

Dr Gee investigated the case of an old lady who, as with many such deaths, was found lying on her hearth, her body wholly consumed by fire except for her right foot. The paintwork in her living-room was blistered in places and soot blackened the furniture. A tea towel hanging near the body was unsinged and firewood inside a nearby open oven was untouched. Dr Gee's theory was that the old lady had fallen on to the hearth and that cinders had set fire to her head. The body had then gone on burning in its own fat like a candle, helped by the draught from the chimney which had drawn the flames up and prevented them from spreading.

Having presented his paper to an audience at Leeds University, Dr Gee was surprised by the debate that followed among his highly educated audience. He later wrote in his notes: 'Dr George Manning described his experience of several similar cases, and indicated that the phenomenon was certainly not as rare as might be supposed from the literature. This view was supported by Dr David Price, who said that he met with this phenomenon approximately once in every four years.'

In a later paper, *Medicine, Science and the Law*, written in 1965, Dr Gee said that he had conducted further experiments and had found that small quantities of body fat could be set alight and that the burning could be sustained by placing the sample in a draught.

Coroners have since leapt on this experiment as the basis for many of their judgments in cases of spontaneous combustion. They have done so despite the fact that Dr Gee's laboratory experiment did not include the use of bone which is obviously much harder to incinerate. Neither did it explain away the spectacularly fierce blazes that characterize spontaneous human combustion cases; Dr Gee's experiment resulted only in slow smouldering.

More recent cases have done nothing to support Dr Gee's beliefs. On 12 November 1974, Jack Angel, a clothing salesman, went to sleep in his motor home in Savannah, Georgia, and awoke four days later with his right hand burned black. He also bore distinct, well-defined burn marks on other parts of his body, including his arm, chest and legs. Yet there was no trace of fire in the van. The trailer was dismantled in the search for a reason for Mr Angel's injuries, without success. Mr Angel's hand later had to be amputated.

The death of a girl who suddenly burst into flames in the corridor of an English college on 28 January 1985 has still to be explained. Jacqueline Fitzsimons, a seventeen-year-old cookery student, was chatting with friends at Halton Technical College, Widnes, Cheshire, when fire engulfed her. Horrified staff tore off their jackets, threw her on the floor and fought to smother the flames. But Jacqueline died from her burns fifteen days later in the intensive care unit of Whiston Hospital, Merseyside.

A major investigation into the tragedy, involving police, fire chief and the government's Health and Safety Executive, was ordered by a coroner. They examined previous 'human torch' cases and other scientific data. Tests were performed on the jacket and trousers that Jacqueline had been wearing but they provided no clues. It was also established that there had been no trace of fat or other cooking material which could have triggered an explosion.

Discussing the theory of spontaneous human combustion, the college's principal, Alan Hough, would only say: 'I do not know what other explanation there is. It's a complete mystery.' A fire service official said cautiously, 'It's a possibility we must look at.' The inquest, however, concluded that her clothing had caught fire during a cookery class and had flared up later because of the draught in the college corridor.

* * *

Cases of spontaneous human combustion like those above have one thing in common: the bafflement of scientists, experts and laymen alike. We are today no nearer to finding a solution to one of the most macabre phenomena of all time than were our ancient ancestors when they trustingly attributed 'human bonfires' to the wrath of the Almighty. As the Book of Job warns: 'By the blast of God they perish, and by the breath of His nostrils are they consumed.'

Divine retribution was a handy explanation for a pre-scientific age. But since the first fully documented cases in the seventeenth century, the sheer volume of case histories means that the phenomenon cannot be brushed aside – even by coroners, pathologists and other medical experts desperate to find an 'acceptable' cause of such deaths.

There are now a growing number of cases testified to by witnesses and by experts. There would be more if scientists and doctors could bear having their professional credibility doubted. Yet those scientists and doctors who have carefully examined bodies have had to admit that there have been cases of death by self-combustion that really cannot be explained away.

Spontaneous human combustion can occur in any circumstance – in a room with little air, in an area with good ventilation, and even outside. Its most common characteristic is the speed with which it strikes. The victims are often discovered still sitting calmly as though nothing had happened. Many victims were seen alive just a few moments before fire struck.

The other baffling aspect of this phenomenon is the extreme intensity of heat. Normally the human body is very hard to set alight, especially if still alive. People who die in fires usually suffer only partial or superficial damage from burns. Experts agree that reduction to a pile of calcined ashes demands ferocious heat which needs to be fuelled and maintained for hours. Even crematoria have to grind up bones that remain after a human body is burned.

Some researchers have also made note of the lack of struggle or cries by victims. Renowned psychic investigator Charles Fort, who devoted his life to collating every single report and document on strange phenomena, wrote at the beginning of this century: 'In their grim submission, it is almost as if they had been lulled by the wings of a vampire'.

This inertia cannot be due solely to intoxication, as was often suggested at this period of history. Back in the nineteenth century, chemist Baron Justus von Liebig, although highly cynical of human combustion, still discredited the notion that there was any connection between self-cremation and drinking. He showed conclusively that, when set alight, alcohol and fatty tissue behave in a different way from cases of human combustion.

Nor can this inertia be due to the victim being overcome by fumes. Combustion of this type appears to be preceded by psychological paralysis which renders victims helpless and leaves survivors unable to give any reasonable explanation as to what happened. In one bizarre case in 1885, a husband suffocated from the smoke of his wife's combusting body. Her ashes lay in a charred hole beside his unburnt corpse.

Yet from that day to the present time, officialdom has been over-cautious in attributing such weird and inexplicable tragedies to anything but normal and natural causes. J. L. Casper, in his *Handbook of the Practice of Forensic Medicine*, complained: 'It is sad to think that in an earnest scientific work, in this year of grace 1861, we must still treat of the fable "spontaneous combustion".' A century later, coroners and scientific theorists are equally cynical, adhering to the research findings of Dr Gee of Leeds University rather than the evidence of history. Few experts dare credit unexplained deaths to spontaneous human combustion. Officially it just doesn't happen. To quote Dr Gavin Thurston, the coroner for Inner West London, 'No such phenomenon as spontaneous combustion exists or has ever occurred.'

So should spontaneous human combustion be dismissed as nothing more than a medieval superstition? Or should we give greater credence to the many case histories of those who witnessed the bizarre experience of self-cremation, those who survived it – and those who did not live to tell the tale?

Coroners often have to deal with evidence that contradicts accepted physical laws and medical opinion. Yet inevitably the cause is put down to knocked-over heaters, flying sparks or carelessness with cigarettes. And in the case of children, playing with matches is often blamed. Surely twentieth-century science can offer explanations other than these for spontaneous human combustion? In fact, there are several theories that might account for the phenomenon. None are conclusive but some appear more credible than others.

One of the least likely is the 'psychic suicide'. This suggests that human combustion might be self-induced by those suffering severe depression or people who are 'at war with the world'. Their reserves of physical and psychic energy can suddenly be released in a suicidal explosion.

Another theory is that organic or mechanical malfunctioning of the body can lead to an accumulation of explosive compounds and the build-up of phosphagens in muscle tissue. A technical paper, *Applied Trophology*, in December 1957, stated: 'Phosphagen is a compound like nitroglycerine, of endothermic formation (that is, absorbs heat). It is no doubt so highly developed in certain sedentary persons as to make their bodies actually combustible, subject to ignition, burning like gunpowder under some circumstances.'

A third theory is that spontaneous human combustion occurs when people burn after their clothes have caught fire. But this can be disproved by the many cases in which only the victims' flesh was burned while their clothes were undamaged.

Other research, such as that by Livingston Gearhart, has attempted to prove that spontaneous combustion is directly related to increased magnetic and electro-magnetic disturbances in the atmosphere. In 1975, Gearhart wrote in the Fortean journal *Pursuit* that solar activity causes the strength of the Earth's magnetic field to rise and fall dramatically. He said he had kept a log of magnetic activity gathered daily by astronomers and geophysicists – and had discovered that a significant number of combustion cases took place on or near a peak in the geomagnetic flux. Gearhart said this proved there was a distinct correlation between high geomagnetic readings and spontaneous human combustion.

One of the most oft-heard explanations for human bonfires is the phenomenon known as ball lightning. Maxwell Cade and Delphine Davis are authors of the comprehensive study of ball lightning, *Taming of the Thunderbolts*, published in 1969. They started writing the book having, of course, heard of spontaneous combustion but professing themselves dubious as to the truth of such cases. They changed their minds when a doctor friend told them 'of a lecture which he attended at the Massachusetts Medico-Legal Society, where several such cases were discussed. When we expressed cautious doubts, the doctor assured us that he had been called to a similar case himself as recently as the autumn of 1959.'

Maxwell Cade and Delphine Davis report the views of several physicists who believe that the huge energies of ball lightning could produce short radio waves of the same kind used in microwave ovens. 'If this theory is correct,' say the authors, 'it is possible for victims to be burned to death, not merely within their clothes, but even within their skin, either by the proximity of a lightning ball or having a ball form within their body, or just by the action of the intense radio-frequency field which, in the absence of their body, would have formed a lightning ball at that place.'

Of all explanations, ball lightning is the most easily accepted because of its natural origins. It would account for the victims being cooked from the inside, starting with different points of the anatomy and burning the body at differing rates – in exactly the same way as microwave diathermy can heat different materials at different speeds.

As with all these theories, however, proof is scant and the explanations would account for only a proportion of known cases. It would be wrong, however, to deny that there is a logical, scientific solution to the horrifying mystery of spontaneous human combustion, one that is yet to be discovered but one that is nonetheless horribly real.

Today, sadly, we have learned of many forms of death that invisibly penetrate the human body. Weapons of war have been devised almost beyond man's imagination: X-ray lasers, microwave projectors, radiation guns, ultra-sound beams – all tools of modern warfare which can literally 'cook' a man to death.

* * *

But do any of the above explain the following case?

Early on the frosty morning of 5 December 1966, Don Gosnell, a gas meter reader, started his day's work in the town of Coudersport, Pennsylvania. One of the first calls of the day was at the home of Dr John Irving Bentley, a retired family doctor. Knowing that the 92-year-old man could get about only with the aid of a walking frame, Gosnell was not surprised when no one answered the door, so he let himself in. In the hallway he detected a faint smell of smoke but took little notice of it.

Gosnell went straight down to the meters in the basement, where he noticed a neat pile of ash on the floor. He briefly wondered how it had got there but did not bother to turn his eyes upwards towards the ceiling. where there was a charred hole through which the ash had fallen from the bathroom above. Gosnell read the meter and walked back upstairs. Now there was a light blue smoke in the air.

Calling out for Dr Bentley, the meter man retraced his steps through the hallway towards the old man's bedroom. It was smoky but empty, so he headed for the bathroom. At the bathroom door he sniffed 'a strange, sweetish smell'. He opened the door and recoiled in horror.

Alongside the char-edged hole in the floor lay Dr Bentley's steel walking frame, blackened but with its rubber tips still intact. Beside the frame was the lower half of the doctor's right leg. A slipper was still on one of the old man's feet, which was burned off at the calf. And that was all that was left of Dr Bentley apart from a pile of ash. Don Gosnell ran from the building screaming, 'Dr Bentley is burned up!'

At the inquest which followed, the coroner listened to the seemingly obvious explanation that Dr Bentley had set himself on fire while lighting his pipe. This failed to tally with the facts, however, since the doctor's pipe was carefully placed on its stand by the bed. Neither did it explain why a fire of such ferocity had done so little damage to the rest of the bathroom, which was virtually untouched by fire apart from a slight blackening on the side of the bathtub.

The coroner recorded a verdict of 'death by asphyxiation and ninety per cent burning of the body'. Hardly an explanation for one of the most macabre phenomena of our time. All the coroner would say after the case was 'It was the oddest thing you ever saw.'

Buried Alive

When a young girl vanished in mysterious circumstances, the prime suspect was John Esposito. Police swooped on his New York home, and inch by inch, searched for clues, convinced that he was involved in the disappearance. And all the while they were being watched by the missing girl herself . . . trapped in a tiny underground cell.

Every move made by the police and shifty 43-year-old Esposito was relayed to little Katie Beers, chained by the neck in the squalid, specially built dungeon. Her frantic screams punctuated the acrid atmosphere from the moment she caught sight of a uniform on her TV screen, and did not stop until long after the last policeman had left the house above. But Katie remained trapped in her filthy prison. No one had heard the hysterical shrieks of this pitiful child.

The terrible torment of Katie Beers began on 28 December 1992 when she set out on an exciting trip to mark her forthcoming tenth birthday. Katie, neglected, unkempt, and four foot tall with dark blond hair, was a familiar figure in the tatty suburb where she lived with her godmother. There was little sunshine in the life of the youngster, who frequently missed school because she was too busy running errands and doing chores. The 'kindly' offer from family friend John Esposito of an outing to a toy shop and a video game arcade as part of her birthday celebrations must have been an thrilling prospect for this modern-day Cinderella.

As she met up with avuncular Esposito that afternoon, she couldn't have imagined the nightmare to come. She did not know that Esposito – whom she called 'Big John' – already had a record for the attempted abduction of a seven-year-old boy from a shopping mall. Neither did she know that her own mother had also lodged a complaint with police against Esposito, claiming that he had molested her teenage son, Katie's half-brother, John.

Now Esposito had little Katie at his mercy, too. After their outing he made sexual overtures to the girl. Shocked and disgusted, she recoiled from his kisses. And when she refused his advances, she was dragged screaming to the bunker at the bottom of the house.

He bundled her into an office where she watched in amazement and terror as he unbolted a set of shelves from the wall to reveal a cupboard with a 210 lb slab of concrete on the floor. He needed a block and tackle to manoeuvre the huge weight which was some 6 inches thick. It in turn exposed a wooden door under which there was a ladder leading down to a 7-foot-deep well. It turned sharply into a cramped corridor, the length of a man. At the end of this tortuous journey was the chamber which was to imprison her.

Esposito, a builder, had constructed the cell eighteen months before. No one knows what prompted him to start building it, but he embarked on the project following the deaths of his older brother and mother, which both occurred in the same year. Not only was the cell sound-proofed but it was sealed off from the house so that even a sniffer dog would have been unlikely to track it down.

When staggered detectives finally unearthed the dungeon, they likened it to the pit in which hapless victims were kept in the horror film, *The Silence of the Lambs*. One police officer said, 'It sent a shiver down all our spines to think that any man could go to such elaborate lengths to imprison a child.' Drew Biondo, a spokesman for the District Attorney, said: 'You had to go through so many machinations it was like King Tut's tomb.'

Katie bit, scratched and struggled, but to no avail. Esposito was stronger and, by now, quite determined. At 3 feet high, 2 feet wide and 7 feet long, Katie's cell amounted to little more than a coffin. Windowless and poorly ventilated, the only shafts of light which pierced the darkness were from a TV screen and the closed circuit monitor her captor had rigged up to show what was going on in the house above. There was a mattress on the floor, but cruel Esposito only allowed her to use it at night. During the day she was chained to the inside of a raised, plywood box in a crouching position, her legs wound up by her face. She not only suffered terrible cramp, but also began to feel gnawing pains in her stomach, perhaps due to hunger, or fear, or both. Her head throbbed and she felt sick.

In a sadistic twist, he forced her to record a message which would cover his tracks. Screaming and sobbing, her frantic words were, 'I've been kidnapped by a man with a knife, and oh, my God, here he comes . . .'

Esposito played the message from a public pay phone to her godmother, Linda Inghilleri, who immediately rang the Spaceplex Family Fun Center in Long Island where she believed Katie was and discovered the girl had indeed disappeared. Esposito was by now 'searching' for her, brimming with phony remorse and fake tears at having lost sight of his young charge.

Meanwhile, Katie was spending the first of sixteen days (a total of 381 hours) in her dank, grim prison.

At night Esposito would appear, bearing salami sandwiches, pizza and soda. Only then did he allow her to use the portable toilet installed in the hole. Frequently, unable to hang on, she soiled herself before he got there, which meant the stench was revolting. One night, they even sat together watching the television crime programme 'America's Most Wanted', featuring her disappearance. She saw her mother and Linda Inghilleri both tear-stained and frantic, pleading for news of her. Esposito continued to make advances. Katie continued to resist.

The depths of mental cruelty to which her captor sank appalled even hardened cops. It wasn't enough that she could see the scouring detectives, so near and yet so far. Esposito, who called her 'his little pet', also showed her newspaper cuttings reporting her own death. He goaded her by saying that she would never be found. He threatened to hang himself without leaving any message as to her whereabouts. She would, he assured her, starve and suffer a lingering, painful death. She didn't know which would be worse, his leering face appearing at night to inflict more torture, or his sudden disappearance, leaving her without food, water and hope. She waited with bated breath and beating heart for the whirr of the power tool that Esposito used to remove the bolts before he squeezed his bulky frame into the small cell.

Astonishingly, however, the resourceful Katie managed to keep her spirits up by imagining it was all a game. 'Sometimes I would think of this as a "Home Alone" game,' Katie told police. 'Sometimes I would think about

Dorothy [in the *Wizard of Oz*]. I would say, there's no place like home. There's no place like home.'

She recounted how she yelled for help when she saw police making routine inquiries in the house above her, even though they couldn't hear her. In her bleakest moments, she even wondered if she was dead as newspapers brought to her by Esposito speculated about her demise. 'I was reading I was dead but I thought I was alive,' she said.

Noticing stains on the sheets, she pondered about the possible fate of other children who had perhaps been there before. Her cage was ventilated but rain and snow found a way in through the same route as the vital oxygen. She shivered in damp clothes, longing for the warmth of a fire, but displayed remarkable fortitude.

In her short life, Katie had suffered more than her fair share of knocks which had given her a good grounding for just such an ordeal. Her mother Marilyn Beers was a cab driver who had handed her over when she was just two months old to godmother Linda, a woman she had met as a fare. It was five years before mother and daughter were reunited. After renting a series of apartments, Linda Inghilleri, her husband Sal and little Katie moved in with Marilyn and son John into a house owned by Marilyn's mother, Helen Beers.

It was hardly 'Home, Sweet Home'. Rubbish littered the rooms which were scavenged by cats, cockroaches and even rats. With her unsavoury home and scruffy appearance, Katie had few friends. She spent much of her time running errands for her rambling family. Linda had by this time lost a leg through diabetes and was confined to a bedroom, and would summon Katie by thumping on the floor. Katie headed off to buy cigarettes, sweets or food. She was also in charge of doing the laundry. Usually she was clad in thin cotton clothes, whatever the weather. Occasionally, she wore no shoes.

'She was so tiny but she was very independent,' recalls Trudy Welsh, from the QT Laundromat, in West Islip, frequented by Katie. 'She used to stand on the wagons to reach the machines. I felt so sorry for her.' Together, they would natter over a cup of coffee like a couple of world-weary housewives, even though Katie was just six years old. 'I used to say "Katie, you're not old enough to drink coffee." And she'd say: "I've been drinking coffee since I was four."'

When the bank foreclosed on Helen Beer's second mortgage, the Inghilleris took Katie to a rented bungalow in Bay Shore. In January 1992, however, Marilyn Beers took Katie back, accusing Sal of sexual abuse. Rarely attending school, Katie flitted between the two families for the next twelve months until her abduction.

Bachelor Esposito kept open house for children and furnished a games room in his home especially for them. Youngsters went there to play pool or video games, or help themselves to bowls of sweets. His bid to be a welfare worker among needy children was turned down when details of his criminal past surfaced. The cheerful neighbour who impressed everyone with his time and patience with troubled children had a dark side, evoked by Katie when she rejected his fumbling advances.

Katie Beers had been his captive and he her tormentor for fifteen days when he thrust a wad of bank notes at her, telling her he was going to kill himself. He mumbled that he would leave a note pinned to his body directing police to her. Then he left with a dramatic flourish. Katie was terrified. Would he really kill himself? Would he remember to leave the note? Anyway, would his body ever be found? The child was in terror at the prospect of dying in the dank, dark hole.

But the next face she saw was that of a kindly police officer. Esposito had finally cracked after being under round-the-clock police surveillance. 'I'll show you where I've got her,' he eventually told detectives. Then he led the police with mounting horror along his terror trail. When the shaft was unsealed, they called out her name. After a while they heard her answer softly: 'I'm here.' One shell-shocked policeman asked: 'How are you?' Courageous Katie replied: 'I'm fine – how are you?'

Blinking in the light which was by now strange to her, she saw Esposito break down and sob after she emerged. Police officers were staggered when she approached him, kindly patted his shoulder and said, 'Don't cry, Big John, everything's going to be OK.'

And everything is OK for Katie now. The slum-and-slavery existence she had known was put behind her. She was placed in a foster home in the care of a decorated Vietnam veteran and his wife. They had three children of their own and another foster child. Washed and dressed, she was at last able to set off for school every day like other children. Professional counselling has helped her over-come her nightmares.

Her mother Marilyn fought for custody, claiming that she was torn apart by the enforced absence. As for Linda Inghilleri, she also wanted Katie back but lost a custody battle. 'I raised her,' she claimed. 'I taught her how to talk, I was with her when she was sick. Marilyn is the biological mother but I'm the one who nurtured Katie.' She later said, 'To me there is no difference between John Esposito and Marilyn Beers. They both claim to love her, but in a sick way. They both shared the same fake tears. But Katie and I have shared a real love, a real home and real tears to be together forever.' While husband Sal awaited trial for alleged sexual abuse, Linda pledged that she would divorce him anyway.

For his part, Esposito claimed that he merely wanted a friend. He tried to convince himself he was saving Katie from the drudgery of life with her two families. He was charged with kidnapping and related misdemeanours and faced a maximum of twenty-five years in jail. Police are certain that no other children were his victims.

Poor Katie Beers was literally buried alive to satisfy the deviant lusts of a monster. Other people have been prematurely entombed entirely by accident. Stories of people being buried alive have provided a macabre fascination for years. It's a nightmare for all those tormented at the thought of being trapped underground. For some it's the encompassing blackness that sets their spines tingling. For others, it's the fact that no one would hear their screams.

One of the worst cases in recent years came from China where an eighteen-year-old known as Chen lapsed into unconsciousness after drinking too much alcohol and was comatose for ten hours. His family thought he had stopped breathing and set about burying him. But after buying a coffin they were forced to hush up the internment because Chinese regulations insist on cremations.

Three days later, the authorities found out what had happened and persuaded the family to cremate their only son. When they opened the coffin they found the body in a sitting position with arms pushed against the side. The fingertips were bloodied from his attempts to claw his way out. The body was covered in blood with clothes tattered and torn. A doctor who examined the body decided Chen had regained consciousness about twenty-four hours after being buried. It seems that the alcohol had made his breathing so shallow it had been impossible to detect.

According to an Egyptian newspaper, *El Gomhoria*, a man was entombed alive by his four children in the family vault because no one wanted to pay for his food and shelter. Gravediggers rescued 72-year-old Hamid Afifi after forty-five days spent in the crypt in the summer of 1991. When he returned to his home, his children believed him to be a ghost coming to haunt them for their wickedness.

An apparent 'return from the dead' had catastrophic effects in one Saudi Arabian family. Two women died from shock when a relative they had buried walked through the door of the family home. Muattak al-Shahrani was committed to the ground after being knocked out by the vane of a windmill. But twenty-seven hours later, the sound of sheep's hooves awoke him and a passing shepherd came to his aid after hearing his cries. Still wearing his shroud, he returned home where his sister and mother collapsed on seeing him.

The fear of being buried alive in a coffin reached almost hysterical proportions during the Victorian era. Some pessimists, suspecting a doctor would miss faint signs of life in pronouncing their demise, even ordered a bell to be hung above their grave with a thin cord leading directly to the coffin below. Such precautions, it was argued, would allow friends and relatives to be alerted in the event that consciousness was regained.

This concern is perhaps rooted more in the Victorian obsession with the macabre and gaslight horror-fiction than any real danger of such an appalling death. And yet live burials do happen. Within the last few decades there have been well-documented cases of the dead rising from the grave to resume working lives. Three of the most remarkable resurrections have occurred on the island of Haiti, where the ancient voodoo religion still holds sway among much of the population. In each case the victims were 'zombified' – pronounced dead and then 'restored' to life – by witchdoctors all within a matter of days. Bizarre though it seems, both zombies and the buried alive phenomenon are now scientific fact.

The man who takes much of the credit for this discovery is Harvard anthropologist Dr E. Wade Davis. In 1980 he astounded fellow academics with the announcement that 'zombieism actually exists. There are Haitians who have been raised from their graves and returned to life.'

Davis had been invited to conduct his own investigation of the zombie phenomenon by Dr Lamarque Douyon, head of the Port-au-Prince Psychiatric Centre. His studies began with the astonishing story of one man, Clairvius Narcisse, who in 1962 had been admitted to the local Albert Schweitzer Hospital suffering from a severe fever. Forty-year-old Narcisse never recovered and within forty-eight hours was dead. Hospital authorities arranged for his burial the following day.

That should have been the sad, though unremarkable, end of the matter. But eighteen years later, Narcisse's sister Angeline was stopped by man she vaguely recognized. His first words made her blood run cold: 'Do you know me? I am Clairvius.' The voice was enough. Angeline instantly realized she was speaking to the brother whose death she had mourned all those years ago.

According to Narcisse, he had been zombified, following a plot by their brothers to auction off some of the family's estate. He had no recollection of the length of time he had been buried in the cemetery but clearly remembered how a voodoo witchdoctor had administered a potion to bring him back to life. He was then turned out with a party of zombie labourers to work on a farm.

A couple of years later, the owner of the land died and Narcisse, who by now seemed to have shaken off the effects of the zombie curse, escaped. He wandered penniless for sixteen years and decided to make himself known to Angeline only when he was sure the brother who had devised the plan to zombify him was dead.

Up to this point in Narcisse's account, sceptics could be forgiven for suspecting him to be a crude publicity seeker. But then the hospital authorities began offering hard facts to back him up. His death certificate was checked; his grave, which had been left obviously untouched for years, was re-dug and the coffin opened. Sure enough, it was empty. Narcisse even suggested the scar on his cheek had been caused as the result of a nail piercing his skin when the lid was hammered down. As additional confirmation, a group of farm labourers in the area where he claimed to have been put to work remembered him and vouched for his tale.

Davis and Douyon had at last uncovered a case founded on overwhelming evidence. Soon, similar, equally fantastic, stories began to emerge. One involved a thirty-year-old woman called Francena Illeus, sometimes known as Ti Femme, who had 'died' in 1976. Three years later, her mother recognized her from a distinctive scar on her forehead as she wandered near her home village. Again, her grave was exhumed and this time the coffin was full of rocks. A third case, of an elderly woman called Natagette Joseph, provided equally persuasive evidence of the witchdoctors' work. Many villagers swore they had been present at her funeral in 1964 and had seen her laid in the ground.

Davis had by now begun to construct a theory which could explain zombieism. He suggested that witchdoctors would use a range of rare and little-known poisons to place their intended victim in a state of suspended animation. To casual observers, and even trained medics, the victim would display all the usual features of a corpse, with undetectable heartbeat, pulse and breathing. Then, once the hapless target had been safely buried, he or she would be dug up within a couple of days for antidotes to be administered. Quite often permanent brain damage would have occurred – hence the popular idea of a zombie – but this could be a positive bonus to the witchdoctor as the man could then be sold as a fully subjugated slave.

Poison as the cause of zombieism had first been suggested fifty years earlier, though until Davis began his work the idea had always been scorned by academics. Now, suddenly, the sinister mysteries on which the entire voodoo religion was founded were being laid bare.

Davis studied toxins from the plant *Datura stramonium*, sometimes known as 'zombie's cucumber' on Haiti and as 'jimsonweed' in the Western world. He considered voodoo links with the Bufo Marinus toad, keenly sought as a producer of 'medicine' for witchdoctors, and explored the use of toxins from two species of puffer fish. Such fish are considered exquisite delicacies in Japan, though any diner who tries them runs the risk of a speedy death if the chef has not fully removed all traces of the toxin-bearing liver and roe. Davis knew that Captain Cook had been among the earliest of puffer victims. And case studies of two unfortunate Japanese 'read like classic accounts of Haitian zombification'. Both these men had been pronounced dead by doctors but made miraculous recoveries before they could be buried.

Davis backed up his theories by obtaining samples of so-called 'zombie-powder' used by witchdoctors. Analysis showed they contained, among other ingredients, pieces of human corpse, nettle, toad and puffer fish. He concluded:

Zombies are a Haitian phenomenon which can be explained logically. The active ingredients in the poison are extracts from the skin of the toad Bufo Marinus and one or more species of puffer fish. The skin of the toad is a natural chemical factory which produces hallucinogens, powerful anaesthetics and chemicals which affect the heart and nervous system. The puffer fish contains a deadly nerve poison called tetrodotoxin. A witchdoctor in Haiti is very skilled in administering just the right amount of poison. Too much poison will kill the victim completely and resuscitation will not be possible. Too little and the victim will not be a convincing corpse.

Davis' work did much to rid Haiti of the mystique of voodoo, used by ruthless dictators such as 'Baby Doc' Duvalier to subjugate the people. Yet even today there lingers on the island a core of belief in the old religion and the power of the witchdoctors. Davis himself recognized that something more than mere toxins and antidotes – some still unclear ritual – was deployed by witchdoctors to ensure the successful raising of a zombie.

Perhaps the Victorians were right after all to worry themselves into the grave.

Rasputin

A midnight frost crusted the snowy paths of St Petersburg as the rangy figure of Rasputin strode towards a nobleman's palace with vigour. Arguably the most powerful man in the Russian empire, Rasputin's fiery eyes were dancing with delight. Tonight he had an assignation with a beautiful princess, one of the country's elite whom he longed to recruit into his retinue. There would be drinking, feasting, some music perhaps and then ... who knows. His pace quickened as he approached the door.

The fact that the husband of his quarry was walking beside him didn't bother Rasputin at all. Many Russian husbands of the day had stood by passively while their wives were gripped, both mentally and physically, by the magnetism of this unholy monk. Rasputin knew the Prince Felix Yusupov to be old-fashioned, discreet, skittish, and probably homosexual. He was unlikely to be a hindrance.

Rasputin, all but licking his lips in anticipation of the night ahead, didn't notice that the prince was in turn occupied with plans of his own. The deeply loyal prince was one of a growing band who were appalled at the way their beloved country had degenerated. This they laid at the door of the powerful, sinister Rasputin. His influence over the Tsarina, wife of Russia's imperial ruler Tsar Nicolas II, was legendary. The disreputable monk was known for getting his own way, even in matters of state, and his ill-informed judgement was plunging the country into chaos. Now Yusupov headed a band of conspirators who had resolved to smash Rasputin's vice-like grip. Tonight they were going to kill the monk.

There were shocks in store for everyone, however. For although Yusupov administered enough cyanide in wine and cakes to kill six men, it wasn't enough to slay Rasputin. Nor were three bullets in the ribs, back and neck. Even a bludgeoning with a heavy metal chain still left Rasputin twitching as he refused to relinquish his grip on life. Only when the body was plunged into the freezing waters of a nearby river could the assassins be sure their prey was finally dead. Despite the iron and steel constitution Rasputin displayed, he could have survived no more than a few seconds in the icy flow. His body was discovered frozen in the River Neva two days later, confirming gossip which had spread through the city like wildfire: that Rasputin was dead.

The bizarre and compelling story of the unholy monk's death was matched only by his life and astonishing climb to power. Grigory Efimovich, who later adopted the name Rasputin (peasant slang meaning 'debauched woman-chaser'), was born in the Siberian outpost of Pokrovskoie in 1871, his father a drunken horse thief, his mother no more than a child herself. There was little joy in his young life as he joined the rest of his village in working the land to eke out a meagre existence. Education was only an afterthought. In fact, his spelling was so bad that even the word 'diary' on his scrawled notes found recently in Russian archives was mis-spelt. Bitterly cold and cheerless, the landscape was as stark as young Grigory's homelife. He was regularly beaten by his father, a known rogue.

But the youngster found a haven from this dreary life at a young age. He found that sex not only kept out the cold but was addictively pleasurable. He became hooked. Legend has it that, as a teenager, he lost his virginity to a Russian general's wife, Danilova Kubasova, who seduced him with a little help from her six hand-maidens in her stately home near his village. It hardly seems credible that a noblewoman would entice this filthy ragamuffin into her chamber but if she did, she was merely the first of many. Perhaps like countless others she fell victim to his hypnotic eyes. More likely, she had heard about the astonishing dimensions of his penis, said to measure some 13 inches.

In any event, Rasputin went on to earn his reputation for debauchery with sexual exploits among village girls. It was during just such an episode that he allegedly saw the light. In fact, he was bathing naked in a pond with three village maidens when his religious conversion occurred. He emerged dripping, proclaiming the gospel in a manner borrowed from a travelling priest he had recently seen. His sudden calling, prompted in part by an ultimatum from local, more respectable clerics, took him away from the village where he had grown up; away from his loyal wife Praskovia Feodorovna and four children and into feudal Russia. He embraced the Khlisty sect, or Flagellants, as they were known. The sect's philosophy of licentious behaviour and odd sexual peccadilloes fitted in perfectly with his own.

There were about 120,000 followers of this bizarre fringe church group around the country. Meetings which took place in forest clearings involved the faithful calling on

God, singing, chanting and dancing in a frenzy by the light of flaming torches. Anyone who could not keep up the pace in this heady, energetic worship was soundly whipped by the leader of the meeting. As the service ended the men and women fell on each other lustfully to satisfy their carnal desires.

Rasputin, coached in the art of seduction and orgies at a Khlisty monastery in Verkhoture, took full part in the services, and more besides, after he left to travel the towns and cities. He seduced a nun in Tsarytsin who was convinced the devil was within her and had pleaded with him for an exorcism. And in another town he visited, he thrashed a nude prostitute with his belt driving her into the street like a dog. Pious society women happily abandoned themselves and were lured into sex with the wily preacher.

But just how could this unkempt figure with dirty hands, matted beard and insolent manner wheedle his way into the affections of so many?

There were those electric eyes which he flashed to great effect. Even photographs testify to their piercing and persuasive qualities. It is said that he could induce an orgasm in a woman simply by looking at her. But Rasputin also became a master of sensational sermons, delivered with passion and zeal. His presence was magnetic. But the firebrand delivery masked some curious gospel which must have left him at odds with the prevalent Russian Orthodox religion. For example, he insisted to his followers: 'It is by repentance alone that we can win our salvation. We must therefore sin in order to have an opportunity for repentance. So when God places temptation in our way, it is our duty to yield.' Much later, he recalled: 'In the Khlisty I discovered the forces that make man work. I realised that so long as you bear sin secretly and within you, and fearfully cover it up with fasting, prayer and eternal discussion of the Scriptures, so long will you remain hypocrites and good for nothings.'

He made evangelical prophecies, performed exorcisms and uttered incantations. He even boasted of performing miracles. His very presence was eerily compelling. Soon his fame spread and people were kneeling before him in the streets, kissing his hands and begging for his blessing.

In 1904, Rasputin's ascendancy was assured when he first went to St Petersburg, summoned by an eminent cleric of the day, Father John of Kronstadt. After the two men met, Father John declared that Rasputin was marked out by God.

In 1906, Prime Minister Peter Stolypin's daughter was badly injured by a revolutionary bomb thrown at her father's house. Doctors were convinced she was going to die. In desperation, Stolypin sent for Rasputin. The dishevelled visionary stood at the end of her bed and prayed. Within an hour she was out of danger.

Rasputin now took a flat in the capital, revelling in his growing reputation as a holy man. Women thronged to his door, anxious to do the bidding of this new mystic master in order to be cleansed of sin or healed. It was only a matter of time before he was invited to the Royal Palace to meet Russia's Tsar Nicholas II and his wife Tsarina Alexandra.

It didn't take long for the keen eyes and ready guile of the monk to discover their vulnerability. It was their young son Alexander. The Tsarevich was the son they longed for after giving birth to four daughters. They planned how he would one day be the head of the Romanov dynasty which would thrive and flourish under his leadership, securing the future of the throne and, indeed, of Russia. He became the pivot of his parents' world. But at birth Alexandra, granddaughter to Queen Victoria, had passed to him the inherited disease haemophilia, which renders the blood unable to clot so that any minor scratch or bump can become a life-threatening condition. The couple cosseted the boy they adored, and summoned the best medical experts in the country. But Alexandra despaired as doctor after doctor seemed unable to stem the flow of blood from tiny wounds or improve the outlook for his health.

Word of Rasputin's strange powers had spread behind the palace walls. Alexandra was intrigued. Could this man be saviour to her son and end the torment of his ill health that dogged her daily? As chance would have it, the four-year-old Tsarevich was in the middle of a haemophiliac attack when Rasputin swept into the Winter Palace in 1908. And somehow Rasputin did indeed stop the bleeding.

Some claim that he used hypnosis, others that he calmed the boy, alleviated his stress and so ended the attack. There are those who insist that Rasputin did indeed have a touch which could magically heal. Whatever the cause of the cure, it was proof enough to the Tsarina that the best hope for her beloved son lay in the hands of the Siberian peasant monk. The fact that he was filthy, ill-educated and brazen mattered not a jot to her once she made up her determined mind.

Already the palace was in thrall to the power of the occult, mysteries and miracles. Further fuel was added to the flames of Rasputin's reputation when Countess Ignatiev, a favoured member of the court, had a vision in which a saint appeared to her and said, 'There is a great prophet among you.' This prophet, everyone agreed, must surely be Rasputin.

Outside the palace, Rasputin was building an empire of his own. He established the Rasputristry, a band of obedient female followers drawn mostly from the middle and upper classes who peopled his apartment and catered for his every whim. They happily stripped themselves and scrubbed him in local steam baths or spent the night with him huddled under his red fox bedspread. His disciples called him Staretz, the Old Man.

Rasputin kept his eagle eyes open for opportunities to boost the numbers of his admiring horde, particularly among society women with powerful husbands. Rumour had it that he even tried to seduce the Grand Duchess Tatiana, daughter of the Tsar. And he exerted more and more influence over matters of state. His suggestions for government and church posts which became vacant were usually accepted. He installed allies, often incompetent reprobates, in authority where they would protect his interests. In the process, he received plenty of roubles for his trouble.

The court became deeply divided over the monk and his cavorting ways. While many society women were convinced he was a saint, there were others who saw him as a dangerous sinner using sinister techniques for his own ends. However, Rasputin had an unfailing ally in the form of the Tsarina, who always referred to him as 'Our Friend'. It was months before any backlash against him could gain momentum because she dispatched his known enemies to the snowy wastes of the countryside if they dared speak out. Even close friends and cousins were given the royal cold shoulder because they had voiced their concerns.

Eventually, however, there was a sufficient undercurrent of feeling against the monk for even the toadying press to denounce him, and the Tsar, always less smitten with Rasputin than his wife, agreed to act. In March 1912, Rasputin was banished from court and returned to his

Siberian home with a band of faithful followers in tow. But while he was away, the Tsarevich took a turn for the worse. His attacks became more frequent and, with each passing day, the Tsarina grew more concerned. Finally, Rasputin was summoned back to the Winter Palace. When he arrived, the Empress of all Russia knelt before him and asked for his blessing.

Shortly afterwards, her faith in him was confirmed again when the boy fell ill on holiday in Poland. Physicians seemed helpless in the face of a septic tumour which left little Alexander stricken. When the crisis was at its height, Rasputin sent a telegram saying: 'God has seen your tears and heard your prayers. Grieve no more, your son will live.' Within days, the boy's serious condition improved. It was, insisted his grateful mother, all thanks to Rasputin.

Rasputin knew only too well he had his enemies. In June 1914, he only narrowly escaped deadly retribution by a knife-wielding prostitute who had once been his mistress. He was visiting his native village of Pokrovskoie when the prostitute, Khinia Gureva, struck. As she plunged a dagger into his stomach she cried, 'I've killed the Anti-Christ.' Then she turned the bloodied weapon on herself.

The injury to Rasputin was dangerous but, in character-istically macabre fashion, failed to do any long-term damage to his superhuman frame. He was merely confined to bed for a few weeks, during which time the distraught Tsarina teleponed daily. Meanwhile, Khinia, whose suicide bid had proved unsuccessful, was sent to an asylum.

While Rasputin recuperated, the growing crisis in Europe erupted and Russia was sucked into the bloodbath of the First World War. It was a critical point in Rasputin's career. Suddenly, telephone calls from the Tsarina dwindled. She was busy on hospital committees and sewing protective clothing for battling soldiers. At last her bright but bored mind was filled with purpose. She had no time to entertain the bearded peasant who had planned to take over her home when he returned. For a while it seemed that the bond between them was breaking, but spookily fate was once again on Rasputin's side. Many influential figures in the court believed that Rasputin might have averted the costly military conflict of 1914 had he been in St Petersburg. His propaganda machine got to work even in his absence and it only took another haemophiliac attack to reinstate the monk at the Tsarina's side.

Since coming to the throne in 1894, Tsar Nicholas had not distinguished himself as a ruler. Although not as brutal as his father, he had earned the hatred and loathing of the poor by his action against a peaceful march for food in 1905. Workers who had trekked to his palace to protest against food shortages and the system which kept them enslaved were met with savagery. The Tsar's own body-guards, the feared Cossacks, cut them down with sabres and gunfire. At least 130 died and hundreds more were injured.

After the massacre, the Tsar repeated the assertion he had made when he took the throne: that he was the divine ruler of all Russia. Democracy was not an option he would consider. This autocratic intransigence became a breeding ground for revolution.

The Great War distracted Nicholas from his country's internal problems. From the comfort of his palace, the Tsar was concerned with Russia's performance in the war. As his cousin Kaiser Wilhelm's army swept through imperial territory, the badly equipped, poorly run forces put up little resistance. He toyed with the idea of leading the army himself.

Rasputin was among those who favoured the Tsar's departure to the front. For while the ruler heeded the holy man on matters of religion and ethics, he was prone to ignore advice on matters of politics and state. With the Tsar out of the way, this would give Rasputin absolute power through his puppet Queen. He also counted on the support of some eminent statesmen including the Ministers of Justice and the Interior, the Procurator of the Holy Synod and the Director of the Police Bureau.

But Rasputin's enemies were equally united. They agreed that the only way to free the country of this malevolent force was premeditated murder. The most eminent of the plotters was Prince Felix Yusupov – a member of one of the richest families in Russia, wealthier even than the Tsar himself. Their families were linked when Felix wed Princess Irina, niece of the Tsar. Although his roots were in the fearsome Tartars, Yusupov was hardly an archetypal warrior. He was handsome and witty, proud of his delicate stature. Despite his marriage, he was bisexual and was known to dress in women's clothes. This free-living spirit was later to befriend the exiled British Royals, the Windsors, in Paris.

Also in the murderous gang was Grand Duke Dmitri Pavlovich, a past amour of the lovely Princess Irina and cousin of the Tsar, home from the front line due to ill health. Another war veteran, Captain Sergei Soukhotin, joined them, along with army medic Doctor Lazovert. Vladimir Purishkevich was the old man of the group. He was over fifty while the rest were ambitious youngsters. An extreme right-winger, he had been responsible for some of the terrifying pogroms of the Jews in Russia.

Princess Irina was the bait used to lure Rasputin to the lavish Moika Palace, home to the Yusupov family for generations. Prince Felix Yusupov faked the invitation for midnight of 29 December 1916, when he knew his wife was detained in the Crimea.

Rasputin must have been tempted beyond endurance as he received warning on the day before his death that a murder plot had been hatched. He chose to ignore it. He picked his clothes carefully for the meeting, dressing to thrill. A white silk blouse embroidered with cornflowers on top of lush, velvet, wide trousers and shiny boots. Around his waist was a dramatic red cord with dangling tassels.

Dr Lazovert donned the uniform of a chauffeur to accompany Yusupov to Rasputin's flat. Rasputin had been lying on the bed, contemplating the evening ahead, when the knock on the door signalled the start of the night's dreadful events. They drove around the back streets before pulling up at the grand Moika Palace. It was vital to elude the Okhrana, the Russian secret police, who kept watch over Rasputin.

Rasputin and Prince Felix made their way to a basement room that had been sumptuously decorated for the occasion. Princess Irina was entertaining friends upstairs and would be along shortly, explained a nervous Yusupov. Upstairs, his fellow killers kept themselves busy winding up the gramophone which played 'I'm a Yankee Doodle Dandy', the only record they possessed.

Yusupov offered his victim wine and cakes, both laced with devastating amounts of poison. Rasputin chose tea and biscuits. Increasingly nervous, Yusupov found to his horror that small talk was wearing thin. Rasputin was demanding to know where the princess was and why she had kept him waiting. Finally, in his agitation, the monk reached for a cake and munched it, then ate another. He had consumed generous quantities of poison – but nothing happened.

Yusupov was horrified. Once again he offered wine and this time the still unsuspecting visitor accepted, swigging generously from the poisoned chalice. He had another, but still showed no ill effects. Instead of collapsing, as they had planned, Rasputin strode up and down the room, seizing a guitar and asking Yusupov to sing and play for him.

Stunned by the unexpected turn of events, Yusupov strummed and crooned, appalled at the incredible stamina shown by his victim. Unable to stand the tension for a moment longer, he finally excused himself on the pretext of hurrying his wife upstairs and dashed to consult with his accomplices. Yusupov snatched a revolver and hid it behind his back, then rejoined Rasputin, who finally looked as if he was ailing. But a further glass of wine seemed to revive him. Yusupov felt he had no choice but to use the firearm. He invited Rasputin to inspect a beautiful crystal crucifix in the room and then shot him at point-blank range. Blood from the wound ran in a red river on to the white polar bear rug. Yusopov is said to have sexually assaulted the body after Rasputin reeled.

As Rasputin's savage roar subsided, the other four plotters rushed into the room babbling in excitement. Minutes later, they pronounced him dead. One produced a knife to castrate the man who had cuckolded so many Russian husbands. The severed penis was thrown across the room. It landed up in the possession of a maid, who kept it in a polished wooden box in her apartment in Paris as recently as 1968. Reportedly, it looked 'like a blackened, overripe banana, about a foot long'.

Three of the plotters then set off to act as decoy, posing as the trio who had left Rasputin's address three hours before now returning after a night's entertainment. Yusupov and Purishkevich remained, discussing the brave new world they were creating with the killing of one evil man.

Whether it was morbid curiosity or genuine unease, Yusupov was drawn back to examine the corpse. He felt for the pulse – there was nothing. But, as he watched, an eye began to twitch. Then the face came back to life before his eyes. In an instant, Rasputin was on his feet, bellowing and wrestling with a shocked Yusupov. The petrified prince fled, leaving a raging Rasputin with an epaulette from his uniform grasped firmly in his hand.

Alerted by the commotion, Purishkevich pursued Rasputin through a courtyard door and towards the gate. He too could hardly believe his eyes. There was Rasputin, whose body had lain inert on the cellar floor, screaming the words: 'Felix, Felix, I will tell everything to the Tsarina.' Purishkevich fired four shots, two of which hit their target. Rasputin was felled again. Then Yusupov, having armed himself with a heavy chain, stumbled on to the scene. Refusing to believe that his enemy was finally near death, he set about the groaning body with the chain, summoning the last remnants of strength he could muster. Finally, he fell unconscious alongside Rasputin and was carted off to bed.

The conspirators now regrouped and heard the astonishing tale of Rasputin's reincarnation. They wrapped the still warm body in a heavy blue curtain and made for the river. It took a mighty effort to heave the leaden cadaver over the wall of the bridge. Only when they heard the splash as it finally plunged into the water could they be sure that their victim was dead. In a final display of ineptitude, they forgot to encircle the body with chains which would have pinned it to the river bed. A sentry on duty nearby slept throughout.

There were mixed responses to the death. Peasants

rejoiced, uttering the old Russian saying, 'A dog's death for a dog'. In the higher echelons of society, there was a more muted reaction, although his supporters, particularly the Tsarina, were devastated. Those linked with the alleged killing had to be protected from the revenge planned by the outraged Rasputristry.

Rasputin's body was found on New Year's Day 1917, the day the Tsar returned to his capital to investigate the mystery. The dead monk's arm was frozen into an upright position as if he were giving the sign of the cross. A post-mortem revealed that he had been shot, possibly poisoned and was almost certainly alive when he went in to the water.

Under the direction of the griefstricken Empress, the body was embalmed and covered with flowers and icons. It was taken for a private funeral on land close to the royal palace at Tsarskoie-Selo. But it was to lie in peace for only a matter of months. Later that same year, the Royal Family was forced from the throne as revolution swept Russia. Soldiers supporting the uprising exhumed Rasputin's coffin and took it to the nearby Forest of Pargolovo. In a clearing they piled up pine logs, forced the top from the coffin and drew the putrefying corpse from its box with the aid of sticks. It went on to the logs where petrol turned it into a pyre so fierce that the flames burned for six hours. His ashes were buried under the snow. Intriguingly, the icon from the Tsarina that had been buried with him was removed and later turned up in an American auction.

Even more macabre was the fact that Rasputin had a premonition of his death and had forecast to the day when it would be. With this in mind, he had destroyed many of his personal papers, not for fear of embarrassing those he left behind, but to hide the extent of his illiteracy. He had even told his supporters that his body would not be left in peace after he was buried but would be consumed by fire. The Empress who had so loved the maniacal monk outlived him by only a few months. She died with the rest of her family as the Bolsheviks took a terrible revenge against years of Imperial excesses.

The episode which had Rasputin all but ruling Imperial Russia as it slid into a terminal decline still leaves questions unanswered today. No one knows if he made love to the statuesque Tsarina who was his devoted slave. And who can say whether he was a clever charlatan or a man with magical powers at the tips of his blackened fingers . . . ?

The German Vampires

He was only nine years old when he first felt the bloodlust. It was then that a perverted dog-catcher befriended him and initiated him into the 'pleasures' of bestiality and of torturing animals. The young Peter Kurten found that his greatest sexual kick could be derived from watching spurting blood and he would often slice off the heads of swans to drink his fill. The Vampire of Dusseldorf's reign of sadistic murder and sexual depravity had begun.

Within a year he had committed his first atrocity. He was playing with two other boys on a raft on the Rhine and, on a whim, decided that it would be fun to drown one of them. He pushed the helpless youngster, who couldn't swim, into the water and gleefully watched him flailing about, laughing at his cries for mercy. When the other boy dived in to try and save him, Kurten pushed him under the raft and held him below the surface until he, too, drowned.

At home there was no refuge from the culture of violence that was to dominate Kurten's life. He was one of thirteen children who lived in appalling poverty in a one-bedroomed apartment. His father was a drunken thug whose alcoholism was compounded by a mental problem. Kurten Senior would delight in beating the children and would sometimes

105

force his wife to have sex in front of them. He was eventually put behind bars for three years after committing incest with his thirteen-year-old daughter.

As a teenager, Peter Kurten continued to obtain his sex thrills from animals, stabbing them at the moment of orgasm to achieve heightened pleasure. Then, out of the blue, he began an affair with a prostitute almost twice his age. She was a confirmed masochist who took pleasure in the sexual abuse her new-found lover inflicted upon her. Suddenly, Kurten saw that the brutality with which he treated animals could easily be re-focused on his fellow human beings. His apprenticeship as sadist and torturer was complete.

A few months after this relationship began, Kurten was caught stealing and received a two-year prison sentence. This served only to reinforce a growing bitterness with the society around him and he would speak later of his anger at the prison conditions for young people. As the months behind bars passed, he retreated further into his depraved fantasy world. He even made sure he disobeyed prison regulations to get himself sentenced to solitary confinement. He regarded this as the perfect environment to conjure up his sick daydreams.

Later on he would tell a court exactly what these entailed:

I thought of myself causing accidents affecting thousands of people and invented a number of crazy fantasies such as smashing bridges and boring through bridge piers. Then I spun a number of fantasies with regard to bacilli which I might be able to introduce into the drinking water and so cause a great calamity.

I imagined myself using schools or orphanages for

the purpose, where I could carry out murders by giving away chocolate samples containing arsenic which I could have obtained through housebreaking. I derived the sort of pleasure from these visions that other people would get from thinking about a naked woman.

After leaving prison, Kurten decided that he would wage a personal vendetta against what he saw as the 'sick' society around him. He embarked on a series of arson attacks which, he later explained, coincided with his first urges to attack and kill . . .

When my desire for injuring people awoke, the love of setting fire to things awoke as well. The sight of the flames delighted me, but above all it was the excitement of the attempts to extinguish the fire and the agitation of those who saw their property being destroyed.

His first attempted murder took place in the woods at Grafenburg, Dusseldorf. Kurten beat a girl severely before and during intercourse then left her half dead on the ground. No body was ever found and the poor victim probably dragged herself home, too terrified to report the fate she had suffered.

Then, on 25 May 1913, the Dusseldorf area was shaken by the worst murder in living memory. An eight-year-old girl, Christine Klein, was found dead in bed. Her throat had been cut and she had been raped. The finger of suspicion pointed at her uncle, who was arrested and tried but acquitted, unsurprisingly, for lack of evidence. The poor man remained dogged by the shame of what happened till he died on the killing fields of the Great War.

The truth behind little Christine's death would remain

hidden for seventeen years. In the end it was Peter Kurten himself who, in clipped, matter-of-fact tones, told his trial judge and jury what really happened.

> I had been stealing, specializing in public bars or inns where the owners lived on the floor above. In a room above an inn at Cologne-Mulheim I discovered a child asleep. Her head was facing the window. I seized it with my left hand and strangled her for about a minute and a half. The child woke up and struggled but lost consciousness.
>
> I had a small but sharp pocket knife with me and I held the child's head and cut her throat. I heard the blood spurt and drip on the mat beside the bed ... The whole thing lasted about three minutes, then I locked the door again and went home to Dusseldorf. Next day I went back to Mulheim. There is a cafe opposite the Klein's place and I sat there and drank a glass of beer, and read all about the murder in the papers. People were talking about it all around me. All this amount of horror and indignation did me good.

With his sickening tendencies, one might have thought that Kurten would relish the chance of going to war and spilling the blood of the Kaiser's enemies. In fact, his army career lasted barely a day before he deserted. He spent the entire conflict in jail for that and other petty criminal offences.

On his release in 1921, Kurten portrayed himself for a while as a good, hard-working German. He married a prostitute – though his method of getting her to the altar was by a threat to kill her rather than any romantic gesture – and took gainful employment as a moulder in a factory. To many he appeared entirely respectable. He was an active trade unionist, a popular figure at parties and a charmer among the ladies. Some noted that he was, perhaps, a little vain but he could be forgiven that.

In 1925, Kurten and his wife moved into the centre of Dusseldorf and once more the lust for blood descended upon him. By now, unknown to his wife, he was enjoying regular flings with a string of mistresses. The women concerned found that they had taken on a demanding lover, a man who combined a sinister cocktail of sex and sadism in a way none had ever experienced before. All of them kept his secret, perhaps too afraid of the revenge he might seek.

They were right to be worried. Kurten's idea of a sexual kick was to stab his mistresses with a knife or scissors and achieve orgasm as he watched their blood pouring out. Soon he switched his blood lust to complete strangers, often drinking the blood of those he killed or injured. In one case he sated himself by pressing his lips to the throat arteries of a victim, in another he drank from a wound on the side of a girl's head. He would even lick blood off their hands and claimed that during one frenzied attack he drank so much that he was sick.

By the mid-summer of 1929, the Dusseldorf police realized that they were dealing with a major serial killer and sexual deviant. The man clearly acted like a mad vampire, but he was also clever. He made sure he didn't stick to the same districts and was careful to vary the style of his attacks to ensure that he kept one step ahead of the detectives hunting him. The tactic worked well. Police files linked forty-six 'crimes of deviancy', including four murders. Yet they had not the faintest clue as to the perpetrator's identity.

By now, Dusseldorf was a city gripped by fear. Most

people were long past the arguments over whether vampires existed. They had seen the evidence with their own eyes and were taking no chances. Children were scolded if they dared skip off alone, women were escorted everywhere by their menfolk, and by nightfall most families preferred to stay safe indoors rather than venture on to the narrow, dimly lit streets.

So it was on the evening of 23 August 1929. But, despite the atmosphere of tension, hundreds of people did brave the night to attend one of the highlight of the city's year: the annual fair in the Flehe suburb. They felt there was safety in numbers and the bright lights, military music, wurst stalls and beer kellers all helped to induce a feeling of warm harmony. It was far from the traditional stalking ground of vampires – but that didn't worry Peter Kurten. Over the next twelve hours he indulged in an orgy of killing and sadism beyond even the worst fears of the police.

Just before 10.30 p.m., two foster sisters, Gertrude Hamacher, aged five, and Louise Lenzen, fourteen, took a last look at the fair and headed home through some nearby allotments. They didn't see the shadowy figure who slipped from behind a row of bean sticks and followed them. Then Louise heard a gentle voice behind her and turned to see who it could be. 'Oh dear,' said the man 'I've forgotten to buy some cigarettes. Look, would you be very kind and go to one of the booths and get some for me? I'll look after the little girl.'

Louise took the proffered money and ran back to the fairground. Wordlessly, the stranger picked little Gertrude up and bundled her behind the beanpoles where she was strangled expertly, with no chance to scream for help. He then slashed her throat with a Bavarian knife. When Louise returned and handed over the cigarettes she was also manhandled into the allotments. In terror she screamed 'Mama, Mama' but her words floated away in the music still welling up from the fairground. Like her sister, she died of strangulation. Her throat was cut purely to relieve Kurten's unspeakable sexual desires.

The following morning, 26-year-old servant girl Gertrude Schulte, met a man who offered to take her to the nearby Neuss fair. Feeling lonely, she foolishly agreed. The man, who called himself Fritz Baumgart, suggested they take a stroll through the woods. A few minutes later he roughly pulled her towards him and tried to have sex. She screamed 'I'd rather die', only to hear her gleeful attacker snap back 'Well, die then.' With that he began stabbing her in the neck and shoulders with a knife and gave one final thrust which snapped off the blade, leaving it embedded in her back. 'Now,' said the monster coldly 'you can die.' Despite her agonies and appalling injuries Gertrude was saved. A rambler heard her cries and called in police and an ambulance. But by then Peter Kurten had vanished.

By now the vampire tendencies were running wild in Kurten's twisted psyche. On one day, within the space of thirty minutes, he attacked and wounded an 18-year-old girl, a 37-year-old woman and a 30-year-old man. He exchanged his Bavarian dagger for a slimmer, sharper blade, then moved on to a cudgel which he used to hammer two more servant girls to their deaths. The only thing that linked the attacks was their unspeakable brutality. One five-year-old victim, Gertrude Albermann, was found to have thirty-six separate wounds on her little body.

Gertrude was the last of the Dusseldorf Vampire's murder victims though the frenzied assaults continued in the city throughout the winter. By now reports of the bloodletting were being devoured across Germany; in the city itself some of the wealthier occupants even decided to leave for country retreats until the monster was caught. Most had no such option. Girls like Maria Budlick, a 21-year-old maidservant, came to Dusseldorf because they were desperate to find work. Maria knew there was a sex fiend at large. She never dreamed she would meet him so quickly.

On 14 May 1930, she stepped off a train and strode along the platform in Dusseldorf central station. A kindly-looking man offered to guide her to the nearest women's hostel and she was content to follow him. But as they entered the Volksgarten Park, doubts began to creep into Maria's mind. She was a stranger in a strange city. Her guide could be a robber or rapist . . . or even the Vampire himself. She made up her mind and told the man she would not walk through the trees with him. He argued with her heatedly, but it was no good. She would not be swayed and she was growing more unsure with every word he uttered.

Suddenly another voice came out of the shadows: 'Hello, is everything all right?' Maria almost wept with relief. As her disgruntled escort left she turned to the gentleman who had come to her aid, relief etched into her smile. Peter Kurten smiled back and invited her to accompany him home for a glass of milk and a ham sandwich.

After the meal, Kurten insisted on escorting her personally to the hostel. As they walked through the Grafenburg Woods to the north of the city she discovered to her horror his real motives. Without warning he grabbed her by the throat, forced her up against a tree and tried to rape her. Maria struggled but she was hopelessly at his mercy. Then, as she felt herself slipping into unconsciousness he suddenly released his grip and hissed into her ear: 'Do you remember where I live, in case you ever need my help again?' Maria managed to sob out a single word: 'No'. It probably saved her life.

Kurten left and Maria managed to stagger out of the woods and back into the city. Incredibly, she did not contact the police but instead wrote a letter to a friend in her home town of Cologne, recounting her dreadful experience. She was probably still in a state of shock, so much so that she addressed the envelope incorrectly. The people of Dusseldorf would soon have good reason to give thanks for that simple mistake.

Within a few days the letter found its way back to Cologne Post Office and was opened so that it could be returned to its sender. The official responsible read the contents and immediately realized the importance of what Maria was saying. He contacted the police and the following day a bewildered and frightened Maria was being gently asked all about her ordeal by a detective. She did well.

She had lied to Kurten about remembering his address and now she showed no hesitation in recalling that it was somewhere in Mettmannerstrasse. Under police escort, she went back there and thought she could identify the house as No. 71. While the plain-clothes men waited outside, she spoke to the landlady and asked if a 'fair-haired, rather sedate man' lived there. The woman beckoned her to follow upstairs to the fourth floor, unlocked a door, and Maria Budlick saw the room in which she had enjoyed her glass of milk and ham sandwich.

The final proof was only seconds away. She walked back downstairs – to be confronted by the face that haunted her every waking moment. Kurten looked stunned, but held his nerve long enough to continue into his room and leave again almost as quickly. Maria, her mind reeling now, managed to run outside and call to the plain-clothes men: 'That's the man who assaulted me in the woods. His name is Peter Kurten.'

At this point there was still no hard evidence to nail Kurten as the Vampire of Dusseldorf. But he realized he had made a bad mistake in letting Maria go free and knew his time would soon be up.

Far from panicking, Kurten strolled to the restaurant where his wife worked and invited her to join him for a meal. As the food lay in front of them he calmly informed her: 'I am the man sought by the police. I am the monster of Dusseldorf.' Frau Kurten didn't touch the dinner but the confession left Kurten unfazed. After eating his own meal he heartily tucked in to hers.

On the morning of 24 May 1930, Frau Kurten called at her local police station to tell all she knew. She informed detectives that she had arranged to meet her husband at 3 p.m. outside St Rochus Church. Plain-clothes officers were briefed and armed, and at the appointed time Kurten found himself surrounded by four of them pointing pistols at his chest. His response was typical. With a broad smile he assured the men: 'There is no need to be afraid.'

When the trial opened on 13 April 1931, Kurten attracted the kind of public attention now reserved for pop stars. Thousands pushed and shoved around the converted drill hall of the Dusseldorf police headquarters to catch a glimpse of the fiend who had terrorized the streets. What they saw amazed them. This was no half-man, half-beast, such as the media had led them to believe. He looked a normal, intelligent, gentle character. A doctor, perhaps, or civil servant. His hair was meticulously groomed into a loose parting, he had the whiff of a subtle cologne about him and in his well-cut suit and mirror-bright shoes he looked every inch the perfect gentleman.

Except that he had admitted to sixty-eight horrible crimes, including nine murders and seven attempted murders. On each of those sixteen victims he had let loose his vampire urges and the court was taking no chances. Throughout his trial Kurten was kept under armed guard, surrounded by a shoulder-high wooden cage.

The prosecution barely need have appeared in court. Kurten's ghoulish account of his own atrocities, delivered in quiet, modulated tones, damned him more effectively than any barrister could. It was left to the Vampire's hard-pressed defending counsel, Dr Wehner, to persuade the jury that his client was mad and so save him from the guillotine. It was a near hopeless task, given that the nation's most distinguished psychiatrists had already pronounced him fully sane. This extract from the court proceedings in which Wehner cross-examined psychiatrist Professor Sioli shows just how fragile the defence case was.

WEHNER: Kurten is the king of sexual delinquents because he unites nearly all perversions in one person. Can that not change your views about insanity? Is it possible for the Kurten case to persuade psychiatry to adopt another opinion?

SIOLI: No.

WEHNER: That is the dreadful thing. The man Kurten is a riddle to me. I cannot solve it. The criminal Haarman only killed men. Landrau only women, Grossmann only women, but Kurten killed men, women, children and animals, killed anything he found.

SIOLI: And was at the same time a clever man and quite a nice one.

In the moments before the jury retired, Kurten was allowed to make a statement. For a while he droned on about his contempt for abortionists and admitted his own crimes could not be excused. Yet in the same breath he tried a last-ditch attempt at sympathy. 'The real reason for my conviction is that there comes a time in the life of every criminal when he can go no further,' he said. 'And this spiritual collapse is what I experienced. But I do feel I must make one statement: Some of my victims made things very easy for me. Manhunting on the part of women today has taken on such forms that . . .' He never finished the sentence. The presiding judge, Dr Rose, outraged at Kurten's pompous self-righteousness, hammered his desk and shouted: 'Stop these remarks.'

It was more than a year later that Kurten at last walked to the guillotine built in the yard of Klingelputz Prison. That evening, 1 July 1932, he gobbled down his last meal of veal, fried potatoes and white wine and spent his final moments in deep conversation with the prison psychiatrist instructed to attend him as he awaited his doom. 'Tell me,' Kurten asked the doctor casually, 'after my head has been chopped off, will I still be able to hear, at least for a moment, the sound of my own blood gushing from the stump of my neck?'

The poor man could only stare back incredulously as Kurten added: 'That would be the pleasure to end all pleasures.'

While Kurten was unusual in his vampire-like habits, his atrocities were by no means unique. Another serial murderer with a liking for human flesh was operating in Germany at the very time Kurten's sadistic desires were taking root. This man, Fritz Haarmann, who was mentioned in the Kurten trial above, knew nothing of the Dusseldorf Vampire. His stalking ground was Hanover. And his prey was young boys – especially if they were homeless with no family to report them missing.

In the spring of 1924, Hanover found itself sucked in to the kind of werewolf scare that should have died out in the Middle Ages. It started with housewives complaining about cuts of meat they had bought. The joints looked, smelled and tasted odd, the women said. There were rumours that a vampire or werewolf was on the loose. Could the meat possibly be human flesh? The police were quick to crush such rumours. Offending joints were pronounced to be pork and senior officers blamed the scare on 'mass public hysteria'.

Then, on 17 May, children found a human skull on the banks of the River Leine. It was the first of many (one pathologist later claimed the river had washed up the remains of at least twenty-seven dismembered murder victims) yet at this stage police still did not want to accept publicly what most of Hanover's frightened citizenry believed as fact. Namely that a serial murderer was on the loose. Incredibly, detectives put out a statement to the press claiming that the bones found had been placed near the river by medical students as a sick prank.

In their desire to quell public anxiety, police chiefs were guilty of a huge misjudgement. But although they should have realized they were dealing with a ruthless sex killer, they could not have known the appalling depravity with which he committed his crimes. For Fritz Haarmann liked to seduce or rape his boy victims before despatching them, vampire style, with a savage bite to their throats.

Haarmann, like Kurten, came from a difficult family background. He adored his mother, who became an invalid soon after he was born, but loathed his father, a mean and moody locomotive stoker nicknamed 'Sulky Olle'. Olle Haarmann tried to get his boy committed to an asylum on the grounds that he had a feeble mind. The doctors refused, saying he was not mentally ill. Rejected by his father, young Fritz soon found himself wandering around Germany getting involved in petty crime. He was seen by other crooks as something of a fat simpleton who tried hard to please. And he got a reputation among police for coming quietly when arrested, often with a laugh on his lips.

In 1918 Haarmann completed a five-year jail term to find himself thrown into the chaos of post-war Germany. He quickly realized that he had his own niche in this sinister, twilight world of villains and con-men, black marketeers and swindlers. He found himself drawn more and more to Hanover's central station to watch the drifters arrive, many of them young and vulnerable and desperate to see a friendly face. Haarmann was that face. He would be down there every night, offering sweets, cigarettes and chocolate to the new arrivals. The relief and gratitude would shine out from their eyes as he offered them shelter and a mattress for the night.

Haarmann was good at lending an ear to these boys, some as young as twelve years old. By listening to their stories he would win their confidence and soon even the welfare workers at the station began to see him as one of their team. Police knew about his underworld and black market connections, but Haarmann convinced detectives that he could be a useful informer. Consequently, his activities as fence and petty thief were left undisturbed while he provided his friends in the police with intelligence on planned robberies and hideouts. As his personal wealth increased, he set himself up as a second-hand clothes dealer and meat hawker. Housewives would come running to buy his keenly priced joints and in an economy still reeling from the war, he got a reputation for always having plenty of stock.

When, in September 1918, the parents of seventeen-year-old Friedel Rothe reported that he had gone missing, detectives did not overly exert themselves. This sort of thing happened all the time. Even when an informer mentioned he had seen someone answering Rothe's description in a billiards room with Haarmann, the officers didn't get excited. They did not even want to question their friend Fritz, though they finally agreed to do so.

Six years later, during the Hanover Vampire's trial, Haarmann would boast proudly: 'When the police examined my room, the head of the boy Friedel was lying wrapped in newspaper behind the oven.'

That close shave served only to convince Haarmann that he was unstoppable. The following year he teamed up with an accomplice, homosexual Hans Grans, aged twenty. Grans regarded himself as Haarmann's social superior, and was happy to let everybody know it. Slowly he began to wield a terrible influence on Haarmann, once even instructing him to murder a boy 'because I like the clothes he's wearing'.

The two men lived in a sidestreet called Rothe Reihe (Red Row) close to the River Leine. They became callously casual about their grisly deeds, often carting around buckets of blood in front of neighbours and chopping up bodies so that everyone could hear. But still Haarmann's cover remained intact. He was a butcher. His behaviour, thought the locals, was entirely normal.

Yet the noose was closing. Newspapers described

Hanover as a town to which hundreds of youngsters would gravitate . . . and vanish. One writer even suggested 600 people had disappeared in the city inside a year. The findings of the skull and the bones by the river at last spurred the police into action. Underworld sources were questioned at length and runaways were asked to identify anyone who had tried to befriend them. More and more, the finger of suspicion began to point at Haarmann.

At last detectives decided to have him watched. On the night of 22 June 1924, Haarmann was on his usual beat in the station when he decided to accost a teenager called Fromm. They quarrelled, began to fight, and the police moved in to arrest the man they knew as one of their best 'grasses'. A search of his flat revealed blood-splattered walls and heaps of clothes of varying sizes. Haarmann tried to stay calm. 'Of course,' he told his interrogators, 'what do you expect? I am a butcher and I trade in second-hand clothes.'

Parents of the missing children were invited to the flat to look at the clothes. One mother couldn't see anything she recognized . . . until she spotted the son of Haarmann's land-lady. He was wearing the coat that used to belong to her boy. The evidence was now overwhelming and Haarmann knew it. He broke down and confessed everything.

The trial of Haarmann and Grans began on 4 December 1924. They were jointly charged with the murders of 27 boys aged between 12 and 18 and the case became the biggest news story in Europe.

Haarmann showed glimpses of his callous ways right from the start. He was shown pictures of his victims and asked if he had been responsible for their deaths. 'Yes, that might well be,' he would say of one photo. 'I'm not sure about that one,' he would claim occasionally. But when a court official held up a picture of young Hermann Wolf, Haarmann turned scathingly on the boy's distraught father, who was sitting in court: 'I should never have looked twice at such an ugly youngster as, according to his photograph, your son must have been. You say your boy had not even a shirt to his name and that his socks were tied on to his feet with string! Deuce take it, you should have been ashamed to let him go about like that. There's plenty of rubbish like him around. Think what you're saying man. Such a fellow would have been far beneath my notice.'

One court reporter filed this moving account of the scenes as Haarmann stood in the dock:

Nearly 200 witnesses had to appear in the box, mostly parents of the unfortunate youths. There were scenes of painful intensity as a poor father or mother would recognize some fragment or other of the clothing or belongings of their murdered son. Here it was a handkerchief, there a pair of braces, and again a greasy coat, soiled almost beyond recognition, that was shown to the relatives and to Haarmann. And with the quivering nostrils of a hound snuffling his prey, as if he were scenting rather than seeing the things displayed, did he admit at once that he knew them.

At one point an exchange between the prosecution counsel and Haarmann filled the courtroom with an electric tension . . .

COUNSEL: How many victims did you kill altogether?
HAARMANN: It might be thirty, it might be forty. I really can't remember the exact number.
COUNSEL: How did you kill your victims?

HAARMANN: I bit them through their throats.

Damned out of his own mouth the Vampire of Hanover was found guilty on 19 December 1924. His last words to the court were screamed with a ferocity that belied the psychiatrists' insistence that he was sane:

Do you think I enjoy killing people? I was ill for eight days after the first time. Condemn me to death. I ask only for justice. I am not mad. It is true I often get into a state when I do not know what I am doing, but that is not madness. Make it short, make it soon. Deliver me from this life, which is a torment. I will not petition for mercy, nor will I appeal. I want to pass just one more merry evening in my cell with coffee, cheese and cigars, after which I will curse my father and go to my execution as if it were a wedding.

Fritz Haarmann's last wishes were granted. He was beheaded the next day . . . and Hanover rejoiced.

The Andes Plane Crash

The Andes is a harsh, unforgiving mountain range where giant snowy peaks fall away to rocky gullies then climb up, crevice by crag, to cloud-scraping heights. When a plane with forty-five passengers aboard crashed somewhere in the region, no one imagined there would be survivors. But there were sixteen who not only survived the impact but a further ten weeks camping out in the mountains. And they stayed alive by resorting to the unimaginable – eating the bodies of their friends.

As hunger took hold and rescue seemed impossible, the sixteen realized their only chance was to eat human flesh. With each passing day they pulled dead bodies out of the snow to carve off hunks of fatted skin. When corpses became more scarce, they scavenged from carcasses and ate brains, tongues, sinews, livers and kidneys. Even lungs were sliced up for a meal.

The human meat was mainly eaten raw. Occasionally it was cooked. Many at first found themselves unable to dine on the dead knowing the food was once a companion who had been sitting just yards away when calamity struck. But even the most squeamish ended up eating like cannibals – because without gorging on the dead, death was certain. After a few days, most were able to hack up the human bodies and scoff their different parts without a second thought.

The gruesome tale began to unfold at dawn on 12 October 1972 at Carrasco, Uruguay. This small country with a population of less than three million lies between Argentina and the foot of Brazil. With rampant inflation and a burgeoning terrorist movement, the Spanish-speaking South American state had its fair share of problems in the 1970s. But it was no banana republic and had a growing army of middle-class, in addition to the long-established beef and dairy farmers. It was from this wealthy, well-educated bracket that many on the ill-fated flight were drawn.

The aircraft, an American-built Fairchild F-227, had been chartered from the Uruguayan Air Force for a rugby team trip to Chile. The amateur team were from the Old Christians' Club, formed by ex-pupils of a Catholic college in Uruguay's capital, Montevideo, which was run by Irish priests who all but introduced the sport to the country. The shamrock-wearing players, once the envy of the country, were now fighting to find form again.

The passenger list included more than just the fit, burly young men who made up the team. There were relatives, friends and a complete stranger on the flight, as well as five crew. At the controls when the plane took off at 8.05 a.m. was Air Force pilot Colonel Cesar Ferradas, a veteran of the trans-Andes route, which is notorious for the number of lives it has claimed. The plane headed off across Argentina, and eventually the wall of mountains that is the Andes were in sight.

But the weather was against them. The Andes stretch the length of the continent from the Caribbean virtually to Cape Horn, some 4,000 miles. In the southerly section, where the Fairchild was crossing, the peaks are most consistently high – Ice Age glaciers which moulded the landscape left no fewer than fifty peaks above 20,000 feet on the border of Argentina and Chile.

Mindful of the extreme dangers of flying over the Andes, where air currents can tug a plane out of control, pilot Ferradas decided to land in the Argentine town of Mendoza. The passengers scattered to find hotels for the night. Ferradas and his co-pilot, Lieutenant Dante Hector Lagurara, considered the possibilities. Given the improving weather conditions, they could attempt an early afternoon crossing of the Andes, albeit at a treacherous time of day when the air currents swirled dangerously. Or, since military regulations meant they would soon outstay their welcome in Argentina, they could abandon the trip altogether. This would not only incur the wrath of the rugby lads but also lose valuable revenue for the Air Force.

They decided to continue. After take-off on Friday the 13th, the aircraft battled against strong headwinds across the mountain ranges. Lagurara was at the controls in regular touch with air traffic control at Santiago, Chile, radioing what he decided was their correct position. Air traffic control gave him permission to prepare for landing by dropping height.

But Lagurara's navigation was faulty. Speeding through the thick, soupy clouds, he had no idea how badly awry his estimates were until they were given the go-ahead for a descent – and then it was too late. The passengers were being bumped and jerked as the plane hit air pockets and sharp winds, plummeting out of the mountain cloud cover. As the grey mist cleared, the crew realized to their horror they were only feet away from the mountainside. Back in the passenger section, survivor Eduardo Strauch recalled:

'All the boys were shouting and throwing balls around inside the cabin. I was looking out of the window because I had noticed the mountains were very near and I didn't think that was right.'

As all the passengers realized the impending danger, some assumed the crash position in their seats, others simply prayed. The lurching Fairchild struggled to climb – but the desperate effort failed. The right-hand wing was sheared off as it scraped the mountain and in turn it sliced off the tail section of the plane.

The first five victims were sucked out into the snowy wastes. Meanwhile, the left wing broke off, leaving the cigar-shaped fuselage helplessly on course for a crash. But the expected smash never came. The plane flopped down on to its belly and slid down a slope before coming to a halt in an icy gorge.

Amid the pain and panic, survivors heroically pulled at trapped bodies in a bid to save their friends. Shaken but unhurt was team captain Marcelo Perez who, along with medical students Gustavo Zerbino and Roberto Canessa, set about saving survivors.

Some clambered out of the rear of the plane to see passenger Carlos Valeta careering down the mountainside, apparently unable to see the wreckage of the aircraft or the frantically waving survivors. He lost his footing in the thigh-deep snow and plunged down the mountain out of sight.

Three middle-aged passengers died instantly. They were husband and wife Dr and Señora Nicola. The other was Eugenia Parrado, whose daughter Susana lay with blood pouring from a head wound and whose son Nando was unconscious and apparently close to death. Pilot Ferradas was also killed. Lagurara was alive, but only just, trapped in his cabin and wailing in agony. It was a day before the screams subsided as he died.

Many had crushed limbs. One of the survivors, Enrique Platero, was walking around with a steel tube sticking out of his stomach. As Zerbino tugged out the tube, a sizeable length of intestine came out with it. On the barked instructions of medical student Zerbino, Platero simply tied up his shirt to hide the gaping wound. The shock of the accident took its toll, as did altitude sickness and concussion, which left many unable to function properly.

Although the plane went down in the afternoon, it soon became clear exactly what those left alive were up against. The wreckage, although hemmed in by mountains, was open to the elements. Snow began to fall and it wasn't long before daylight faded, leaving them subject to appallingly cold conditions with temperatures of around minus 40°C.

In cramped conditions, with the screams and moans of the injured filling the air, the thirty-two survivors prepared to spend their first night on the mountain. For sustenance there were liberal amounts of wine bought at the unscheduled stop in Mendoza. Confident that rescue services would reach them before long, the frozen, frightened bunch took huge slugs of alcohol.

Three more people died in the night. The two medical students, with no more than thirty months' training between them, realized how pitifully inadequate their skills were in the face of such devastation. Now they all took a more organized view of supplies. Apart from the wine, now dwindling in supply, there was a bottle of whisky, one of brandy and one of crème de menthe. For food, they had eight chocolate bars, five bars of nougat, toffees, dates, plums and a packet of biscuits, two tins of mussels, some salted almonds and three jars of jam. With extensive snow

127

cover there was no sign of edible plants growing on the mountain. It was clear that without an immediate rescue food would be in short supply.

Water was just as much of a problem. There was precious little heat from the sun to melt down the acres of snow into water and it was never enough. So they had to force snow into their mouths through lips which rapidly became blistered and sore. Afterwards, they likened it to thrusting a burning poker on to their tongues. But the ache in their empty bellies began to obsess them. Initially, no one mentioned the ready supply of meals lying clothed and half-buried in the snow around the plane: the bodies of the dead travellers.

Nando Parrado, who had first been thought to be fatally injured, came round from his coma and vowed to escape the torment of the peaks. When he voiced his intention of walking to civilization, the others told him he would starve. 'Then I'll cut meat from one of the pilots – after all, they got us into this mess,' he retorted, before going back to nurse his worsening sister, Susana.

Nobody condemned him for his barbarous thoughts, nor did anyone lick their lips in hunger. At this stage, the survivors were concerned at why a rescue was taking so long when they had already seen two planes flying overhead. Neither, it transpired later, had spotted them. Their morale was sent plunging to new depths when they discovered, on a rigged-up radio set, that the search for the crashed plane had been abandoned. If they were going to live, it would be by their own efforts alone.

After ten days without food, the twenty-nine survivors were fainting with hunger and their paltry rations were running low. They fantasized about their favourite meals: sumptuous cakes, sweets and tasty traditional dishes. Some began to mention the unmentionable. Could they eat the bodies of their dead friends? Adolfo Strauch said afterwards, 'The most awful thought came into my head and I didn't know if I dared say it. I whispered to my cousin: "I think we are going to have to eat the bodies or we are never going to get out of here." I wanted to see if he thought I was off my head but he replied he had been thinking the same.'

As the murmured idea became planted in each of their minds, they decided to call a meeting to debate it. They were strict Catholics. How could they eat human flesh? Yet their rigid religious values actually helped in their dilemma. Survivor Pancho Delgado explained: 'If Jesus had shared flesh and blood with His apostles at the last supper, it was a sign we should do the same – take the flesh and blood as an intimate communion between us.'

Canessa argued Yes, why not? They would soon be so weak they would be unable to survive, given the bitter conditions. 'It was horrible,' he said later. 'There are your dead friends and you say, why is this happening to me? Why is life so tough? But you think this is the only way. If you don't do it, would someone else do it to you?' The reasoning that swayed many towards the distasteful act was that, if they themselves had perished, they would wish to be eaten so that their friends could live.

Finally, Canessa left the shelter of the plane, armed himself with some broken glass and sliced at a bared buttock. He cut twenty slithers of flesh and dried them in the sun before challenging his comrades to help themselves. They watched as he sampled the raw flesh. He prayed as he slipped the first morsel past his lips. The taboo was broken. Nineteen others followed his example while four remained firmly in the plane. Daniel Fernandez explained, 'I felt disgusted by the first mouthful, it wasn't

129

easy. It was the human flesh of a friend. I was eating a friend. I didn't know who it was but that was what I was doing. It was so difficult.'

Try as he might, Coche Inciarte felt unable to eat the flesh of others he had known. 'I couldn't swallow. What I did manage to get down I threw up again. It was a physical rejection. My body rejected it and I vomited. It was a waste. I had to say to myself, don't be stupid; eat or you will die.' He finally consoled himself with the thought that it was a miracle that anyone had survived the crash and it would be absurd to turn their back on that miracle by starving themselves to death.

The priority was then to cover the corpses with snow to keep them fresh for eating. There was little by way of fuel but they did try roasting the flesh on a fire made from broken crates. They discovered the taste of the meat improved immensely, giving it a texture like beef. It made the ordeal of eating human flesh much more tolerable – even though it crossed their minds that some nutritional value would be lost through cooking.

Two of the boys who at first refused meat eventually changed their minds. Although far from happy at the prospect of cannibalism, they were persuaded of its merits when they witnessed the increased health and strength in their meat-eating companions. Finally, just two were surviving on the meagre rations recovered from the luggage in the crashed plane. Married couple Liliana and Javier Methol, intending to have a second honeymoon, held out despite pressure from the rest to succumb. They busily made plans for the future with their three children safely back home. But the couple grew weaker as the rugby players grew stronger.

It wasn't long before the stark choice of death or eating

meat became apparent. They chose life by consuming flesh. And they joined the others in making a pact ... if any among them died, then they agreed that their comrades should banquet on their bodies.

But the horror was far from over. Seventeen days after the first disaster came tragedy number two. After night fell and while many slept, a deadly avalanche engulfed the carcass of the plane. The only warning was an ominous rumble. No one had time to act. The snow swept through the makeshift wall of seats painstakingly built by the young men to shield themselves from the cold. It filled the cavity of the plane to within two feet of the ceiling.

One of the rugby players, Rob Harley, had jumped up on hearing the rush of snow and escaped the paralysing tide. He quickly burrowed to free as many of his pals as he could. With their faces smothered, the youngsters lay with their lungs bursting pinned down by the weight of ice-encrusted snow. Working swiftly, Harley brushed snow from as many faces as he could find. Several boys found they could force themselves to freedom with their first gulps of air. But despite the heroic efforts, eight more died in the avalanche, including team captain Perez and Liliana Methol. Now only nineteen were left alive. And three more were to perish in the achingly long weeks before they were rescued.

The weather was so poor they were unable to leave the freezing, sodden plane for days. They had no option but to carve off slices of wet flesh from those eight bodies inside the fuselage to abate their hunger. Only days before, the body that became their meal had been walking, talking and longing for escape. It was almost more than they could bear.

The survivors forced themselves to look ahead. They planned a trek to Chile to seek help. They would undertake

131

the expedition as soon as the weather improved. But waiting for the change in the weather became an agony in itself. They knew it was pointless setting off until the first thaw of spring. But each day was an endurance test. Unified though the group was, with bonds being forged that were to last for decades, there were daily niggles which they could barely contain.

The weather did begin to get warm for a few hours at midday but the biting cold was still an enemy. They fell into a routine of searching out bodies, lining them up in an outdoor larder and settling down to wait. Those victims who were most loved by the survivors would be the last to be eaten, they all agreed. That meant Javier Methol would not be forced to eat his wife or witness the others doing so. This was the grim reality they were now facing.

By now, they were accustomed to eating flesh. Gustavo Zerbino explained, 'When you are 11,000 feet up with no animals, no trees, your mind changes. What seems impossible becomes acceptable. I kept thinking: "I need to do it, I need to do it." And then I did it. Terrible for a day or two but then it became normal. But we are not cannibals. Cannibals kill to eat. We ate to live. And we joked. We talked about going for pizzas. We imagined glorious meals. We described favourite restaurants. Anything for hope.'

After a few trials, the expedition team was chosen. All hopes were pinned on the physical and mental fitness of the strongest: Nando Parrado, Roberto Canessa and Antonio Vizintin. To prepare, they were given extra meat and the best, most comfortable places in the plane at night.

Sixty days after the crash, the trio set out amid the waves and cheers of their companions. Ahead of them was a climb that would have daunted even an experienced, well-

In April 1935 a Tiger shark regurgitated a human arm, sparking a bizarre murder mystery. Sydney police search Gunnamatta Bay where 'Sharky' was caught.

The Rev. Jim Jones, architect of the grisly Jonestown Massacre.

Donald Neilson, hunted by police who knew him only as the Black Panther.

Hooded horror... how the Black Panther went in search of victims.

Lesley Whittle, the teenage heiress who was kidnapped and chained deep in an underground prison.

One of the shafts leading to the underground maze where Lesley Whittle's body was found.

Berkeley Square in the 1860s: the Mayfair home of ghosts and ghouls.

The remains of Dr John Irving Bentley, of Pennsylvania, found in his bathroom in 1966.

Katie Beers was chained in a tiny underground cell for sixteen days.

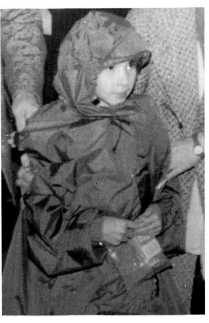

John Esposito, the family friend who became a sadistic abductor.

'Mad monk' Rasputin held the Tsarina's court in his mystic stranglehold.

The dapper Peter Kurten of Dusseldorf, who 'united all perversions'. *(Popperfoto)*

Movie recreation of an airliner crash in the Andes – where the survivors turned to cannibalism to live.

Don Nichols and his son Dan, the Montana mountain men.

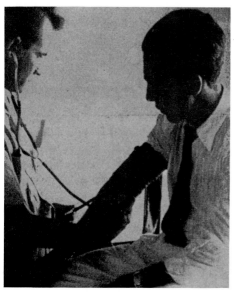

Antonio Villas Boas exhibited symptoms suggesting radiation poisoning after his abduction by aliens. *(Mary Evans Picture Library)*

Dennis Nilsen lured young men to his home, murdered them, then lay with their bodies to re-enact his sick fantasies.

Accused of witchcraft; in this case, the hysteria was in Salem, USA. *(Mary Evans Picture Library)*

In 1991 the soft-spoken American Jeffrey Dahmer was revealed as a real-life 'Hannibal the Cannibal'.

equipped mountaineer. Here were three raggle-taggle climbers dressed in layers of clothes taken from the dead to protect them from the cold and football boots shielded by plastic bags. Ahead of them lay a 13,000-foot peak. Each carried rugby socks packed with flesh to last them a week. The trio knew if they did not break out of the mountains, everyone would be doomed. So thoughts of failure were banished. However, the ascent was harder than they could have imagined. Snow made distances deceptive. They climbed relentlessly on the first day and still found themselves little more than half way up the treacherous slope.

They painfully scaled the mountain in three days, to be rewarded by a breathtaking panorama at the summit. But with that wonderful view came the realization that the lush green fields of Chile were not just on the other side, as they had thought. There would be many days' hard trekking before they re-entered charted territory. Later, Nando Parrado described the decision about whether to go on or give up as the hardest he has ever taken.

At the summit, the trio realized that one of their number would have to return if the remaining two were to have a chance of making it at all. Vizintin agreed to go back to the wreckage so that the others could have his meat supply. Canessa and Parrado trudged forward. The former, felled by stomach cramps, blisters and hideous tiredness, begged to stop. Nando goaded him on.

Back at the plane, the high spirits at the departure of the expedition evaporated as they witnessed the frustratingly slow progress made by the rescue team before they vanished into the clouds. The survivors' spirits plummeted still further when they saw the third member of that rescue team reappear on the horizon, heading back towards them.

133

When he regained the crash site, Vizintin explained that the trek to civilization would be far longer and far more arduous than they had thought. The survivors were utterly demoralized.

There was little to do other than sit and wonder. They passed the time whittling meat off discarded bones, as food was becoming scarce. As the strength of the sun during daylight hours increased, they had the luxury of being able to dry their soggy clothes. But it also meant that the remaining bodies were exposed to warmth for the first time and would quickly rot. The fitter amongst the group organized an expedition of their own up the mountain to retrieve the bodies first lost when the tail came off the stricken plane. They split one head open with an axe to discover that the brains were already putrid. Nevertheless, they returned with a body strapped to a make-shift sledge constructed of aircraft cushions, tobogganing speedily back to base. Another day, one returned carting a severed arm over his shoulder to add to the larder. Now the unwritten rules about eating flesh were broken, there was no room for squeamishness.

Twice the group thought they heard aircraft overhead. They devised a plan in which the fittest of the bunch would dance in a circle so the movement would attract the attention of passing pilots. The route for the dance was marked out with discarded human bones. But neither aircraft passed close enough to see the tiny figures or spot the white plane covered with snow. They resorted to eating fingers and lungs. And tempers frayed as they imagined the whereabouts of the expedition team. Each hour was more gruelling and hellish than the last as the group speculated on whether rescuers would arrive today, tomorrow ... or never. Roy Harley described the torment. 'We saw day after day after day go by and our friends were dying all the time. No one came to find us. The turning point was when the third month came and we realized we were still stuck on the mountain. That began to destroy us.'

They did not know it, but rescue was indeed at hand. Although Canessa was flagging, Parrado saw a route into a valley and fixed on the downwards path with almost terrifying intensity. Sure enough, the snow gave way to streams, green tufts and, for the first time in months, they saw birds and small animals. Nine days into the expedition, amid landscape that was comfortingly hospitable, they realized their meat supplies were starting to rot and gorged themselves on ten large hunks, virtually all the remainder. That night they slept soundly with their bellies full of flesh. They awoke, guessing that this was the day they would be saved.

And then came the sight they had dreamed of – another human being. A Chilean peasant caring for cattle caught sight of them from across a stream. He was perplexed by the sight of the bearded, emaciated pair. At first he believed them to be tourists – but why did they run and stumble towards him so frantically? He rode off to get help and the following day the pair were taken by horseback to a peasant shack where they ate and drank their fill. It was a further day before rescue services could be alerted and pluck survivors from the wreckage. Seventy-two long, harrowing days had passed since the plane had gone down.

The world embraced the survivors. Still elated at their return to civilization, they told how they had kept alive by eating cheese and lichen. It wasn't until a Chilean camera crew flew to the scene of the wreckage and found two half-eaten legs that the truth emerged.

The survivors chose to explain away their decision in

religious terms and found backing from the Roman Catholic Church, which regarded it as a transfusion of life from one to another. Far from being a sin, it had been their duty to stay alive, South American bishops agreed.

But the memory of nourishing themselves on a fellow human lingered with all sixteen survivors. Alvaro Mangino explained: 'At first I was embarrassed, although everyone said it was all right. But deep inside I felt guilt which took me many years to get rid of and to realize that what we had done was both natural and rational.'

With the grief of so many neighbours mingling with the joy of those who returned, the subject was still taboo among many in Uruguay. Nando Parrado explained:

Nobody has ever asked me in this neighbourhood about eating human flesh in twenty years. I have been asked all over the world except in this neighbourhood. Over the years journalists have asked the same thing; it fascinates people. What does it taste like? I only say like normal meat. We had to eat almost every part of the body, which is very difficult to understand for somebody sitting comfortably in his house.

What made us survive? Our education, our culture, as members of a team, as Catholics, perhaps. Most of all our ignorance. We did not know how bad things were, we just hoped.

The survivors remained close to one another, keeping in constant touch over the decades. Parrado went on to be a television personality, Canessa a heart surgeon with political aspirations while Carlitos Paez fought drug and drink addiction.

One lasting bond unites the survivors to this day. Carlitos

Paez explains: 'With regard to eating human flesh, I'm not ashamed of anything I did. If I had to do it again I would without hesitation. The only thing I would never do is say who we have eaten. I think that would deeply upset relatives of those who died – and that is something I am simply not prepared to do.'

The Mountain Men Kidnappers

Kari Swenson was attractive, intelligent and strong. An Olympic bi-athlete skier, she was capable of pushing herself beyond normal human bounds of stamina and endurance. She was gifted with a strength of character and a resource of willpower that shone through as she battled fatigue and the elements to train for her Olympic dream in the majestic peaks of the American Rockies.

If Kari had not been so strong, she would not be alive today. If she had not been so intelligent, she could not have survived the incredible horrors that she was forced to endure on those mountains. If she had not been so attractive, she might never have had to . . .

Kari Swenson's ordeal began on a brilliant summer's day in the heart of what remains of North America's great wilderness. The names on the map she carried resounded with echoes of an adventurous past; they rang with romance. She was out jogging along a pathway through the 'Big Sky' state of Montana, on a trail in the Rocky Mountains between Bozeman and Yellowstone National Park. It looks down on the crystal waters of Lake Ullery. It was as near to paradise as Kari had ever found.

She was twenty-four, with red, shoulder-length hair and shining blue eyes. She had recently returned from Chamonix, France, where she had finished fifth in the 10-kilometre skiing finals. A graduate in microbiology from Montana State University, Kari worked part-time as a waitress to save money for a return trip to Europe. She spent every moment of her spare time running on the mountain tracks to improve her Olympic chances. She wore training shoes, red shorts and a skimpy T-shirt. Nothing more. The sweat glistened on her brow and her heart pounded as she fought her way ever higher into the hills. Joyfully she came to the crest of a ridge – and found herself staring down the barrels of two rifles. Her heart seemed to stop.

'There was no expression on their faces,' said Kari. 'They just stared at me. They both had long hair and stringy beards. They were very dirty.'

The pretty athlete was terrified. It was a long time before she could summon the courage to relate her story; but when she did, it held a courtroom enthralled, though repelled, by the macabre nature of her ordeal . . .

I asked the two men what trail I was on and they told me the name. But as I turned to go they stepped in front of me. One of them, the older one, came up to me and said: 'We don't get many women up in the mountains that we can talk to. We just want to talk to you for a while.' They asked me my name and I lied and said it was Sue, or something. I also told them I was married and would be missed by my husband. They were both lies.

Suddenly one of them grabbed my wrist. The older man said: 'If you decide not to stay you'll have one hell

140

of an adventure story to tell your grandchildren.' I thought I was going to be raped and murdered.

Kari was led away by the two men, whom she soon learned were father and son. They took her to their camp, the sight of which made her quake still more. Raised on poles were the carcasses of animals, while the skins were suspended from lines strung between the trees.

In desperation, the terrified athlete appealed to the more silent of her abductors. 'I looked at the younger one,' she said, 'and told him: "You're young – you don't want to become involved in this."' She had barely got the words out before she felt a numbing pain and everything went black. The father, overhearing the girl's pleas to his son, had knocked her unconscious with a single haymaker blow to the head.

Kari was woken the next morning by the sound of rifle shots. She found herself chained to a tree in the middle of the camp, covered by only a thin sleeping bag. She saw the young man emerge from the woods swinging a dead squirrel by the tail. 'Breakfast,' he said, proffering the bloodied rodent. Kari refused the treat.

Further indignity was to follow. Kari was asked to remove her red shorts. Certain that she was about to be raped, she refused – until they persuaded her that their motive was not sexual but for camouflage purposes. The father took them from her and began dying them with charcoal from the edge of their camp fire in an attempt to make them less conspicuous. As the older man was engaged in this strange task, the shivering girl again begged his son to free her. 'No,' he replied. 'You're real pretty. I want to keep you.'

That simple statement of intent sent fresh shivers

through her. She cast her mind back to what she thought must have been a nightmare. This was a story she knew. These were scenes she recollected. This was a horror she had somehow seen before.

Then suddenly it came back to her. Long ago, Kari had read a book about a kidnapping. It was the story of a warped young man who could not form normal relationships with women. So instead of wooing a woman he abducted one. He kidnapped the girl of his dreams and kept her like a precious hoard in his dungeon, where he loved her and treasured her – but never set her free. The book was by novelist John Fowles and was ominously entitled *The Collector*.

Kari had read that book and now she suddenly realized the meaning of her captor's statement, 'I want to keep you.' In the silent heart of the Rocky Mountains where no one but her tormentors could hear, Kari Swenson wept her heart out.

The date was 16 July 1984. It was the second day of the young athlete's captivity and down in the valleys below the alarm had already long been raised. Down below was sanity and civilization – but little understanding of life at the snow line, where the air cuts like a knife and the Kodiak bears rule, where man has failed to conquer. Certainly no one in the towns lying between the rugged ranges had an inkling of the primeval forces that drove Kari's kidnappers.

The elder man was Don Nichols, the younger his son Dan. Neither had read *The Collector* but they had both retreated from civilization in the same strange way as author Fowles's anti-hero. They had forsaken the American twentieth-century dream for the life of old-style backwoodsmen: frontiersmen in a terrain they shared with the wolves and the Kodiak bears.

* * *

The mountain men's retreat from civilization began in White Sulphur Springs, an old Montana gold rush town which had once seen some of the toughest characters to cross the prairies. Its infamous past had given way to quieter pursuits. It was now a sleepy cowboy hamlet of about 1,500 people, served by three bars, two diners, one bank, one store and one gas station.

In 1969, a divorcee named Berdina Nichols moved to Sulphur Springs after splitting with her husband Don when their 'hippie' dream of back-to-nature farming in another part of the state turned sour, killed off by mining and construction development. The relics of this dream were a very few dollars, a daughter Barbara, aged fourteen, and a four-year-old son, Dan.

After the break-up of his family, father Don moved to another wilderness region of North America and settled in Jackson Hole, Wyoming. There he brooded on how the pervasive influence of civilization had wrecked his life. He became the ultimate loner and evolved his own personal philosophy and lifestyle. He held a job as a machinist, as well as undertaking motor repairs for neighbours. Every spare moment would be spent in the empty, mountainous countryside that surrounded his home town. And every weekend he journeyed to Sulphur Springs to be reunited with the son he still idolized and to whom he wanted to impart what he termed his 'mountain policy'.

Don Nichols was more than a doting father, however. He took his son Dan into the mountains to witness his wilderness creed at work first-hand. He taught Dan that sharing nature's harshness and its bounty strengthened a man. It gave him the power to live on a higher moral plane than the city men in suits who made the money and the law.

143

In the Rocky Mountain range in Montana – America's 'Big Sky' state – they cast aside the basic ethics and morals that bound the civilized folk in the valleys below. They were shooting, fishing and hunting as God had intended. They could take what they wanted. If necessary, they would kill for it.

'Most rules and laws are not made for the common man,' Don Nichols was to tell a hushed courtroom. 'They were made for someone to get richer, so someone could shove someone else around. That was not for me. I lived by the sun and the stars and the water.'

The young Dan lapped all this up. He idolized his father and yearned for his longer visits, when Don would take the boy up into the mountains for six weeks and more at a time. There he encountered no distractions as he infused the boy with the certainty that life with his family, authority and schooling was for an inferior race.

Doubtless, the experiences young Dan enjoyed in the green valleys and on the slate-grey peaks were the envy of his school friends. He and his father tickled trout in mountain streams, cooked them over flames started only from dry twigs, and washed them down with coffee brewed from acorns. He learned how to stalk and trap deer, then gut and skin them with his hunting knife. He could even spear salmon as they leaped upstream.

Dan returned from these expeditions with tales that held his classmates in awe. But they disturbed his teachers, who strongly discouraged such fanaticism. Eventually they protested to Don Nichols that he was destabilizing his boy. The father responded by keeping Dan away from school for two months beyond the start of the 1973 school year.

On their return to town, Don was arrested at gunpoint by his boy's new stepfather: ironically, a policeman who had since married Berdina Nichols. The boy's natural father was sentenced to a month in jail for failing to return his boy to school. But the punishment served only to reinforce Don's passionate hatred of all rules of law and to increase his determination to take Dan away with him into the wilds for ever.

Dan's teachers never realized the level of the brainwashing the boy was suffering. His father would beat him on the legs and on the forehead 'to give him discipline' and supposedly better equip him for the rigours of the wilderness. As he grew into his teen years, Dan was evidently awkward in company, had few friends and no girlfriends. As his father grew further from reality, his son grew increasingly to despise the adults who kept him chained to a desk and to the hearth back in Sulphur Springs.

In October 1983, at the age of eighteen, young Dan determined to ascend the mountains for the last time – and never return. 'Pa wanted to live in the mountains for good and so did I,' he said later. 'At first I didn't want to but then I realized it was the only place for me, too. I wanted to be with him for ever, for as long as he lived. We went to Jackson Hole at first and the two of us were living in a car. I got a job washing dishes. One day Pa said to me: "This ain't no life." And he was right. So I never went back to no diner. We headed up into the mountains and I felt the sun on my face. I was happy.'

At that time Don Nichols lugged around a chain wherever he went. It was 6 feet long and he wrapped it round himself like a mountaineer's coil of rope. Young Dan never thought to ask for what purpose his father carried his strange burden. Sure, it had its uses for trapping, for building shelters, for fording rivers. But it had a further use, which even young Dan never dreamed of . . .

The mountain men, father and son, lived like creatures from another age. Seldom did they venture down into the townships, and only then to stock up with dried beans, whiskey and ammunition. They migrated with the beasts from one wilderness area to another, from one season to another. They trapped snow geese on their flights north and south. They hunted deer and smeared their own faces with their blood. Their hair became matted with the charcoal from camp fires. Their hats reeked with the raccoon fat that protected them from the rains. The pair of them stank.

These were the men that Kari Swenson encountered as she reached the ridge of a hill on her lonely workout in July 1984. It was then that Dan Nichols realized the ultimate use of the chain that his father carried with him night and day. It was to trap him a 'bride'.

As Kari Swenson lay chained to a tree on the first morning of her captivity, people back in town were already mobilizing in the hunt to find her. Initially, the fear was that she had been attacked by a bear; a wounded grizzly had recently been sighted in the area. Had Kari crossed its path?

Alan Goldstein and Jim Schwalbe were among the first to volunteer for the search party. They were both friends of Kari and were ready at dawn on 16 July to venture up the mountains. Schwalbe, aged thirty, bore a heavy pack of survival and first-aid equipment. To protect himself from wild animals, Goldstein, thirty-six, carried a Walther pistol, as issued to West German police.

The pair set off at 6 a.m. Kari awoke in chains at 6.30. Two hours later, more by chance than by good tracking, Goldstein and Schwalbe blundered into the camp of the mountain men. Dan Nichols was close to the captive Kari and told her in a nervous tone: 'Pa taught me never to let anyone creep into your camp.' He slid his hand into a pack and drew out a Magnum pistol.

'Stay away, stay away,' screeched Kari. 'They've got guns.'

Alerted, Don Nichols dashed into the clearing shouting: 'Shut her up, shut her up, shut her up.'

Panicking, his son turned the gun on Kari and fired a single shot.

'I'm hit,' she screamed as the bullet tore through her shoulderblade and embedded itself in the tree to which she was chained.

Dan seemed dumbfounded as the blood seeped through her T-shirt, the crimson stain growing ever broader. 'Oh my God,' he whined. 'I shot her. I can't believe I shot her. I didn't mean to shoot her.'

Goldstein remained close to the tree-line while Schwalbe dashed to the side of the bleeding girl. Don covered him with a .22 gauge hunting rifle as he investigated the severity of her wound. The girl moaned softly. Apart from that, all was silent for a few moments. Then suddenly Goldstein shouted out: 'Drop your weapons. You are surrounded by two hundred armed men.'

It was so obviously a bluff that Don turned on the distant figure with a look of withering scorn. The mountain man slowly raised his rifle, took careful aim and fired. Used to downing fast-moving game, Don found his motionless quarry an easy target. 'He dropped like a light,' the hunter recalled at his trial.

The bullet hit Goldstein's forehead and exploded through his skull, shattering it and exploding his brain against the bark of the surrounding trees. Schwalbe was fleeter of foot.

147

He turned on his heels and, before Don could take a fresh bead on him, he had fled the camp, stopping only briefly beside the still-twitching corpse. 'My back muscles shivered every step of the way,' he recalled. 'I had passed Alan's body, making sure he was dead, and then I just took off. With each step, I felt sure that I would feel a slug between my shoulder blades.'

Back at the campsite, Young Dan became hysterical. 'She's gonna die, pa,' he squealed, 'she's gonna die.'

'She'll live,' his father growled back at him, slapping him about the face until he stopped crying. 'Now let's get out of here.'

The mountain men forgot their macho image and beat an ignominious retreat. They bundled together their meagre possessions, tossing Kari out of the sleeping bag in which she was trembling with fear and cold. Within minutes they had fled the scene, leaving the poor girl to her own resources. Kari crawled over to the embers of the campfire and tried to blow new life into the charcoal. She found that her breath was getting shorter and realized that one of her lungs had been pierced by the bullet. Panic set in. Agonizingly, she blew into the coals, but they grew dimmer and dimmer. Kari faced death in the Rockies.

Then came the sound of a helicopter. The rotor blades whirred overhead before fading again beyond the tree-line The frantic girl reached for the red shorts that Don had tried to blacken, and she waved them above her head. The sound of the chopper grew louder. As nausea overcame her, the helicopter hovered directly over the campsite. As it landed in the clearing, Kari passed out.

Within hours the nation's media was receiving news agency reports of the girl's deliverance. Only a bare glimpse of Kari's grisly ordeal was revealed as the poor girl lay in a hospital bed. But the story of father and son abandoning society to pit their wits and their wiles against society captured the imagination of city dwellers and suburban man. The idea of them abducting a woman, caveman style, added an extra, morbidly fascinating twist to the tale.

Pressmen swarmed into the area, all intent on the scoop of a lifetime. Equally, because of media interest, the law enforcement agencies were forced to throw massive money and manpower into the hunt. SWAT teams were drafted in; all-terrain vehicles tore up the mountain tracks; helicopters criss-crossed the ranges. There was one man, however, who was more determined than any other to hunt down the fugitives. He was a tough Montana lawman by the name of Sheriff Johnny France, himself an adventurer, formerly a rodeo rider and now cast in the role of modern-day bounty hunter. At forty-four years of age, he knew the hills instinctively – and he understood the cunning of the men he was hunting. As the search dragged on fruitlessly into weeks and months, it became a one-man crusade by Sheriff France.

The lawman became obsessed with his quarry. He walked more than twenty miles every weekend, taking in some of America's toughest terrain. Sometimes France was accompanied by a posse but mostly he stalked the mountains alone. The hunt had become a personal vendetta for the sheriff determined to see justice done.

France became increasingly frustrated as the weeks went by. Whenever he thought he had found Don and Dan they always seemed just one extra step ahead of him. One week he would come across a vegetable plot they had planted before moving on; another time he would find bits of hide and bone where the two men had dined off wild animals.

But not once did he catch sight of Don and Dan Nichols. Such was his growing frustration that France became outraged when he found carved into a tree the words: 'Danny and Don Nichols lived in these mountains: 14 July 1984'. That date was the day before the kidnap and close to where Kari was abducted. But France was determined to win. He told people: 'I'm a mountain man, too, and I'll catch them.'

On 15 December, exactly five months to the day since Kari had been kidnapped, the lawman got a tantalizing call from a relative twenty miles from Big Sky. She told him she had seen smoke from a campfire. France was back on their trail.

He immediately called in a helicopter and mustered more officers, while he himself set off to Norris on a snowmobile. The day was already ending, and as France tracked the mountain men in the snow, he knew it was a last desperate race against time. Incredibly, France saw the Nichols men before they saw him. They were casually cooking venison, but whipped round, their eyes flashing, when France casually asked them: 'Have you seen any coyote?'

Don Nichols reached for his gun but France raised his rifle, calmly saying: 'You're under arrest.' The game was up for the mountain men but Don Nichols couldn't resist one last jibe. 'What took you so long?' he asked France.

Dan and Don Nichols were tried in Virginia City in May 1985. There were separate trials, with Dan's attorney claiming that the son had been brainwashed by his father and that, never having meant to harm anyone, could not be found guilty of attempted murder. Instead, the jury found Dan guilty of kidnapping and intimidation. He was sentenced to twenty years in a youth camp.

When Don Nichols came to trial, he claimed the shooting of Goldstein was self-defence, saying their pursuer had aimed his gun at them first. He tried to evoke compassion from the jury by describing his joy at living in the mountains away from the city rat race. The jurors took six hours to find him guilty of both kidnapping and murder.

Don closed his eyes and tried to bring his beloved mountains back to mind. As he was led to the cells to face a life sentence like a caged animal, he knew he would never see them again.

Ironically, after making a full recovery, Kari Swenson spends most of her time walking and skiing in Don's mountains.

UFO Encounters

There is no greater fear than the fear of the unknown. And for hundreds of innocent humans, that unknown has erupted into the most traumatic experience of their lives – from the Great Beyond of space. The terror from the skies, a speciality of science fiction writers, has become all too real for these victims. Their encounters of the too-close-for-comfort kind with aliens from other worlds has left them scarred, both mentally and physically. For some, it may also have meant their deaths.

A perfect holiday in the romantic setting of Niagara Falls was drawing to a close for Betty and Barney Hill as they drove through New Hampshire towards their home on the clear moonlit night of 19 September 1961. Betty watched the dark shadows of trees dancing in the glare of the car's headlights as Barney happily motored through the Connecticut River valley.

Glancing up into the night sky, Betty was intrigued by one particularly bright star, bigger and more brilliant than the others, which, strangely, seemed to be keeping pace with their own vehicle.

Finally, she persuaded Barney to take a look for himself. He pulled the car over and took out a pair of binoculars so he could get a better view. What he saw almost sent him rigid with fear. There was a fuselage, but no wings. Flashing lights, but no engine sound. A large, moving, flying object, but no rational explanation. In the darkness of the lonely road, he and his wife were being pursued by an alien spaceship.

Barney and Betty leapt into their car and continued on towards Cannon Mountain as the object disappeared from sight behind a hill. Then, suddenly, it reappeared directly in front of their car, only 100 yards away. Barney slammed on the brakes and the engine cut out. He didn't know if it had stalled or if unseen forces were at work. Whatever the reason, their car refused to restart.

The terrified couple got out of the car, but Barney found himself compelled to take a closer look. As he walked towards the craft, which was now clearly visible and glowing with a hypnotic pulsating light, Barney could see creatures behind a row of windows. They were watching him as intently as he was fascinated by them. He did not hear Betty plead, 'Barney, come back. Don't go, you damn fool.'

As he got closer he could make out their humanoid shapes and shiny black jackets. But the worst thing was their eyes – ice-blue, slanted and malevolent – which sent a chill of horror down his spine. Then Betty somehow managed to break him free from his spellbound fascination and the couple climbed back into their car as their tidal wave of terror slowly ebbed away.

Sadly, however, it was only the beginning of their nightmare. Somehow they had 'lost' two hours and when they realized what had happened they were 35 miles farther south than they should have been. Both felt numb and confused, aware that something had happened, but not quite sure what. Neither could account for the missing time or distance.

Ten days later, Betty began to have horrible nightmares, dreaming of strange beings but never quite being able to remember the details of what had taken place. Barney suffered curious pains in his stomach and groin. Desperate, they sought the help of Dr Benjamin Simon, one of America's foremost mind doctors. He put them through weeks of intensive interrogation under hypnosis, and eventually the full horror of that weird meeting of worlds emerged.

The couple had not, as they thought, managed to flee. They had been abducted in a trance-like state and had been subjected to a series of medical examinations inside the alien craft. Betty revealed how the creatures took samples of her skin, hair and nails. Stripped naked, she was examined from head to foot by an alien with a cluster of needles, causing excruciating agony which only eased when another alien rubbed his hands together in front of her eyes.

Barney recalled being taken into an examination room where a sort of cup was placed over his groin. He felt the coldness of the object but no real sensation of pain. They took out his false teeth and examined them, but were frustrated when they tried to do the same to Betty, whose teeth were real. They communicated as if by telepathy, although they did speak an unintelligible language which sounded like a babble to Barney. When they had finished, he felt strangely happy and reassured that they would come to no harm. Just before being freed, the couple were given a hypnotic suggestion that they would remember nothing about their time aboard the UFO. Years later, Betty drew from memory a 'star map' shown to her by the aliens which indicated their star of origin as Eta Retuculi.

Scientists and UFO-logists have remained divided in their opinions of the Hills' testimony over the years but the couple always appeared totally sincere when relating their experiences during interviews. They have never wavered in their account by a single word.

Theories abound which attempt to explain the phenomenon of UFOs. Why have UFOs been confirmed on radar when they have been invisible to the naked eye? Why do some people innocently fall victim to the visitors from Outer Space, while others may spend a lifetime desperately scanning the skies for proof positive that UFOs exist and never see a thing?

UFO expert and author, John Keel, believes that a large part of the phenomenon is hidden from us. 'We can only see the objects and the entities under certain circumstances,' he says. 'Perhaps only certain types of people can see them at all. There are strange forces which are almost beyond our powers of comprehension.' Whatever the explanation, anyone who has actually seen a UFO – or, worse, had a close encounter with one – will never forget the experience. For many, as in the cases which follow, it can change their lives for ever . . .

A bolt of blue light fired from an alien spaceship shot across the night sky, hitting forestry worker Travis Walton squarely in the chest. According to his terror-stricken friends, he was picked up and tossed backwards 'like a limp rag doll'.

The journey had begun like almost any other for Travis and his forestry gang as their pick-up truck bounced down the remote winding road into the gathering gloom of the Apache-Sitgreave National Forest, near Snowflake,

Arizona, on 5 November 1975. Until, that is, they rounded a bend, to be confronted by a terrifying sight that was to change all their lives. Never in their wildest dreams would any of the men have expected that danger was fast approaching – from another world.

Mike Rogers, who was at the wheel, saw it first. Hovering 15 feet above a clearing in the woods was a glowing, yellowish object. Rogers stamped on the brakes and the pick-up skidded to a halt, bathed in the eerie yellow gold light. All the men were transfixed except Travis Walton. He leapt out of the vehicle to take a closer look, ignoring the pleas of his friends to get back in the truck. 'The guys were calling me, saying "Get away from there, get back here",' says Travis. 'I guess that egged me on. I was frightened but I was showing off a bit, too.'

Then the searing bolt of light flashed across the night sky, picking Travis up off his feet and throwing him backwards. In the truck, fear took over, forcing the burly loggers to think only of their own lives. Rogers gunned the accelerator and the pick-up screamed off into the night like a bat out of hell.

Travis later recalled: 'When the bolt hit me it was like an electric blow to my jaw and everything went black. I woke up and thought I was in hospital but I could see three figures who weren't humans. They looked like foetuses, about five feet tall, and they wore tight-fitting, tan-brown robes. Their skin was white like mushrooms, but they had no clear features.'

When Walton's friends reached town they alerted police and a massive search was launched. But when they returned to the scene of their close encounter the strange craft had vanished – along with Travis. The police even began to suspect the six loggers of murdering their friend and concocting the bizarre story to cover their tracks. Then five days later, out of the blue, Travis reappeared. He telephoned his sister from a phone box in a neighbouring town, disorientated, shaken and with no recollection of where he had been for the missing days.

Later, under hypnosis, he was able to reveal his strange experience. He said:

> I know people won't believe me, but I was in their spaceship and I met those creatures. We all saw the saucer that night but I was just so excited I wanted to get a better look and ran out from the truck. When they took me aboard I guess I panicked and tried to smash a kind of transparent tube to use as a weapon, but it wouldn't break. I saw one human-like man who just smiled at me. The others scampered away. I could feel that we were moving and I knew we were in a spaceship. Then things went black again. When I woke I was on the highway, feeling shaky. I recognized I was in a village a few miles from my home and I called my sister.

Travis never changed his account of those fateful five days and his story was subsequently made into a major film, *Fire in the Sky*, starring actor James Garner. Before taking the role, Garner spent hours talking about the incident with Travis. He concluded: 'I believe him. If I didn't, I wouldn't have touched the role with a barge pole.'

A Brazilian farmer ploughing his fields in the cool of an early October evening in 1957 fled in terror when a massive egg-shaped object began to hover over his tractor. Antonio Villas Boas only managed to run a few paces before someone – or, rather, something – grabbed his arms.

Boas was carried screaming towards what he could now clearly see was an alien spacecraft by four kidnappers, each about 5ft 4in tall. 'My speech seemed to arouse their curiosity for they stopped and peered attentively into my face every time I spoke,' he said.

Once inside the strange craft, Boas was examined by an excited group of aliens who chatted away 'in a series of barks, slightly resembling the sound of a dog'. Boas was then forcibly stripped naked and a glass flask with a nozzled tube was applied to his skin. He watched, amazed and terrified, as the flask began to fill with his blood. Then it was moved to his chin, and again blood was withdrawn. The skin was grazed, leaving a wound which a doctor later identified.

When they had finished their examination, Boas was left in a room which filled with a choking gas, forcing him to vomit in one corner. Then the horrible ordeal took a bizarre and, for Boas, exciting twist. A door opened and a naked, blonde woman joined him on the couch where he was recovering. She had large blue eyes which seemed to slant outwards, a straight nose, high cheekbones, almost invisible thin lips and a sharply pointed chin. Despite the trauma of his abduction, Boas could not prevent himself from having sex with her. He felt the aliens must have given him some powerful aphrodisiac to make his 'performance' possible.

When it was over, the woman pointed at her stomach and then at the sky. Boas took this as a sign that he had been used by the aliens for an experiment in Earthling reproduction and that, somewhere in space, he might be the father of a hybrid child. He was to pay for his pleasure, though. The following day his arms and legs broke out in sores, and his face became speckled with yellowish spots. The symptoms strongly suggested radiation poisoning or, at the very least, exposure to radiation.

Housewife Madge Bye was making her way quietly to a church service on Christmas morning in 1965 when the festive calm was suddenly shattered by a loud 'crackling' sound coming from above her head. Before she could look up she was hurled against the churchyard wall and pinned there 'as though by invisible fingers of sound'. She was frozen into a temporary state of shock.

The weird cracking sound also paralysed a child's pet dog. When the frightened youngster tried to carry her dog indoors, she too was affected, her limbs starting to shake violently and uncontrollably. It was just one in a series of strange phenomena reported in the skies above Warminster, England, around this time. Reverend P. Graham Philips said he and his family had often seen a 'brightly glowing cigar-shaped object' hovering above the town. Another local, botanist and geologist David Holton, spoke of seeing a flock of pigeons suddenly killed in flight for no apparent reason. He examined the birds as soon as they hit the ground and, amazingly, found that rigor mortis had set in almost instantly. 'There can only be one explanation which is at all possible,' he said. 'This is neither natural nor supernatural. It is extra-terrestrial. All the evidence points that way.'

The mystery of the dead birds had an eerie parallel in July 1975 when fifteen ponies were found dead on Dartmoor. Their bones were crushed, their ribs were cracked and their flesh had rotted away to leave bare skeletons in only forty-eight hours. UFO investigators combed the area with Geiger counters and metal detectors after police and animal experts declared themselves baffled. They found no evidence of radiation but their leader John Wyse said: 'I think the ponies were crushed by an anti-gravity field of a flying saucer when it took off.'

On the other side of the Atlantic, top UFO investigator Dr J. Allen Hynek was called in when a number of farm animals were found mutilated in Minnesota in 1973. There were no human footprints near the dead animals and no sign of Earthly predators. Internal organs had been removed as if by surgery and some of the twenty-two dead cattle had been drained of blood.

Flames belched from the large diamond-shaped UFO which confronted Vicky Landrum, her grandson Colby and her best friend Betty Cash as they drove home to Dayton, Texas, on 29 December 1980. Mrs Landrum laid later: 'I really thought it was the end of the world.'

The two women got out of their car to marvel at the strange craft lighting up the night sky as they were held, trance-like, for fifteen minutes. 'I felt my eyes starting to burn and I called Betty to get back in the car but she was standing there entranced,' said Mrs Landrum. Every so often they heard a loud rushing noise, like air brakes, and larger flames spewed from the UFO, scorching down towards the road. Each time it lifted slightly then settled back. Eventually, it rose slowly before disappearing at high speed into the night sky.

All three began to feel sick within an hour of getting home. The two women's skin turned bright red and their eyes began to burn and weep. Large lumps began to form all over Mrs Cash's body, her hair fell out in handfuls, and she suffered agonizing headaches. She was soon too weak to get out of bed and was admitted to Houston's Parkway Hospital. During four weeks of intensive tests, doctors tried to find out what was wrong with her. 'They kept asking if I was a burns victim,' she said. 'Skin was peeling off my arms and legs and face. I was blistered all over. My ears and eyes were so swollen my own family did not recognize me.'

Mrs Landrum also suffered terrible eye problems and her hair fell out in tufts. Colby, who stayed in the car, suffered stomach pains and for weeks was haunted by terrible nightmares which left him screaming in fear.

UFO investigators reported that a similar diamond-shaped craft had been seen thirty minutes earlier by three people driving 20 miles further east. Mrs Landrum was hypnotized to try to unlock more information about the weird encounter. Clutching at the front of her blouse and sweating with panic, she gasped: 'We can't get through, it's blocking the road. The whole thing's burning up . . . Oh my God, it's coming closer, we're going to burn up.'

Dr Leo Sprinkle, a professor of counselling at Wyoming University, said: 'There is no doubt she had a real experience. I believe the craft was under intelligent control.' A radiologist who examined their records said the women were apparently suffering the symptoms of radiation poisoning. Betty Cash later developed breast cancer. Many experts agreed they had been exposed to some sort of unshielded nuclear source – whether it was extra-terrestrial or an unidentified man-made creation.

The two women sued the US government for $20 million, claiming that if officials refused to believe in UFOs then the object must have been man-made. But the case was dismissed on the grounds that the military had no such object in their possession. One question the courts could not answer, however, was: If the object was not man-made, just who was operating a nuclear device in the night skies above Texas?

One case has baffled both police and UFO experts for years. It concerns a down-to-earth miner who vanished while on a simple errand to buy potatoes from a shop only 200 yards from his home in northern England in June 1980. Zygmunt Adamski was a quiet Polish exile whose spare time was spent almost entirely caring for his wife Lottie, who was confined to a wheelchair. When his half-naked body was discovered on top of a coal tip five days after he set out on his errand, local police were confounded by a series of seemingly inexplicable events.

How did Adamski come to be on top of a coal tip where smooth sides showed that no one had climbed it? Why was his semi-naked body so spotlessly clean?; despite his filthy surroundings he looked as if he had just walked out of a shower. Why were his trousers ripped to shreds and his shirt missing? And how did he vanish from a tightly knit community for five days without anyone seeing him?

Some of those questions could have their answers in the bizarre events recorded by Police Constable Alan Godfrey, the first officer called to the scene. He revealed that he had been transfixed by what looked like a flying saucer only hours before the body was discovered. It was an object about the size of a bus, floating five feet off the ground. The bottom half of the shape was spinning and he could see rows of windows and a dome on the top. He couldn't alert his station because neither his car radio nor his walkie-talkie would work. He kept quiet for fear of ridicule – until the body was discovered.

The mystery deepened when it was discovered that, although Adamski had apparently died of a heart attack, parts of his corpse were found to have been burned with a corrosive substance scientists could not identify. Many people believe to this day that he had been frightened to death by creatures from Outer Space.

At the inquest, coroner Mr James Turnbull said: 'This is quite the most mysterious death I have ever investigated. As a coroner I cannot speculate. But I must admit that if I was walking over Ilkley Moor tomorrow and a UFO came down, I would not be surprised. I might be terrified, but not surprised.'

Perhaps Zygmunt Adamski had become one of the few – maybe even one of many – who have paid the ultimate price for their close encounter with beings from another world.

Those who have not experienced a close encounter with a UFO remain, like the Biblical Thomas, doubting. Yet, with more than 100,000 million stars in our galaxy alone it is surely not beyond possibility that other life forms exist somewhere in the Great Beyond of space.

For betting men, it is worth noting that even bookmakers are taking the possibility of aliens contacting Earth a little more seriously. They have slashed the odds of it happening from 500-1 to just 33-1. But then those who actually have encountered aliens from Outer Space don't view the visitations as a game of chance. Those who have witnessed the unthinkable remain vigilant, earnest . . . and scared.

Dennis Nilsen

At a glance it seems a picture of suburban tranquillity. Two friends spending the evening in front of the television, a bottle of Bacardi by their side. There's occasional small talk about the programme they are watching, a verdict on the latest news, or quip about a well-known celebrity. Then it's time for bed. For one there is a single bed with worn grubby sheets, but cosy and inviting for all that. For the other, it's a numbingly cold crater beneath the floorboards with only an old curtain for protection against the cobwebs and the grime.

Only now can anyone looking in begin to detect the deeply sinister episode unfolding in this absurd aura of normality. For only one of the men is alive. He is civil servant Dennis Nilsen. Sitting opposite him is the corpse of one of his victims. As the evening draws to a close, Nilsen manhandles the leaden body in the chair on to the floor. There he meticulously re-wraps the pale lifeless form and replaces it under the floorboards of his North London garden flat where it has been stored. There it will remain until the next day, or perhaps the following week, when lonely Nilsen is once again overcome with the urge for company.

Nilsen was the killer who chilled a nation, Britain's most

prolific serial killer this century. He claimed some fifteen lives – nowadays he disputes the number – in just over four years. Only one of his victims was missed, a Canadian tourist called Kenneth Ockendon, for whom TV and press appeals were made following his disappearance. The rest came from the shadowy world of single young men drifting in and out of homosexual circles looking for love or money, or simply a place to spend the night.

It was while they slept that Nilsen struck. He had no interest in the thrill of a physical fight to the death. After all, it could have led to injury or discovery. No, the bespectacled clerk, who considered himself something of an intellectual, waited until they were soundly sleeping or deeply distracted until he made his deadly move. Armed with a tie, he lassoed their necks as they slept and squeezed the life out of them. Even today, not all the victims have been identified.

At one stage, his compulsion to kill led to a line of bodies taking up every inch of gloomy room under his floorboards. He eventually disposed of them by chopping them up and putting them in a garden bonfire which flared into a furnace as the flesh sizzled and spat.

After he moved house, he no longer had access to a garden, so he was forced to dissect corpses more fully, removing maggoty innards to dump on waste ground, while flushing much of the remaining skin and bone down the toilet. It was the inadequacies of the drainage system that finally led to his arrest on 9 February 1983.

Nilsen lived in the top flat of 23 Cranley Gardens, Muswell Hill, North London, an address that has since gone into the archives of horror. Then, it stood out only because it was dilapidated and run-down in a road where owners took pride in their property. The house was, in fact, owned by an Asian woman who lived abroad, and it was divided into six flats and bedsitters. Nilsen lived at the top of the house with his faithful mongrel, Bleep.

The four other occupants of the house – a barmaid and her builder boyfriend, a dental nurse from New Zealand and a Dutch welfare worker – knew little about Nilsen except that he was devoted to his dog and went by the name of Des. But that didn't stop them posting warning signs on his door the day the plumbing gave up the ghosts of his past . . .

The downstairs toilet refused to flush, and despite pouring acid down the pan, whatever was causing the blockage remained stubbornly in place. When word of the plumbing problem reached Nilsen through his obliging fellow tenants, he knew he had to work fast. Any full-scale probe could mean someone entering his poky, acrid-smelling flat where flies buzzed incessantly. The odds were they would find the body of a man killed the previous week and hidden by Nilsen in his wardrobe. He got to work.

With plastic sheets protecting the floor, he painstakingly laid out the body of the man in the middle of the front room. With precision, he grasped a kitchen knife and severed the head. As soon as he had finished mopping the spurt of blood that accompanied the butchery, he reached for a sturdy cooking pot and popped in the head, which still bore all the features of the man it had once been. Filled with water, the pan went on the stove to simmer while Nilsen went off to the supermarket for some fortifying Jamaican rum. But with a few drinks inside him, Nilsen lost the appetite for his grisly task. He went to bed, leaving the headless corpse spread on the floor.

It was Sunday – three days after the killing – before he finished dismembering the body. He used the freshly sharpened blade to saw through the waist and he put the legs and lower body in a bag and stored it in a drawer. Then he hacked off both arms and put them and the rib cage in black plastic sacks. He added the boiled head before finally closing the door on the stomach-churning remnants of twenty-year-old Scottish drug addict and drifter Stephen Sinclair.

Whatever plans Nilsen had for subsequently disposing of the body were to be thwarted. For as he set off for his desk at the Jobcentre in Kentish Town on Monday, his neighbours decided to resolve the difficulties with the drain once and for all. A plumber who had called over the weekend had decided it was too big a problem for him to tackle alone, so the agents called in Dyno-Rod, whose engineer, Michael Cattran, arrived on Tuesday evening. With the help of one of the residents, he swung himself down into the sewer to survey the scene by torchlight. All around him were chunks of rotting grey flaccid matter. Was it this unknown gunge that was causing the foul stench?

Deep inside, Cattran had a nagging suspicion of the truth, although it sounded too ludicrous even to mention. He decided to telephone his boss for advice. The hubbub in the house while he made the call alerted Nilsen to the dilemma that now faced him. Cattran actually showed him the disgusting contents of the sewer with a flash of the torch.

It took plenty of drink before Nilsen plucked up the courage for the last filthy job he would do in his final twenty-four hours of freedom. Under cover of darkness he took a bucket, edged carefully through the manhole and collected the slabs of human flesh he himself had flushed there. He could not have known that barmaid Fiona Bridges, already spooked by the business of the drains, had heard his plodding feet and noted the scuffing sounds as the drain cover was removed.

Cattran was astonished and dismayed when he returned the next day to show his boss the extraordinary bilge and found the sewers clean. It wasn't long, however, before Fiona Bridges joined them and described the eerie noises of the night before. Then Cattran had the nous, or the stomach, to do something Nilsen had not. He put his arm up a pipe and retrieved a piece of decomposing flesh. The police were called. Within hours, a forensic report revealed that it was human. By the time Nilsen returned home, detectives were waiting for him.

Who knows what was going through the mind of this man with a secret lust for death that was to make even the most hardened copper blanch? At first he made a half-hearted attempt at innocence. He had already tried to throw people off the scent by reporting a foul smell in his drains to the landlords in the manner of an outraged tenant. When detectives said they were there because human remains had been found in the drains, he replied, 'Good grief, how awful.'

At the first sign of pressure from the police, however, he caved in. He took them into his squalid flat and told them there was a body in a bag in his wardrobe. The stench of rotting flesh was confirmation enough. In the hours that followed, they heard details of one of the most appalling serial crimes from one of the most unlikely-looking villains ever. It was hard to know whether he was mad, or bad – or perhaps both.

Dennis Nilsen was born on 23 November 1945 in the fishing

port of Fraserburgh, Scotland. He was the second son of Olav Nilsen, a Norwegian serviceman brought to the coast of Aberdeenshire by the Second World War – and by a local girl, Betty Whyte, who, despite enemy bombardment, was having the time of her life thanks to the remarkable influx of young men. When she met Olav it was instant love. But it was the sort of love that springs readily in times of war, only to subside when normality resumes. They had three children, Olav Junior, Dennis and Sylvia. But the handsome soldier was a wayward husband and father, and former beauty queen Betty had enough common sense to realize the wedding was a mistake, and the courage of her conviction to end the marriage.

But if Dennis grew up without a father, he received enough love and attention from his grandfather, with whom they all lived, to make up for it. Fisherman Andrew Whyte was best buddies with the youngster and they had great adventures together at the harbour and among the dunes. Bizarrely, however, it was through this loving and strong relationship that Nilsen had his first brush with death – thought by many to be the root of his lifelong obsession.

When Andrew Whyte died of a heart attack at sea, aged sixty-two, he was brought home and laid out so that his many friends and relatives could pay their last respects. Little Dennis, just five years old, was asked if he wanted to see Grandad. Of course he did; he always wanted to see him. But when he was carried to visit the man he adored, it wasn't the lively, laughing fellow he had known. Here was Andrew Whyte, still and silent yet looking like he always had. Dennis was told he had gone to sleep. The youngster's heart was thudding, but he could not identify which emotion was causing his pulses to race. There was unspoken grief, the tremendous sense of occasion, and a complete ignorance of what had happened. That powerful image of death closely linked to a sense of thrilling excitement loomed large in his mind for years.

A shy, colourless boy, Dennis kept himself to himself. He had a small circle of friends, none of them close. But when it came to helpless animals he was inspired and inspiring. He would rescue injured birds or mammals, nursing them gently back to health if he could. When his mother got a council flat, it gave him a chance to indulge his passion by keeping pigeons. A wartime air raid shelter behind the flats was the ideal loft and the three handsome birds thrived. Dennis was never happier than when he petted the cooing birds, his fond pals. But his joy was short-lived. A budding lout from the same block of flats decided to get his revenge on Nilsen for some imagined slight and it was easy to see where the youngster was most vulnerable. One day he arrived home from school to find the treasured birds with broken necks. His grief must have been considerable. But once again he clammed up, refusing to talk about it.

Nilsen has since told a tale of being almost drowned in the sea at Fraserburgh when he was ten and being rescued by an unidentified teenage boy who masturbated over him. It is possibly true, or perhaps the product of his lurid imagination.

As a teenager, his interests turned to the army and he joined the local cadet force. His mother met a new man, Adam Scott, remarried and they moved to Strichen, where she was to have four more children. With his liking for uniform and structured comradeship, it was a natural step for Dennis to join the army as a boy soldier at the age of fifteen.

Soon afterwards, he had a motor scooter crash, suffering injuries which kept him in hospital for several days. He wasn't wearing a crash helmet at the time, and his mother Betty later wondered whether this knock to the head might have caused lasting damage.

In the army, the young Nilsen, then working as a chef, became increasingly aware of his attraction towards men and carefully disguised any leanings towards homosexuality in case this made him an outcast among his comrades. In fact, he had sex for the first time with an Arab boy while serving in Aden. But it was an unsatisfactory liaison – the risk of being discovered and unmasked was too great.

Nilsen often used to like experimenting with mirrors. He would often lay a full-length mirror beside him on the bed and study himself. For his fantasies to run riot, he found it was better if he excluded the head from the reflection. Then it dawned on him that the stiller the body was, the more exciting the experience. He took pleasure in the notion that the body beside him (in this instance, his own) was asleep . . . or dead.

He used body make-up to whiten his skin and make it seem more cadaverous. Then came blue colouring on the lips so that he could at last include his face in the fantasy. He made his eyes bloodshot by rubbing them hard, and used a home-made dye to simulate blood running down his T-shirt. Saliva dribbled from his mouth. In his mind, his own dead body was being sexually assaulted and it led to physical gratification. Later, he was to insist that making himself up to look dead was nothing to do with death itself: 'It was to do with making myself look as different from me as it was possible to imagine to be.'

Two attempts at a stable relationship with other men foundered. In the army, he fell for another young soldier who was not gay but befriended Nilsen because he, too, was lonely. His next relationship was after he left the army at the age of twenty-seven. With this partner he experienced anal sex. It left him hopelessly infatuated but his lover was a promiscuous London homosexual who made it clear he was not going to settle down with Nilsen, or anyone else.

Nilsen then spent a largely unhappy year in the Metropolitan Police. He was disappointed that the force failed to offer the same convivial comradeship he had found and revelled in as a soldier. When he left, colleagues were mystified as to why he abandoned a promising career. None of them knew him well enough to realize that his uncompromising brand of politics – part socialist, part nationalist – left him at odds with authority.

In the summer of 1974, Nilsen finally embarked on a civil service career, as a clerical officer for the Department of Employment. He was based at the Denmark Street branch in London, which specialized in finding staff for the catering trade. He now channelled his rebelliousness into union activities and fought tirelessly and pedantically for the rights of fellow workers. His avid dedication made him somewhat tedious to his colleagues, but there remained a respectfully polite, albeit distant, relationship between them.

Away from work he had a series of meaningless flings with men picked up at gay pubs, until he finally found the opportunity for permanence which he craved. He met a young man called David Gallichan outside a London pub, and asked him to move in. Gallichan had all the hallmarks of the type singled out by Nilsen for attention. He was young, away from home and alone.

Nilsen used a £1,000 legacy left to him by the natural father he had never known to rent a garden flat in the suburbs. When he saw 195 Melrose Avenue in Willesden, with its large back garden and cosy kitchen, he knew it would be perfect. The pair moved in and acquired first a dog, then a cat called DD and finally a budgie. Gallichan, nicknamed 'Twinkle' by Nilsen, had little interest in a physical relationship. But there were displays of affection; when Nilsen fell ill with painful gallstones, it was David who nursed him back to health.

Later, Gallichan recalled that although Nilsen was messy in the kitchen, he was obsessively clean and bathed or showered three times a day. He was mostly content, but isolated from his family. There was little to mark him out as a killer.

At first jobless, David Gallichan eventually got work as a catering assistant for British Rail. He met other men with whom he had affairs. Although the relationship lasted for two years, Nilsen did not have in Twinkle the docile partner he desired. When the relationship finally broke down and Gallichan moved out, leaving Bleep, the dog, with Nilsen, the civil servant felt bitterly let down. David recalled, 'It was the only time I saw a different side to him. He was cold and dismissive. It was as though I had insulted him and he wanted me to go immediately.' Nilsen was injured because his hopes and dreams of a stable relationship had not been fulfilled and he felt insulted that someone he considered less than his intellectual equal had walked out on him.

In the year that followed, there was little to improve Nilsen's declining spirits. Try as he might, he found no prospect of a long-term relationship to replace Gallichan, while at work his ardent involvement in union affairs scuppered any hopes of a better job.

Against this background, he embarked on a New Year

celebration at the end of 1978 which was to determine his future – and seal the fate of fifteen innocent acquaintances. He struck up conversation with a man who drank with him and eventually slept naked with him, although there was no sex between them. As the youth slept soundly, Nilsen awoke and later confessed that he was terrified that his new-found companion would leave. As dawn broke, a clarity of thought entered his by-now addled brain. He seized his tie and put a stranglehold on his bedfellow. Nilsen wished this lad to stay for a while and stay he would, whether he wanted to or not. In fact, the attempt at strangulation failed. Although the young man's body was limp, he started to breathe, so Nilsen finished the job by thrusting his head into a bucket of water, filling his rasping lungs.

With the aid of cigarettes and strong coffee, Nilsen sat and contemplated the body, trying to absorb the enormity of his crime. He ran a bath, but instead of trying to wash his own sins away he bathed the body. With difficulty, he dried the corpse, placed it in his bed and lay down beside it. Aroused, he groped the body although an attempt at anal sex failed. At first, he was fastidious in the care of his captive friend, daily dressing him in new pants, vests and socks.

It took him five days to work out just how he could dispose of the body. The cavity underneath the floorboards seemed the perfect place. But rigor mortis had set in, stiffening the limbs of the victim sufficiently for the body to be stood up against the wall. Only days later could Nilsen work enough pliability into the corpse to insert it underneath the floor as he planned.

Seven days later, Nilsen was consumed with curiosity about the body beneath him and hauled it up to take a second look. It was dirty, so Nilsen himself stripped and once again bathed the corpse. Pale and lifeless, the sight excited him and he masturbated on the stomach. Before retiring exhausted for the night, he hung the body by its ankles from the ceiling. The next day he shoved it unceremoniously back underneath the floor.

For a year he kept his killing urge under control. Then he struck up a conversation with a Canadian tourist, Ken Ockendon, in a London pub. The pair hit it off immediately and enjoyed animated conversation for many hours before returning to Melrose Avenue. Nilsen used the cable of his stereo headphones to strangle Ockendon, tortured as he was with the thought of the amiable young man returning home in the near future. Once again, Nilsen started the bathing ritual and went on to be intimate with the dead body in bed. Before leaving for work, he placed the cold body in a cupboard.

The extent of his love affair with death is revealed in his actions that day. He bought an instant camera which he used to photograph the corpse from various angles. He later destroyed the sick snaps on the bonfire which engulfed the bodies of his victims. He also admitted watching TV with the body spread across him. Again, he managed to climax in close proximity to the cold body. Ockendon, too, was destined for a temporary grave under the floor, from which he was hauled out to provide an evening's companionship on about four more occasions.

Years later, Nilsen was interviewed by psychologist Paul Britton about his crimes and a few minutes of the interview were broadcast on national television. In those moments he revealed: 'The most exciting part of the little conundrum was when I lifted the body and carried it. It was an expression of my power to lift and carry him and have control. The dangling elements of his limp limbs were an expression of his passivity. The more passive he could be, the more powerful I was.'

And so the pattern was established for further slaughters at Melrose Avenue. A new face, a few drinks, a short sleep, the strangulation, followed by a bath (usually for both men), some sexual activity and a body lying cold and accusing the following morning.

One of the victims was Martin Duffey, a sixteen-year-old from Liverpool who had a troubled childhood but a promising future in catering. No one knows why he decided to visit London when he did instead of attending the cookery course as he had planned. He slept rough for two nights before running into Nilsen.

Another was Billy Sutherland, a tattooed Scot, some-time male prostitute and heavy drinker. But if Billy was wayward and a thorn in the flesh of his local constabulary, he had a good heart. He was devoted to his mother and close to his brothers and sisters. Sutherland asked Nilsen for a night's shelter after they had spent the evening boozing. He never woke up again.

Malcolm Barlow was unlucky enough to have an epileptic fit practically on Nilsen's doorstep. This clearly invoked the side of the civil servant that was compelled to aid the underdog, and Nilsen tended Barlow after calling an ambulance. Barlow, a virtual simpleton, returned the following day to say thank you. That simple gesture was a fatal act.

Graham Allen may have been dead before Nilsen struck. Halfway through eating an omelette the visitor lapsed into unconsciousness either through choking or a silent fit. It didn't stop Nilsen moving in for the kill, brave enough with this comatose victim to use his bare hands.

One nameless victim was so physically appealing to Nilsen that it was a week before his body was put under the floor. The killer enjoyed seven days of domestic harmony, returning from work to find a companion and the promise of sexual contentment waiting.

There was still more to cheer Nilsen. He finally won promotion to the Jobcentre in Kentish Town, London, and enjoyed the increased responsibility as well as the company of his new boss, Janet Leaman. But for each high spot in his life, there was a wave of depression to match it. A birthday when one card alone would grace the mantleshelf, written by his mother. Christmas or Easter when families would reunite and Nilsen was lonely, for some reason unwilling to join his own clan's festivities north of the border. It was this recurring emphasis on his solitary existence that may have been the catalyst for each killing.

There was also the problem of disposing of the bodies, which became increasingly pressing with the arrival of warm summer weather. Nilsen's shopping basket must have raised some eyebrows, filled as it was every week with sticks of deodorant, cans of fly killer and endless boxes of air freshener. At Melrose Avenue he contrived to keep other tenants out of the garden so that he could build his body-burning bonfires with relative ease. They were firmly constructed with a durable, box-style opening in the centre. Nilsen would rise early, drag the decomposing cadavers from the house to the garden, bundle them into the middle of the fire and strike a match. Intense though the flames were, the fires which burned for hours failed to arouse suspicion.

Not all the young men who went into Nilsen's flat were throttled. The most remarkable story of the one that got away involved Carl Stotter, who lived to tell his tale to an Old Bailey jury which was eventually to find Nilsen guilty of six murders and two attempted murders.

It was by now May 1982 and Nilsen had moved to Cranley Gardens. He and Stotter met in a North London pub and returned by taxi to the attic room for the night. Stotter, a self-confessed homosexual, part-time model and go-go dancer, recalled at the trial that they held hands on their way back from the pub. Without a second thought, the teenager walked into the web so carefully woven by Nilsen. There were a couple of strong drinks, then a session on the stereo headphones listening to a favourite theme tune for a kill: 'Oh Superman' by Laurie Anderson.

Nilsen not only tried to choke Stotter but also thrust his head into a bucket of water in a bid to finish the job. But Stotter didn't die. Nilsen pulled back from murdering him, possibly because he was so overtly gay. Stotter came around to enthusiastic licks from Bleep over his face. Nilsen was the soul of concern. As Stotter recalled an appalling nightmare in which he had been unable to breathe and was then almost drowned, Nilsen listened sympathetically and said he had thrown a bucket of water on the young man because he had been in shock. Stotter's head was throbbing, his tongue was enlarged and he had burn marks around his throat. He did not emerge from the flat for three days. But although he sought hospital treatment he did not go to the police. Only after he read the extent of Nilsen's crimes did he come forward.

The ordeal left him suffering from panic attacks that were severe enough to stop him working. In a bizarre exchange of letters which took place after Nilsen was jailed, Stotter discovered the civil servant's reason for sparing him and contrasted it with the police version. 'He said that what passed between us was a thin strand of love and humanity. The police, though, said he had no more room to house another body.'

During his interrogation and trial, Nilsen remained unemotional. Although he was helpful and clearly relieved to unburden himself, he showed little remorse or regret. It was for his defence council at the trial to prove that he was mentally deranged. The arguments about whether bouts of abnormality or cold, ruthless, even planned murders took place raged in a rapt courtroom. It took the jury a day to make up its mind on the issue. They decided that it was cold-blooded murder. On 4 November 1983 Nilsen was jailed for life.

Since then he has enthralled the country. His name was on everyone's lips again in January 1993 when a few moments of a filmed interview with him were televised. In it he spoke about the dissection of bodies and how he removed people's innards when the smell was too putrid to bear. 'There isn't a lot of blood. If I stab you right now or you stab me your heart is beating. There would be blood spurting and splashing all over the place. In a dead body there is no splashing at all. The blood congeals and becomes part of the flesh. It is like a butcher's shop.' And he expounded his astonishing theory that the dead were now a part of him: 'The bodies are all gone, everything's gone. But I still feel spiritual communion with these people.'

Indeed, little was left of most of his victims, which is why the police still struggle to put a final figure on the death toll. Nilsen contributed to the investigation, but although traces of bodies were found, they had mostly been reduced to ashes and dust. He was unable to understand the revulsion which greeted his actions after death. Hacking up dead bodies was to him simply a job that had to be done to remove a problem.

The police were able to reconstruct one of the victims, Stephen Sinclair, a man thought by many to be a psychopath in the making. This last victim was numbed with drink and drugs when the stealthy killer flexed the ligature – this time, a tie knotted to a piece of string. Sinclair had only recently attempted suicide. That knowledge gave Nilsen food for his vanity and arrogance. Later he professed he had done Sinclair a favour and cared for him after death as no one had bothered to care for him in life.

As he lay down on the bed next to the cooling corpse, he surveyed with pleasure the whitening dead body and dusted his own living one with talcum powder to match. The satisfaction of being a voyeur over, it was time to go to bed. Nilsen called Bleep to her regular place at the foot of the bed, switched off the light and, turning to the corpse, with affection said, 'Goodnight, Stephen.'

Today, in Scotland Yard's macabre Black Museum, where weapons and skulls and hangman's nooses adorn the walls, there stands a morbidly fascinating exhibit. It is an old-fashioned gas cooker, uncleaned since the day it was removed from the kitchen of Dennis Nilsen's home. Atop the stove sits a large, battered cooking pot which Nilsen used to boil up curries and carry them round the corner to a local school hall which doubled as a day centre for the local old folk. There the kindly young man would serve them up as the staple diet for charitable functions. The pot, unhealthily stained and still encrusted with the remnants of such meals, was also the pot in which Dennis Nilsen boiled the heads of his victims.

The Devil's Disciples

Midnight. The witching hour. High above, nightmare clouds scud fitfully across an angry sky, and a lonely owl shrieks in triumph as it swoops to shatter its prey. It is not just the witching hour; it is truly the witching night – Hallowe'en.

It's a night when good Christians say their prayers and take to bed. Not that there are many good Christians in this wild, remote part of south-east Scotland. The empty kirk stands silhouetted against the faint starlight, gaunt against the grumbling sea. It is an awesome place on a naked, dark and rocky promontory overhanging the water. Creatures of the night sniff their way around the gravestones. There are plenty of new graves in this year of grace 1590.

Suddenly there is a movement. Into the grey North Berwick churchyard steps a young woman, slight and moderately pretty. But now her manner is furtive. Gillie Duncan is the first to arrive for the sabbat, as her unholy master ordered. She will not be alone for long; others of her kind are making their secret way to the meet. Some, she knows, will fly there. Others will sail in sieves. For herself, she has not mastered flight. She has walked all the way from Edinburgh.

Satisfied at last that all is well, Gillie lets out a cry. At the signal, others start sneaking into the clifftop churchyard; soon the revelry will begin. Bitter though the night is, Gillie wears just a light coat above a simple smock. It is the best a maidservant can afford.

Soon, she knows, she will be wearing a lot less. As the consort of the god on earth, she will lead the rites as the coven members dance. Then she will lie naked over the altar as her master has his way with her, followed by whichever of the other men present desire her. And that would be all of them, if past experience was anything to go by, she muses. For the other women, if not the secret, black and midnight hags of old King Macbeth, are not as attractive as Gillie. Some are old, and most are over forty!

Thus was set in motion a train of events that was to shake Scotland to the core and bring torture and agonizing death to scores of innocent (and not so innocent) people.

When Moses handed down his dictum 'Thou shalt not suffer a witch to live,' he was unknowingly triggering one of the most brutal waves of organized terror, of pitiless torture and cruel and violent death the world has ever seen. It was to be a horror that would leave Europe scarred, screaming, wailing and dripping with blood . . .

The witch hunt.

Four centuries ago, it heralded an era of savagery unsurpassed until Hitler. For no law in the history of mankind has been harsher in the keeping or crueller in its penalties than the interdiction on sorcery. How many hundreds of thousands perished in stomach-churning agony by rope, sword, fire or even more hideous means will never be known. But certainly no prey has been harried and vilified with such relentless hatred as witches. Hanging, burning, torture, drowning, even lingering death walled up in dungeons – nothing was considered too terrible for those thought to be in league with the Devil.

England had its share of sadistic witch hunts, as witness the brief but gory reign of terror of Matthew Hopkins, the self-styled Witchfinder General. But England tended to be more merciful. Torture, by mechanical means at least, was banned and victims faced a relatively swift end dangling from a rope. Only one witch is known to have been (legally) burned to death, and then only because in killing her husband she had committed petty treason, the punishment for which was the fire.

Far grimmer was the fate of witches in Scotland and across the sea in Europe, where inquisitors tortured and burned their way around with an enthusiasm and callousness to human suffering that was equalled only by the Gestapo of Hitler's Nazis.

In Germany, the tortures grew ever more diabolical – it was nothing to sit a victim on a burning brazier, or hang him by his wrists on a wall while fires were lit below to char him slowly. Witches were regularly burned alive – often on a barrel of pitch, but if an example was to be made, green wood was used to make the process slower. Others found themselves chained up inside a straw 'cottage', which was then set alight. The German executioner at Neisse even foreshadowed the concentration camps by inventing an oven so that he could roast a number of victims together – including toddlers of two and four years old.

In Scotland there was added mental torture. One poor woman, Alison Balfour, was forced to endure being pressed in a kind of iron maiden for days, while watching her father stretched, her son crippled by savage blows that crushed his legs and her daughter maimed with thumb-screws. The fact that this latter was all of seven years old can only have heightened the agony.

Another favourite technique here was to steep a hair shirt in vinegar. The unfortunate who had to wear it would then have his skin pulled from his body. And – a particularly nasty one for the Scots – they had to pay a fee for each act of torture perpetrated against them!

This, then, was the backdrop to the year's High Sabbat in North Berwick. Treason and ill-wishing were on the agenda. For the God on Earth, the object of veneration of all the witches, was none other than Francis Stewart, Earl of Bothwell, nephew of Mary Queen of Scots and cousin of King James VI, later to become James I of England.

In the noble earl's heart was the death of his cousin the king, whom he saw as the obstacle between him and the throne. Already, he had used his witches to cause a storm to wreck the fleet of James and the young bride, Anne of Denmark, the king was bringing home from Scandinavia. The storm had been ferocious. It had sunk a treasure ship, but had not killed the king.

Now those witches were meeting again at the wind-swept kirk where Gillie waited to greet her companions. Agnes Sampson was the first to arrive. A sage and sensible Edinburgh midwife, she was Gillie's good friend. Altogether a hundred witches were arriving from covens throughout North Berwick. They included, Gillie noticed, six men. She would be busy later on . . .

The sabbat began with a dance, in which the participants formed a ring, facing outwards and moving 'widdershins' (or against the sun). The music was provided by Gillie, playing a jew's harp, and the dance was led by John Fian, a schoolmaster of Saltpans (now Prestonpans) near Edinburgh. Fian was the right-hand man of the master of the lowland covens. At the appropriate time, Fian opened the kirk itself, by blowing into the locks, and lit the candles that surrounded the pulpit. They burned blue. Satan was present.

Satan appeared as a 'muckle black man with a black beard sticking out like a goat's, a high-ridged nose like the beak of a hawk and a long tail'. Whisky and atmosphere obviously had an effect on the minds of witnesses, for, in fact, Bothwell simply wore an animal skin and claws. The witches gave their names to the Devil, turning six times before him (nine times for the men). Then they lined up to kiss the master's naked buttocks.

Finally the group got down to business.

At the Lammas Sabbat in Achison's Haven earlier that year, Bothwell had ordered the witches to raise a storm. Accordingly, Fian, Agnes Sampson, Agnes Thompson and Gillie Duncan baptized a cat, named it James, attached various parts of a dead body from a freshly robbed grave to it and threw it into the sea. The plot failed, possibly because the cat escaped and swam ashore.

Undaunted, the witches took another cat, attached even more bits of a dead body to it and, taking no chances, rowed out to sea before drowning it. At any rate, there *was* a storm, and one ship was sunk. But James and his bride, on separate vessels, escaped and returned to Scotland.

Sterner measures were clearly needed. Agnes Thompson, Euphemie McLean, Barbara Napier and Gillie Duncan were instructed on how to brew a foul concoction by roasting a toad and catching the poison that dripped out.

This brew would bring about the king's destruction if he came anywhere near it. To be doubly sure, Bothwell gave Agnes Sampson a wax image that would be enchanted and burned, causing the king to waste away. He then ordered them to rob graves to collect the macabre ingredients of their witch brews, and after his ritual copulation with Gillie and others, left them to their whisky and debauchery.

The case of Bothwell and the witches was discovered completely by chance. Gillie Duncan's employer was one David Seaton, deputy bailiff in the small town of Trenent, near Edinburgh. He noticed that Gillie spent many nights out of the house, ostensibly helping sick people, for which she had a talent. To a convinced man of the kirk, being out at night could only mean immorality . . . or worse. Seaton suspected sorcery.

The method of inquisition of witches had been laid down a century previously by two Dominican monks in Germany, with the blessing of the then Pope, Innocent VIII. Their book, the *Malleus Maleficarum*, said that witches were to be tortured until they confessed, and then they were to be put to death.

Accordingly, Seaton's first act was to subject Gillie to the torture of the pinniewinks, the same kind of thumbscrew that had given such pain to Alison Balfour's daughter. Several hours of the slow tightening of the screws produced blood, screams, pleas for mercy and eventually badly mangled and broken thumbs. But no confession.

Next Seaton turned to a nasty little method of torture that involved twisting a rope like a tourniquet around the victim's head, and tightening it. Gillie withstood an hour of this excruciating agony, before she was stripped naked to be examined for witch marks – ostensibly, an extra nipple from which the Devil sucked. In fact, many a 'witch' was done to death for an unfortunate wart or mole. At this point, some kind of blemish having been discovered, Gillie opted to avoid the painful persuasions she knew would follow. She broke down and told Seaton everything he wanted to hear and more. Only at this stage did Seaton see fit to bring in the authorities.

The witch hunt had begun.

The scene now shifted to the palace of Holyrood, where the witches were examined by a new team of inquisitors. Since the confessions involved young James so closely, the monarch turned up in person to examine them. Agnes Sampson was the first to confront her stony-faced examiners. From the start she refused to admit any part in the sabbats. And even as the pinniewinks smashed her thumbs and the rope was tightened round her head, she screamed and struggled, but denied her part in coven activities. Finally, the examiners lost patience and she was loaded with chains and dragged to a dungeon to be searched for witch marks.

One was found in her pudenda and, like Gillie before her, Agnes realized that, innocent or guilty, she was doomed. Writhing in agony, she confessed all to avoid further torture. She described the dancing at the North Berwick kirk and told the inquisitors about Gillie's skill on the jew's harp. At this, the king ordered Gillie forward and demanded she play for him. She amazed the king with her dexterity on the instrument. Agnes, say the records, went on to confess sundry things that were so fantastic that James dismissed her evidence as nonsense.

Then a strange thing happened. Agnes begged the king to hear her privately, and whispered in his ear an apparently verbatim account of a conversation he had had with his queen on their wedding night. James went pale and agreed that her evidence should be heard.

Agnes went on to reveal the secrets of the witches' cauldron – how she had hung a black toad by its heels for three days, collecting the venom that dripped out in an oyster shell. She told how the conspirators tried to get the king's valet to lend them an article of his master's clothing to aid the enchantment, but had been thwarted by this worthy. She revealed the nasty business of the cat and the grave-robbing they indulged in to secure enough parts of recently deceased babies to make the spells work. And she revealed that the Devil had had his way with her and the other witches, though for her part she did not enjoy it.

Agnes apparently cut a fine figure at her trial. She was evidently the 'wise woman' of the group, and she was described as being 'of a rank and comprehension above the vulgar; grave and settled in her answers'. Finally, she confessed that Bothwell had consulted her to discover how long the king would live. She could not have known for certain that the costumed master at the sabbats was Bothwell himself.

The trial of Agnes Sampson did not take long. The sentence was inevitable – she was to be taken to a stake on Castle Hill, led along on a witches' bridle (an iron collar with points facing inward). There she was to be 'wirreit' (strangled) – probably by being strung up in her collar. Lastly her body was to be consumed in the flames.

Agnes was lucky. She did not suffer the dreadful doom of being burned alive, even though high treason against the king himself was involved. Neither did she have limbs lopped off as she stood helpless at the stake. And at least she had her day in court ... Her namesake Agnes Thompson died shrieking and protesting her innocence under torture.

Dozens of others were pulled into the net, and one after the other they pointed the finger at Bothwell. The accused were not the dregs of society – the outcasts, the lonely, the poor, the drunkards and the ignorant, as tended to be the case with such crimes in England. The Earl of Arran was among those fingered by successive witches who passed briefly through the court on their way to the strangling pole and the fire.

The ultimate horror of being 'burned quick' (alive) was reserved for Euphemie MacLean, who was the daughter of lawyer and statesman Lord Cliftonhall and the wife of Patrick Mosscrop, another eminent Edinburgh lawyer. She was charged with treason among various other crimes, and she suffered the full rigour of the law, possibly as a warning to those of her high social status.

Only one of the witches seems to have avoided her fate. Barbara Napier was implicated in all the activities of the Lothian covens and was found guilty of all the witchcraft charges. She was found not guilty of high treason, however, and so was sentenced to be strangled before burning. On the day of execution her friends protested that she was pregnant. A medical examination confirmed this, and she was reprieved, though whether she was ever let out of prison or whether she died in a stinking cell is not recorded.

James, however, was upset about Barbara's acquittal on the main charge of treason, largely because it concerned his personal safety. So angry was he that he ordered an Assize of Error to be held, at which the jury who had acquitted her of high treason (although they had found her guilty of enough to have executed her several times over) were to be tried for negligence. James himself addressed the assize, and presented more evidence to show that Napier should have burned. Having got this off his chest, he accepted the humble apologies of the jurors and set them free.

Last came the examination of the most important of the

witches. John Fian was single, highly sexed and nominally a Protestant (in order to keep his job as schoolmaster). Without doubt, however, he was a believer in the old fertility gods of his forbears. He first dabbled in the occult to prepare concoctions that would allow him to have his way with various women who attracted him.

He was taken without a struggle at his lodging in Saltpans and put in a dungeon, where he was urged to reveal his guilt. This he declined to do, so his persuasion started with the 'thrawing' of his head in the rope tourniquet. The torture lasted well over an hour and his skull was on the point of being broken, yet still he would not confess. The reason may have been that his fear of Bothwell was greater than his fear of his tormentors.

The next 'persuader' that the king ordered to be used on Fian was a monstrosity known as a 'bootikins'. A variation on the Spanish Boot, it consisted of four flat planks of wood fastened together to enclose the lower leg. Wedges could be driven in by mighty blows of a mallet, gripping the leg ever tighter until bones shattered and marrow sprayed over victim and torturers alike. A crude implement by the sound of it, its advantage over the mechanical vice of the Spanish Boot would have been only a matter of taste.

Fian withstood just two such blows. After the third he signalled that he would confess to anything if only he was spared further torment. Unfortunately, he was unable to speak. His fellow witches, ordered to examine him, discovered pins sticking his tongue to the roof of his mouth – possibly another 'trick' of the torturer. The pins were removed.

Now able to speak, Fian had plenty to say. Released from the bootikins and taken again before James, he told of his spells to entrap women and of Bothwell's plots to kill the king. At the end, he signed the confession and went glumly to his cell, where he spent the rest of the day in silent and abject misery. That night the jailer's keys went missing – and so did Fian. But when the hue and cry was raised, the pursuers found him calmly waiting for them at his lodgings.

What happened in Fian's few hours of freedom is not known. The most likely scenario is that Bothwell's men bribed the guard to let him escape, after which he was taken to a most uncomfortable interview with his master. Bothwell, furious with his acolyte for revealing his presence in the plot, ordered him to return and retract his confession. Back in custody, Fian announced that his earlier evidence was false, and that he would say nothing more.

The king was not satisfied. In Fian and his master Bothwell, he saw the Devil not just plotting at his life, but actually at his heels. He ordered the torturers to start work in earnest.

Records of the day say that Fian endured a 'straunge' torment, reckoned excessive even for those horrific times. First his fingernails were ripped off one by one with pincers. Then two needles were thrust into each nailbed up to and beyond the joints. To no avail. The wretched Fian, now mumbling and incoherent, was put back in the bootikins where he 'did abide so many blows in them that his legs were crushed and beaten together as small as might be; and the bones and flesh so bruised that the blood and marrow spouted forth in great abundance, whereby they were made unserviceable forever'.

At last the king's temper snapped and Fian was put in a cart and carried away to Castle Hill where, surprisingly perhaps, he was mercifully strangled before his body was thrown on the fire.

The wretches tried and executed were undoubtedly witches – insofar as they were followers of the older religion of wicca. How much of the more lurid evidence, given as it was under the most extreme duress, was true we shall never know.

Bothwell was obviously the king's target. After all, Bothwell was known to have made several attempts at 'kingnapping' – snatching the king in order to bend him to one party's will – and was plotting with the English and the Spanish against James. It was therefore important to the king to nail Bothwell, and tying him in with sorcery was as good a way as any.

Finally Bothwell himself was arraigned. However, the wily earl had the power and the good sense not only to bribe the jury, but also to fill the city with heavily armed desperadoes. Not surprisingly, he was acquitted. A further attempt by him to kidnap the king failed and he was forced to flee the country, first to Spain and then to Italy, where he eventually died, still plotting.

James now became an expert on witches, writing a demonology, and pursuing covens up and down the country. On gaining the relatively safe position as king of England, however, he appeared to lose interest in the subject. Later in his reign, he moved towards putting an end to witch trials, and freed many innocent victims of other witch delusions.

But it was not so elsewhere. All over Europe the persecution continued, growing ever more vicious as the Roman Catholic Church felt its authority challenged, both by the ancient Celtic religions that would not die away and by the rise of Protestantism. Heretics of any kind were burned, tortured and maimed.

Not that the Protestants were any less passionate in

their abhorrence of anything that smacked of unbelief. As religious wars ravaged Europe and different powers held sway over various territories, ordinary inhabitants prayed only that their country would come under Swedish control – the only combatants with the virtue of tolerance.

Back in England, even as James himself became more lenient towards witches, away from the capital the law was translated as local justices saw fit. Witch scares saw executions in Essex and Lancashire during the king's reign, and the terror continued through the reign of Charles I. But it was in the anarchy and religious bigotry around the time of the Civil War that England's most notorious witch hunter flourished.

Matthew Hopkins was a small-time lawyer of Manningtree in Essex. His 'career' began in 1645, when he became involved in the case of Elizabeth Clarke, the victim of a wild accusation of 'ill-wishing'. Since the only legal torture allowed was to keep a suspect without sleep, he did this to notable effect. Elizabeth soon named someone else, Anne West, as a witch, and both confessed to whatever was asked of them.

Hopkins then proclaimed himself the 'Witchfinder General' and set off around the Home Counties with his accomplices John Stearne and Mary Phillips. They operated on a commercial basis, being paid per execution. Their methods consisted of tying suspects on tiny stools to endure an agony of cramp, deprive them of sleep and to starve them. While something of an ascetic himself, Hopkins's assistant Stearne was not above adding rape to the list of indignities suffered by local women.

As Hopkins widened his net to take in the whole of East Anglia, so the hysteria became ever more demented. His presence in a town would bring forth a flood of denunciations. The jails were crammed at various periods of his operations, and there is no doubt that he was responsible for the deaths of well over 300 people. Not only were there denunciations, but gullible villagers came forward to be put to the witch tests – and were found guilty and hanged.

Hopkins refined the hitherto traditional swimming test. The theory was that a witch, having denied the holy water of baptism, would be rejected by all God's water. So a suspect would be tied hands to opposite feet and thrown in a pond. If the water accepted her (she sank) then she was innocent (though dead). If, however, she floated, the water would have rejected her and she would be considered guilty and subject to the full rigour of the law.

The terror of Hopkins and his gang ended with his death in 1647. There are two accounts of how he met his end.

He had certainly over-reached himself by accusing people of influence, and indeed a Parliamentary Commission was set up to investigate him. So one story is that he was astute enough to know his day was past, and retired with his loot to Manningtree, where he died in his bed. But far more satisfying is the account that he himself was accused of witchcraft. Put to the swimming test, he floated. Whereupon the law that he had invoked so often to the destruction of so many was finally turned on him, and he ended his days choking on the end of a rope.

The disgust felt for Hopkins may have signalled the end of the English witch hunts. But the last great 'English' witch trials took place in New England, America, in 1691–2. The name of the town where they took place become synonymous with horror...

Salem.

Again there can be little doubt that many of the settlers

in the harsh new continent would have been followers of the witch cults, despite the narrow Protestantism they professed. Most authorities today believe that the Rev. George Burroughs, one of nineteen hanged as witches, was a coven leader, and did play the part of God on Earth. But the hysteria in Salem Village (now part of Danvers, Massachusetts) spread around the neighbouring towns and settlements until several hundreds were arrested, more than a hundred came to trial and some twenty-nine were hanged, with one man being crushed to death – the old penalty for refusing to plead in court.

The Salem witch hunt started when the nine-year-old daughter of the local minister played at fortune-telling with her eleven-year-old cousin and her father's Indian slave, Tituba. She became so affected that she started having fits and accusing local women of bewitching her. The girls loved the attention so much that others quickly joined their circle and the denunciations became ever more fanciful.

Finally, as in the case of Hopkins, the terror ended when they accused the wife of the governor of involvement. The assizes were disbanded, the jails emptied and the judges were forced to publish an apology for what they had done.

Even today, witch crazes emerge from time to time. Newspaper headlines scream of vile sexual rituals and of obscenities perpetrated against children in the name of Satan. Is it purely the salacious that interests most people? Or do the witch hunters still have work to do in the wicked twentieth century?

Does Satan still stalk . . . ?

Jeffrey Dahmer

By day he was the mild-mannered, helpful, anonymous little man who worked conscientiously in the local chocolate factory. By night he was a crazed homosexual cannibal who kidnapped, slaughtered and sexually abused his victims, and for two years kept a city in the grip of terror.

It was on a warm July night in Milwaukee in 1991 that horrified police uncovered the secret life of America's most twisted serial killer, Jeffrey Dahmer. His small apartment had been turned into a slaughterhouse for his hapless victims. Bizarre and macabre tales of brutal murder and perverted sex were to emerge in a shocking story of unspeakable horror.

Dahmer was a real-life Hannibal Lecter and, like the character made famous in *The Silence of the Lambs*, was not satisfied with merely killing: he was a necrophiliac who ate choice parts of his victims, kept other parts as grotesque and grisly souvenirs and disposed of the bodies in acid baths, drains and sewers.

Film of police and forensic experts carrying vats of acid, decomposing body parts and bones was broadcast day after day to shock even an American public long inured to the horror of lunatic killers. Dahmer had put Milwaukee on the map for something other than beer and football.

When questioned by police, Dahmer readily admitted to the murder of fifteen young men in the state and to two further murders in Ohio – but there still had to be a protracted trial, because he claimed he was insane. A jury had to be asked to decide whether he was a twisted madman or a calculating killing machine. The trial itself was the most gruesome America had ever witnessed, with a national audience of millions on TV lapping up stories of bizarre sex, sick killings and grisly fantasies. If it had been a movie, it would probably have been banned.

As it was, the case of Jeffrey Dahmer ended with a verdict of guilty. The jury judged that he was not insane. They disregarded testimony of psychiatric experts who said he was a psychotic who suffered from unstoppable urges brought about by the mental condition of necrophilia (which made it impossible for him to obtain sexual gratification except from corpses) and the judge sentenced him to consecutive prison sentences totalling over 1,000 years. The state of Wisconsin has no death penalty.

As in the case of many other notorious serial killers, Dahmer's capture came about by accident. Two patrolmen, Robert Rauth and Rolf Mueller, were sitting in their car late one evening when they saw a black man running towards them, a pair of handcuffs dangling from his wrist. The story he babbled out was to lead to the unmasking of one of the most evil and gruesome criminals in history.

The man, Tracy Edwards, spilled out a wild accusation against a resident of the nearby Oxford Apartments who, he said, had threatened to cut out his heart and eat it. He had run for his life. Edwards, it turned out, had narrowly avoided becoming Dahmer's eighteenth victim.

Edwards told the police he had met Dahmer in a shopping mall and had agreed to go back to his flat to drink some beer. When he tried to leave, Dahmer had threatened him with a knife and snapped the handcuffs on his wrist, holding the other end himself. As he related his lucky escape to a hushed court later, he was too nervous even to look at the man in the dock, such was the incredible power Dahmer exerted over his victims.

Edwards said he had been held in Dahmer's lair for several hours, during which time the Milwaukee monster had lain on top of him, listening to his heart. But then he had got restless, swaying and chanting and seeming to go in and out of a trance. It was then that Edwards had seized his chance to escape.

The two cops, well used to answering emergency calls in the run-down section of town that was their beat, took Edwards back to the ordinary-looking block of apartments and rang the bell of one of Dahmer's neighbours. 'Police, open up,' they ordered the neighbour, John Batchelor, through the intercom. He let them in and looked at his watch. It was 11.25 p.m.

The cops then knocked on Dahmer's door as the terrified Edwards waited a safe distance away down the corridor. They were prepared for anything inside the flat – but what they found would turn out to be beyond their wildest imaginings. The door was opened by a slight man with dirty blond hair, wearing a blue T-shirt and jeans. The first thing the cops noticed was a strange, nauseating stench, and pots bubbling on the stove containing an evil-looking goo. In the sink were unwashed dishes with traces of the gooey substance on them . . .

When the two cops radioed in to police headquarters to 'run a make' on Dahmer, they were told he was still on probation following his release from jail for a sexual assault on a thirteen-year-old boy. Dahmer quickly found himself lying face down on the floor as handcuffs twisted his arms high behind his back.

It was then that Officer Mueller opened the refrigerator – and leapt back in horror. 'Oh my God!,' he remembered yelling. 'There's a goddamn head in here. He's one sick son of a bitch.'

Dahmer's murderous spree had come to an abrupt end.

No one had suspected the man in No. 213 of being anything worse than perhaps a little odd. As detectives and forensic experts began pouring into the flat, however, it became apparent that he had been indulging in an orgy of murder for well over a year. Police found a 47-gallon barrel of acid in the apartment, with the decomposing remains of at least three dissected human torsos. Decomposed hands and genitals were kept in pots in kitchen cupboards, along with human skulls and rotting fingers and toes. A collection of Polaroid pictures was discovered showing fifteen different victims in various states of undress and, in the words of a forensic report, 'in different degrees of surgical excision'.

Pictures from gay magazines hung on the bedroom walls and a collection of kinky and pornographic videos littered the living-room. The only normal food in the flat were crisps, mustard and beer. He had not only been killing his victims, but after satisfying his lust on their dead bodies, he had been eating their flesh as well. He later told police that he had fried and eaten one man's biceps. He said that after tenderising and marinating in steak sauce, the meal tasted 'just like beef'. Hamburgers made from strips of human flesh and muscle were found in his fridge. The evidence was taken away by police in special anti-toxin suits.

* * *

Dahmer's father Lionel was a research chemist in Bath, Ohio. He married his sweetheart, Joyce Flint, in 1959 and Jeffrey was born nine months later. As far as is known, his childhood was not particularly traumatic, although his hobby appeared to be collecting dead animals from the highway and skinning or dissecting them. At school he was a class clown – though not in a wholesome way, as classmates were later to recall. His favourite joke was to imitate mentally retarded people. Another pastime was drawing chalk outlines of dead bodies on the floor, homicide-style. He had trouble maintaining relationships because he was considered 'weird'.

When he was eighteen, his mother and father split up and he moved into a motel to fend for himself while his parents fought for custody of his eleven-year-old brother. During the bitter battle, Dahmer's father was to refer to his wife's gross cruelty and neglect and her history of mental illness. No one knows exactly what turns a man into a serial killer, but in Dahmer's case a family history of mental illness might have been a factor.

Dahmer went from high school to university but soon dropped out to join the army. He had dreams of being a military policeman but instead became a medical orderly. He served in Germany but was finally drummed out of the army for alcohol abuse. However, the rudimentary knowledge of anatomy picked up during his time as a medic was to serve him well in his later career as a killer.

Back in America, he drifted from job to job, finally returning to Milwaukee in 1982 to live with his grand-mother. Here he began his pattern of strange sexual behaviour, exposing himself to young children, and finally being charged with the sexual abuse of a thirteen-year-old boy. In one of the many ironies that surfaced in the Dahmer case, the boy's brother was later to become one of the monster's victims.

When found guilty of the sexual abuse charge, he wrote a particularly lucid letter to his trial judge asking for clemency. 'The world has enough misery in it without my adding more to it,' he wrote. 'That is why I am asking for a sentence modification, so that I can continue my life as a productive member of society.'

The year was 1988 and Dahmer had already killed four times.

Dahmer was sentenced to eight years in jail, but amazingly was released as a model prisoner after serving just ten months. He was assigned to social worker Donna Chester, a kindly 35-year-old who saw him as just another minor sex offender trying, through counselling and re-habilitation, to find his way back into society. Ms Chester had another 121 cases on her books and after two years applied for a waiver that made visits to his home unnecessary.

It was a decision that Milwaukee police chief Philip Arreola was to criticize bitterly when Dahmer's dark secret was finally revealed. 'We try to put these people away for a long time,' he fumed. 'Then they get let back on the streets. We can see the tragic results of a system that has ceased to function.'

A few days after that angry statement, Arreola had to eat humble pie when he was forced to admit that three of his men had confronted Dahmer and had even been inside his flat without realizing anything was wrong.

The confrontation in question took place in May 1991, when a fourteen-year-old refugee from Laos, one Konerak

Sinthasomphone, was seen running out of Dahmer's flat naked, apparently drugged and bleeding. Neighbours, most of whom were black, called the police, but allege that when the three officers arrived they were more or less told to 'stop bothering the white guy'.

Yet Sinthasomphone had been drugged with sleeping tablets (Dahmer's favoured way of rendering victims helpless while he strangled them) and there were tiny drill marks in his forehead.

The macabre reason for these strange marks was that Dahmer fantasized about creating zombie-like lovers who would never leave him and would obey all his bidding as sex slaves. He began experimenting on them by trying to carry out crude lobotomies with a Black and Decker drill and acid. One wretched victim lay conscious in his death agonies for a whole day before expiring.

Amazingly, in the case of runaway Sinthasomphone, the three police to whom he appealed for help returned him to Dahmer, who told them he was a lover with whom he had quarrelled. Within hours, Dahmer strangled him, had oral sex with the corpse and then dismembered it, all the time taking Polaroid snaps. The policemen involved were later fired.

As the subsequent trial of Jeffrey Dahmer proceeded in the imposing Milwaukee courthouse, family after family turned out to curse the monster who had slaughtered their loved ones. One young woman, whose nineteen-year-old brother had been butchered in the Oxford Apartments, had to be restrained by court officials as she made a dash for Dahmer, screaming, 'You motherfucker – I'll kill you.'

Towards the end of the trial, Dahmer stunned everyone by asking to make his own statement, an articulate apology composed in his prison cell. Asking for 'no consideration' and declaring he would rather have faced the death penalty, he said:

It is over now. This has never been a case of trying to get free. I really wanted death. I hope God can forgive, I know society and the families never can. I promise to pray every day for their forgiveness. I have seen their tears. If I could give my life right now to bring their loved ones back, I would. This was not about hate. I never hated anyone. I knew I was sick or evil, or both. Now I have some peace. I know the harm I have caused. I can't undo the terrible harm, but I have cooperated as best I could. I am very sorry. I know I will be in prison for the rest of my life. I will turn back to God. I should have stayed with God. I tried and failed and created a holocaust. Only the Lord Jesus Christ can save me from my sins.

He further promised to cooperate with psychologists and became a human guinea pig so that they could study his bizarre mind and perhaps discover what turned a human being into the ghastly killer and cannibal that he had become.

'I pledge to help the doctors find some answers,' the statement continued. 'I know my time in prison will be terrible but I deserve what I get because of what I did.' Dahmer, who admitted to detectives that he had studied satanic scripts, read a passage from the Bible and declared: 'Jesus Christ came in the world to save sinners, of whom I am the worst.'

He apologized to the victims' families, the probation officer he had hoodwinked, and even to the policemen who were fired because of him. He also apologized to his father and his stepmother Shari, who had sat through the trial, heads bowed in silence: 'I love them all. I take all the blame for what I did. I hurt many people. I decided to go through with this trial for a number of reasons. I wanted to show they were not hate crimes. I wanted the world to know the truth. I didn't want any unanswered questions. I wanted to find out what it was that made me bad or evil. Perhaps if there are others out there, this might have helped them.'

Dahmer was sentenced to 1,070 years in jail. He will be eligible for parole in October 2922.

After sentence was passed, Dahmer was taken to the maximum security Columbia Correctional Institution, Wisconsin's toughest jail. Today, in a weird echo of *The Silence of the Lambs* supercriminal Hannibal Lecter, he sits all day, isolated in a round-the-clock observation cell. He has no contact with other prisoners.

He is allowed a brief exercise period alone every day and even though he says he no longer wants to kill, guards are taking no chances. All his food is passed to him through a drawer in a wall. He is guarded night and day by armed men in a control room and he always has to wear the bright orange jumpsuit he was given as he walked in through the doors of the jail.

Unlike Hannibal Lecter in the film, who maintained a library of sorts in his cell, Dahmer is allowed only six books, four magazines, ten pictures and fifteen letters in his cell at any one time. Every week around two dozen letters are addressed to him from women who want to meet him.

Serial killer expert Judith Becker, who testified for the defence at Dahmer's trial, says it is too soon to be able to gauge the effects of prison life on Dahmer. Although he is reported to be cooperating with medical experts – as are other killers in jails around the USA – it would be difficult to read the mind of such a man at any time.

After all, Milwaukee's other monster, Ed Gein, the role model for the hunted murderer in *The Silence of the Lambs*, was working as a babysitter while he spent his nights killing women or digging up bodies to provide the skin for the new 'suit' he was meticulously sewing for himself; Ted Bundy worked for the Samaritans in Seattle between murders; John Wayne Gacy performed as a clown at children's parties and David Berkowitz went on to counselling other prisoners. One thing serial killers seem to have in common is their ability to disguise their traits when not in killing mode.

Dahmer himself had fooled Donna Chester and three policemen, and the sleeping pills he used to drug his victims were all prescribed by his doctor. Judith Becker says: 'Dahmer indicated to me that he hated what he had been doing and talked about a nuclear explosion that had gone off inside him since he was caught. He's talked about killing himself, but that will be difficult where he is. He says he is sorry for what he did and feels pain for the relatives. He says the fantasies have stopped, but there's no way of knowing if they will start up again.'

So there is a suspicion that Dahmer is still managing to some extent to manipulate the system, but how he copes with prison is something that will fascinate the medical and psychiatric profession for years to come. The chances are that he will become a model prisoner with the ability to be perfectly friendly to guards and inmates alike.

One man who will be particularly interested is Robert Ressler, who headed the FBI's special research group on serial killers before he left to set up his own investigation agency. The research outfit, based in Quantico, Virginia, is the one for which the young agent played by Jodie Foster in *The Silence of the Lambs* worked. Ressler, who has interviewed such notable killers as Sharon Tate slayer

Charles Manson, Kennedy assassin Sirhan Sirhan and 'Son of Sam' David Berkowitz, wants to add Dahmer to his case files. 'How can a man be sane and commit these horrendous acts?' asks Ressler. 'Any information we can collect on individuals like Dahmer is like gold dust in tracking down others out there who might be doing the same thing.'

Judith Becker adds: 'We could learn a tremendous amount from studying Dahmer because necrophiliacs are extremely rare. I have not read anywhere of the successful treatment of this disorder.'

Even the most highly qualified experts cannot agree on the kind of demons that live in Dahmer's twisted mind. Early in life he exhibited a strange and bizarre fascination with death when he collected dead animals. Some experts claim that the emotional distance between him and his parents might have contributed to a feeling of abandonment. They say this was what sparked his killing spree; he told doctors that the reason he killed his victims was that he did not want them to leave him. The same experts reckon that being locked up for life with other criminals who won't be leaving might actually appeal to Dahmer.

However, James Fox, a professor of criminal justice at Boston University and author of the book *Mass Murder: The Growing Menace*, disagrees:

These guys enjoy what they do. They might get a little guilty afterwards but the fantasies that drive them on are so powerful that they have to do it again soon. Dahmer won't be able to do it again now he's in jail. He doesn't even have any of his souvenirs (the photographs and body parts that he kept in his apartment) and that could be why he wanted the death penalty. He has nothing left to live for. Souvenirs are important to the disorganized serial killers because they remind them of the best times they ever had. Dahmer's murders were driven by fantasies of destruction, tied up with a sexual desire.

Long after the Dahmer trial, Apartment 213 in the Oxford Apartments on Milwaukee's North 25th Street – Dahmer's chamber of horrors – still lay vacant, as did the entire second floor. The management even took the name from the front of the building to discourage ghouls and sightseers. Jurors from the trial received counselling, and victims' families pressed ahead with lawsuits against Dahmer and the city.

Jeffrey Dahmer was only the fourteenth necrophiliac to be convicted in American legal history. The world will be the better without him. But perhaps no one will ever know what it was that drove him to commit his gruesome crimes. What is certain is that prisoners in Columbia Correctional Institution will never be queuing up to share a cell with him.

Vampire Queen

Behind every legend lies a story; behind every myth a half-truth. And sometimes the truth that spawns the legend that feeds the myth is so terrible that it defies the power of the storyteller to embellish it. From time to time there arises a being so depraved, so inherently wicked, that while the evil lives on after the death of the malefactor, history cannot hope to reveal the total horror.

Such a story is the legend of Dracula, loathsome lord of the 'undead', cursed to spread his poison from beyond the grave and feed his malice with the blood of living beings.

The inspiration for Dracula – the real Dracula, not the furtive creature of Bram Stoker's novel, nor the foul, flighty entity scripted by Hollywood – was in life more sinister than Stoker or any other civilized human could understand.

This monster, far more terrible than that most chilling of horror heroes, lived 400 years ago in medieval Transylvania, now part of Romania. Dracula's real-life role model was steeped in sadism, blood-lust, cruelty, cannibalism, necrophilia and – lesbian sex.

Yes, Dracula was a woman.

Forget the bats, coffins and silver bullets of the Dracula

we know from fable. Enter, if you dare, a world so terrifying that madness lies beyond its borders. For Stoker had to play down the horror he had stumbled across. Even a Gothic novelist needs a level of popular credence. And who could believe in such a pit of depravity as Countess Elizabeth Bathory?

Vampire legends were rife in medieval central Europe. There was a widespread belief in the dead rising from their graves. The legend was fuelled by occasional exhumations that revealed corpses to have moved, to have gnawed on their own hands and to have a look of such petrifying malice on their faces that witnesses were sent mad. But the stark and chilling truth was that these people were buried alive – be it through the lack of medical understanding of the time, the severity of the legal system or the kind of religious fanaticism that inspired the dark cults that then flourished.

Life, for the peasant at any rate, was worth little. When a popular uprising of 1514 was put down, the serfs were impaled on spikes, dismembered, disembowelled or burned alive. The leader of the revolt, George Dosza, was slow-roasted on an iron chair, after which his lieutenants were made to eat his flesh before being broken on the wheel and hanged.

This was the nightmare world into which Elizabeth Bathory was born in 1560, and such was the cruelty she saw meted out every day. The gentry had total power of life and death over their servants. And the mighty Bathory family had hundreds of servants in their many estates.

Young Elizabeth received a scholarly education; she could write Hungarian, Latin and Greek at a time when the king himself could barely write his name. But the education she received from her family and her peers was altogether different.

At the tender age of ten, she saw a visiting gypsy musician hauled up before her father in the middle of a party, accused of selling his child to the Turks. It was a charge made only for the castle's amusement, as in truth nobody would have cared about the fate of a gypsy's offspring. The unhappy wretch denied the charge, but when a sum of money was found on him which he could not adequately explain, his fate was sealed. Death was the grim sentence.

Elizabeth found the whole episode amusing. Later, she was so intrigued by hearing the man moaning and bewailing his fate during the night that she rose with the dawn next day, avoided her governess and hid in the courtyard to watch the execution.

She was beside herself with anticipation as the wretch was dragged out. Breathlessly she watched as a horse was led out and tethered. Then a soldier with a long knife slit open its belly. Fascinated, Elizabeth watched as the gypsy was thrust inside the shrieking animal, the belly of which was then sewn up, leaving only the man's head exposed. She almost swooned as she watched the two thrashing around in their death agony.

Elizabeth had dipped her toe in an ocean of blood. She was to bathe in it often for the rest of her life. Three years later, yet another peasants' uprising was put down. Elizabeth was in the crowd when fifty-four rebellious serfs had their noses and ears sliced off before being hanged. She was learning to be ruthless with disobedient servants.

But it was a relative who opened the door to her stunning depths of depravity.

There was a good deal of intermarriage among the nobility of the day, resulting in ever-increasing numbers of deformities and idiots. In the Bathory clan, her brother

Stefan was a lecher and a drunk, an uncle was a mad epileptic who devoted himself to weird ritual and devil worship, and her aunt Klara was a notorious bisexual who got her kicks from lesbian orgies and the sadistic torturing of servants.

The doctors of the day recognized the weakening of family blood lines, and their remedy was to order patients to drink the fresh blood of healthy peasants. Elizabeth was to spend a lot of time with her aunt. She discovered a taste for blood at the same time as she learned her first torture techniques and opened a new chapter in her own sexuality.

Not that she was entirely lesbian in her desires, although her sexual sadism was directed solely against her female servants. She was engaged to the gruff, semi-literate Count Ferenc Nadasdy, who was five years her senior and was to become a national hero for the leadership of his country's troops against the marauding Turks. But Elizabeth never let herself be thwarted by such concepts as fidelity.

At her aunt's and at her future mother-in-law's, she used to dress as a boy and play sexual games with well-favoured servant lads. But the wedding with Nadasdy was delayed because she went too far in her games and found herself pregnant. So her husband-to-be stayed on at the wars and Elizabeth was sent to a remote Bathory estate for her confinement. The child was given to a local peasant, along with a sum of 'hush money'.

When she finally married in 1575, Elizabeth was fifteen and developing into a real beauty. But that wasn't enough to hold her young husband's attention, and he soon returned to his army life. So the new countess used the services of a particularly well-endowed servant as her personal stud, and spent even longer periods with her twisted aunt Klara...

A blood legend was about to be born.

Elizabeth ran her new home, Castle Sarvar, with a rod of iron – along with a whip, a brand and any other instrument that came to hand. Her disciplining of the staff was brutal, even by the savage standards of the time. Thirty years later, eyewitness testimony at the trial of her closest associates would refer to her love of stripping her girls naked and beating them or sticking pins through their lips. If a girl found a coin and did not hand it in, she would be made to stand naked before the whole castle staff, while the coin was heated in a fire and pressed into her hand.

She did much of the beating herself, but seemed to get just as much satisfaction from watching her trusted older servants causing pain and death. According to one of these, Dorothea Szentes, her method was to have the hands of the girls bound tightly behind their backs. Then, as they stood or crouched helpless and vulnerable, every part of their bodies would be beaten savagely. And her blood lust was quenched only with the victim's death.

The 'punishments' grew ever more gruesome as Elizabeth indulged her passion for torture. She stuck pins under the fingernails of servant girls, inviting them to pull them out if the pain was too great. But any girl who pulled out the pin had her fingers cut off with a pair of shears.

'Star kicking' was another trick she learned from her aunt. Pieces of paper were put between a girl's toes and set alight, whereupon the girl would see stars and kick. One girl suffered severe burns when the countess set her pubic hair alight with a candle.

Elizabeth's husband, too, was wont to join in the fun. Although he never tortured his victims to death, he saw nothing wrong in maltreating peasants. It was he who had

215

one girl stripped, smeared in honey and left outside for twenty-four hours, where she was bitten and stung by all manner of insects. He also refined star kicking by first dipping the paper in oil.

In every one of Elizabeth's homes she maintained a torture chamber, usually in the laundry room, as there was inevitably a lot of cleaning up to do. And every one of her girl servants got to know the inside of these chambers. The slightest infringement of any rule resulted in terrible punishment. According to later testimony, girls would find themselves being tortured as often as ten times a day.

Elizabeth was of a blood line that had been weakened by intermarriage, so she would have followed the quaint medicinal beliefs of the day and would have been drinking blood on prescription. But she brought new terror and death when she devised the scheme of bathing in blood in order to keep herself young and beautiful.

Her fourth child, Paul, was born in 1598. Not surprisingly, the youthful Bathory beauty was beginning to fade, and the countess took to gazing into a mirror for hours at a time. One day, suffering from a particularly bad bout of depression, she was having her hair dressed by a servant girl who accidentally gave it a tug. Furiously, she turned and slapped the face of the girl so hard as to draw blood. Even more angry now, she was about to strike again when she noticed that her skin, in the area that had been touched by the young maid's blood, had become whiter and more translucent.

She had found her fountain of eternal youth. From now on, her life was to be literally a bloodbath.

In 1604, a year after the death of Queen Elizabeth I in England, Count Nadasdy-Bathory, by now a military hero, died and his widow's reign of terror became boundless.

Into the household came one Anna Darvulia, a lesbian and a sadist, whom Elizabeth undoubtedly loved. She joined the other three long-time henchmen of the blood countess: Helena Jo (Paul's wet nurse), Dorothea Szentes and Janos Ficzko, a crippled dwarf and the only male allowed an active role in the sexual sadism. These three stalwarts later pointed to Darvulia's arrival as the time the most abominable atrocities began.

Newcomer Anna brought in the freezing torture: dragging girls naked, as always, into the bitter cold snow and pouring water over them until they froze to death. It became a particular favourite with Elizabeth – it kept the blood fresh for several days. Another punishment for a maid who failed to press the countess's clothes correctly was to have the hot iron thrust into her face until it became a huge scorched wound. On still other occasions Elizabeth would thrust her fingers into a girl's mouth and pull until it split. One girl who tried to escape on a journey was dipped in a river and left to freeze to death. One twelve-year-old who was apprehended in flight was bundled into a kind of iron maiden, a cage filled with spikes, and dangled from a rope. She was so small that the spikes missed her, so Elizabeth had the ropes jerked until the spikes did their deadly work and stripped the skin off the girl's bones.

Elizabeth had an iron maiden in most of her many houses and castles. Some were simple cages with a spring mechanism that released the spikes inside, others were works of art. In keeping with her twisted sexuality, some were even modelled in the form of a slim, lovely girl with tresses on the head and pubic hair below. One of these had a jewelled necklace and precious stones for navel and nipples. But it hid a deadly secret. One of these stones triggered a second mechanism that made spikes shoot outwards. Elizabeth's game was to have an unsuspecting servant girl, inevitably nude, polish her 'ornament' and wait in breathless anticipation until the girl touched the wrong button and died screaming and bloody in the maiden's embrace.

It was at about this time, too, that Elizabeth's perverse tastes broke new boundaries of barbarism. She began biting the flesh of girls as she tortured them. If it was acceptable to gain strength from drinking blood, it was just a small step to eating flesh. On one occasion, she was ill and confined to bed. She ordered one of her old women to bring a girl and strip her in the usual way. Then, as she was held by the bed, Elizabeth bit mouthfuls of flesh from her face, shoulder and breasts.

She now started storing the bodies under her bed for night games of a different kind. But while her necrophilia was long suspected, she had another reason to store bodies in her room. There were so many that she was having difficulty disposing of them.

On one occasion, her son-in-law was on a visit when his dogs unearthed a skeleton in the garden. On another, bodies were piled up so high in the house – because there was not enough trusted staff to remove them – that the place began to stink and had to be abandoned for a while.

According to one of her servants at a judicial investigation in 1611, a diary in Elizabeth's handwriting had been discovered that showed she had been responsible for the deaths of 650 girls and women over the years. In fact the number is probably on the conservative side. She had been torturing and killing servants virtually unhindered for thirty years. At their trial, her accomplices revealed they had thrown bodies into fruit pits, a small canal in the garden and in the path of roaming wolves. The local church had long since refused to bury them.

In fact Pastor Ponikenusz, whose flock included Elizabeth's household and surrounding villages, had denounced Elizabeth in a letter to his superior. He wrote: 'We have heard from the very mouths of the girls who survived the torture process that some of the boys were forced to eat the girls' flesh, roasted on a fire. The flesh of other girls was chopped up fine like mushrooms, cooked and spiced and given to the young lads who did not know what they were eating.'

The fact that her revolting habits were well known, yet no action could be taken against her, argues that the times were far more barbarous than we can today imagine and that the Bathory family, especially when linked to her husband's Nadasdy clan, was too powerful to challenge.

What finally led to Elizabeth's downfall, however, was her switch to murdering people of 'quality'. Under Darvulia's tutelage, only peasant girls were used in the kinky torture and murder sessions. However, suitable victims were becoming increasingly difficult to find as rumours about her spread. The supply was simply drying up. When the vile Darvulia succumbed to a stroke, Elizabeth started to lure the younger daughters of the lesser nobility into the castle, where they met the same fate as had the peasants.

Darvulia was replaced by the widow of a tenant farmer, Erzsi Majorova, who started recruiting noble girls until they, too, realized the dangers of living in the countess's entourage. Yet Elizabeth's bloodlust was uncontrollable. The only recourse was for Majorova to kidnap peasants and scrub them up to look sufficiently like ladies to fool the countess.

By now, even the family could ignore things no longer.

Elizabeth's expenses in satisfying her strange appetites must have been horrendous. In addition, the crown began to take an interest in her affairs. This concern was not entirely in the interests of justice, for it owed the Bathory estate a massive sum of money that had been put up by her husband during the wars. The crown itself was hard up and would have loved to find the countess guilty of some capital offence, so that the debt could be wiped out and Bathory properties seized.

So, in late 1610, Elizabeth's family, together with the local law lord and one-time lover of the countess, Count Thurzo, plotted to have her taken away to a convent where she could disappear from sight. The reasons were political rather than humanitarian, as soon became apparent.

However, it was not to be. Imre Megyery, the man selected by Elizabeth's husband before his death to run Castle Sarvar and be guardian and tutor to his son Paul, had denounced her to parliament. Alarmed by the number of people of quality who had disappeared around her estates, parliament decided to investigate, and by December, King Mathias II felt he had enough evidence to prosecute. He wanted the woman beheaded. Again on pragmatic rather than humanitarian grounds.

Now a new dimension arose. Thurzo, like Elizabeth, was a Protestant, while the king and the majority of the noble houses were Catholic. It was not therefore in the interests of the Protestant cause to allow the Bathory estates to be broken up. So when parliament ordered Count Thurzo to investigate the Bathory case and punish the guilty, he acted swiftly – and in his own interests. Thurzo acted during parliament's Christmas recess, when few could question his methods and motives. He planned to present parliament with a fait accompli after the recess.

In a midnight raid on Castle Cachtice – one of her many residences – where she was spending Christmas, Thurzo's men caught the countess in the act of murder. She was in a blood frenzy crouched over the still bleeding body of yet another victim either daubing herself in blood or else drinking it as it welled out. Immediately the castle was searched and a mass grave was unearthed below a tower. The reign of terror was over.

Thurzo held an immediate trial. On 2 January 1611, Elizabeth's four principal accomplices stood before their accusers. Ficzko, Szentes, Jo and a fearsome peasant woman called Katharina Beneczky were all asked the same eleven questions. All four admitted the charges, but declared that they had been acting under orders. All four gave evidence against the countess. But she was never there to defend herself, nor was she ever tried.

A week later the four were sent to a higher court, still under Thurzo's control, where more evidence about Elizabeth's blood-sucking and werewolfism (biting and devouring the flesh of her girls) was given. Still she was not tried, even though the king ordered that she should be. Her accomplices were not so lucky . . .

At the end of the trial, it was found that there was not enough evidence against Beneczky, so she was jailed until more could be gathered. Her ultimate fate is unknown – very likely she was left to rot in her dungeon. Ficzko, because he had been involved in relatively few crimes, was beheaded, after which his corpse was drained of blood and burned. The old women Jo and Szentes had their fingers, the instruments of so many crimes, torn out with red-hot pincers. They were then thrown alive on a bonfire. A fortnight later the farmer's widow, Majorova, was likewise tried and executed.

Thurzo's scheme was to execute enough of the underlings to distract attention from the principal villain, Elizabeth herself. Throughout this blood-letting Elizabeth remained under house arrest, her fate undecided. Finally, however, she overplayed her arrogant hand. She threatened Thurzo with the vengeance which would be exacted by her family, unaware of their connivance in her arrest.

The count's patience snapped. 'You are like a wild animal,' he shouted. 'You do not deserve to breathe the air on earth, nor see the light of the Lord. You will disappear from the world and never reappear in it again. I condemn you to lifelong imprisonment in your own castle.'

The king was finally persuaded that it would be bad for the country to put Elizabeth on trial, as it would besmirch the name of her husband, the greatest recent war hero. Thurzo's sentence stood.

Workmen were called in to wall up the doors and windows to the small room in which Elizabeth was to be confined in Castle Cachtice. Only a ventilation shaft and a small opening through which food could be pushed connected her to the world. The once all-powerful Elizabeth Bathory was never to leave the room in which she was immured, nor see any sight other than her four walls.

Was Elizabeth Bathory really the figure that inspired Bram Stoker? Was there any truth in her belief that bathing in virgins' blood would maintain her youthful looks? And what was her final fate within her four-walled tomb?

All we know for certain is that late in August 1614 a new jailer arrived at the castle. A young man, he had only heard stories of the great beauty who still dazzled well into her forties by dint of her macabre practices. He wanted to see for himself the truth of the rumours.

Peering through the small grill, he saw the countess lying

crumpled on the floor. Elizabeth Bathory, perhaps the most evil woman the world has ever known, was dead.

And, deprived of her blood baths, she was hideously ugly.

Beverley Allitt

Chris and Joanne Taylor sat clinging to each other in the hospital canteen. Their world was in tatters. Only minutes before, they had been woken by the hospital's night services manager, who had told them that their second son, seven-week-old Liam, had stopped breathing. Now they had to make the biggest decision of their lives – whether or not their baby should die.

Liam had been admitted to the children's ward in Grantham and Kesteven General Hospital on 21 February 1991 as a precaution, because within weeks of his birth there he had developed a persistent heavy cold that became a severe chest infection: bronchiolitis. It wasn't a life-threatening situation. He was not in any danger, and the health visitor simply wanted him monitored to be on the safe side.

Inside the optimistically named 'Mr Happy's Room' on the children's Ward Four, Chris and Joanne were greeted with a heart-breaking scene. Doctors and nurses crowded around the tiny incubator where Liam lay dwarfed by drips and emergency oxygen equipment. Chris and Joanne recoiled in horror when they were told their beautiful baby had suffered respiratory failure and was barely alive.

As the specialist gently told them the harrowing news

that Liam had suffered a severe lack of oxygen when he stopped breathing, they looked at the child in disbelief. Earlier, they had gone to bed happy in the knowledge that Liam was in safe hands. Nurse Allitt, who became known as 'his nurse', had promised to take special care of him, even working a double shift at their request. She had become an ally and a friend and they trusted her.

Liam had been on the mend. Now they were being told that his life hung in the balance and that even if he did live, the terrible damage to his brain meant he would endure a lifetime of suffering.

At 6.30 a.m. Joanne sat beside Chris as he cradled his chubby son in his arms, the drips and monitors removed. They kissed his head, still damp where the hospital chaplain had christened the child Liam James Taylor.

Stunned, they waited for the end, which doctors said would not be long in coming. For seven-and-a-half hours they each took turns in cuddling him as he fought to cling to life. Little Liam had been in the hospital for less than forty-eight hours before he lost his battle.

Chris and Joanne agreed to a post-mortem. The death certificate had stated that Liam had died as a result of pneumonia and suspected septicaemia. But the pathologist found that Liam's heart muscles had died. Doctors were baffled by the findings. It was almost unheard of for a child of that age to die from what was effectively an old man's disease.

Liam was cremated in March 1991. A white marble headstone marks his grave today. In a poignant touch his parents had their pet name for him etched in the pure stone: 'Pudding Pants'.

In the weeks that followed, Chris and Joanne tried to

come to terms with the mystery surrounding his death, their questions unanswered by doctors who themselves could find no answers. No one could have known that his death would be the start of a series of evil killings that would make Nurse Beverley Allitt go down in history as one of Britain's most notorious women killers. No one who knew her could have seen the monster in the making.

Bev, as she was known to her friends, had always wanted to be a nurse – especially, a children's nurse. She talked of nothing else, even as a child. She was popular among the inhabitants of Corby Glen, the tiny, typically English village where she lived. They thought of her as a trustworthy girl whom they often allowed to babysit their children.

Allitt lived with her two sisters and brother at their parents' pub, The Fighting Cocks. She was a plain, over-weight and dumpy girl. A schoolfriend recalls: 'Although her looks never drew much attention, Beverley was always one of the brightest youngsters. She had plenty of ability so it was a bit of a surprise when she narrowly failed the entrance exam to Grantham Girls' High School. 'The former friend added ominously: 'She used to mother the smaller kids. You got used to seeing Beverley playing with the toddlers, pushing their prams or walking them up and down the road.'

Allitt joined the Girl Guides and, in summer, would pack a picnic and walk for miles through fields and woods with friends. There was little in the way of nightlife for girls in their teens in Corby Glen, but once a month on a Friday night the village came alive with a disco in the church hall. Allitt and her friends would spend their pocket money on 50 pence entrance tickets, buy cans of Coke and packets of crisps and dance with each other to Bananarama and Duran Duran. For a couple of years, from the age of fourteen, it was the highlight of the social calendar.

Allitt's schoolfriend said: 'Beverley never had a boy-friend. But we often had a laugh with the boys. None of them would dare tease her about her weight. I got the feeling they were actually a bit frightened of her because most of them were smaller than her. Bev could always take care of herself. She wouldn't want to get into fights and would always back off. But you got the impression that she could handle herself.'

In June 1985, Allitt left Charles Read Secondary Modern School with seven CSEs and one 'O' Level pass in home economics. Still overweight and rarely wearing make-up or a pretty dress, she preferred baggy jumpers and jeans. At seventeen, she went out with a boyfriend for the first time in her life. Village boy Steve Biggs became besotted with her after meeting her in a pub where regulars described her as a 'nice, quiet girl'. The shy, softly spoken roadworker became totally dominated by Allitt in a strange, almost unreal relationship of two-and-a-half years of rows, rejec-tions, rare sexual adventures and, briefly, engagement and talk of marriage.

Steve said: 'I decided that Bev didn't like sex much at all. She never took her clothes off in front of me and I don't suppose you can call what happened between us making love. We had sex – and there's a difference. When Bev said it was over, then it was over, and she used to tell me to stop and I just accepted it because I was in love. Each time it only lasted five minutes at the most. She would normally say: "Get off, you're hurting me."'

Twice the couple went on holiday. But what should have been romantic interludes ended in misery for Steve when

Dracula was a woman, history now tells us. Her name was Countess Elizabeth Bathory. *(Mary Evans Picture Library)*

The smiling nurse pretended to help. In reality, Beverley Allitt was putting paid to the most innocent victims of all.

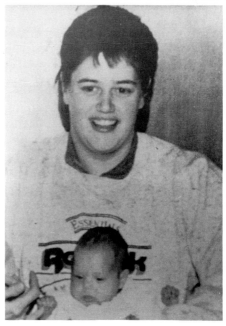

Since medieval times, some men have been thought to have the ability to take on the guise of vampires and werewolves. *(Mary Evans Picture Library)*

Michael Sams was a one-legged train-spotter who kidnapped and killed.

Stephanie Slater was snatched by Sams and kept in a 'coffin' while he issued ransom demands.

Adolfo de Jesus Constanzo believed he was the 'chosen one' of a vicious and violent sect.

Lindy Chamberlain was accused of murdering her own baby. She was cleared after a sensational trial.

Ayers Rock in Australia's Outback. It was here that the Chamberlain baby was snatched by a dingo.

Herman Mudgett's 'Torture Castle' contained dungeons where he painfully put paid to his victims.

Pol Pot was an evil despot who destroyed an entire nation for a fanatical ideal.

Just a tiny proportion of the millions who died to fuel Pol Pot's mad dream.

The Waco compound where men, women and children lined up for a fiery fate.

'Messiah' David Koresh claimed his doomed disciples would find God.

William Burke *(left)* and William Hare *(below)*, the notorious, murderous body-snatchers. *(Mary Evans Picture Library)*

Leonard Lake and ex-wife Cricket. She starred in some of his early, vile videos.

Allitt refused to sleep with him or even hold his hand in public. Yet he remained besotted, allowing her to lay down all the rules. Desperately in love, he once decided to call Allitt's bluff.

'I said I wanted to finish with her. I said I was going but Bev slammed the door, tore at my hair and shouted, "You're not going anywhere." She grabbed my hair and dragged me onto the floor. I was on my knees shouting at her to get off and let me go. She had upset me so much I was crying.'

The relationship was doomed. In the spring of 1990, Allitt phoned Steve out of the blue at his home in Corby Glen and told him it was all over.

Meanwhile, Beverley's aspirations to become a nurse had never left her. Almost immediately after leaving school, she had started a pre-nursing course at Grantham College. But she had to wait a frustrating six months before there was a vacancy for a student nurse at the Grantham and Kesteven Hospital, where eventually she was to bring such misery.

The three years she trained there passed uneventfully and she worked hard to become a State Enrolled Nurse. She spent the last six months of her training in the children's ward in preparation for the job of her dreams, a children's nurse. It seemed, however, that her dreams were about to be shattered when she was turned down for that very position by a hospital 30 miles away. She was told she did not have enough experience with handling very sick children.

Fate took an unexpected twist for her and the children of Ward Four, however, when the Grantham and Kesteven Hospital unexpectedly offered her a six-month contract to work with children. They were suffering from a severe staff shortage; even though a post had been advertised for an experienced nurse, they had had no replies. Beverley was thrilled – at last she had a chance to prove herself . . .

Just three days after Liam Taylor's death, another tragedy hit Ward Four when eleven-year-old Timothy Hardwick died within hours of admission. He had been born with such severe brain damage that he was blind and had never walked or talked. Doctors also found he was suffering from cerebral palsy and epilepsy.

It was because of an epileptic fit that he was rushed to hospital on the evening of 5 March 1991. He responded quickly to the drugs doctors gave him and seemed to be rallying round. Then suddenly, without warning, his condition went into irreversible decline and by 6.30 p.m. he was dead.

But it was to take the deaths of two more children – Becky Phillips and Claire Peck – in similar circumstances before the police were finally called in. In all during the months of February, March and April 1991, there were a total of twenty-four incidents on Ward Four, resulting in the deaths of four children. Nine others suffered from fits, cardiac arrests or respiratory failures which brought them to the brink of death. Kayley Desmond, Paul Crampton, Henry Chan, Bradley Gibson, Katie Phillips, Christopher Peasgood, Christopher King, Patrick Elstone and Michael Davidson, aged between eight weeks and six years of age, were the hapless victims.

The pattern was the same in every case. Children admitted for relatively minor ailments became chronically ill, seemingly out of the blue. Then they recovered, only to suffer a horrendous relapse and, in the case of four children, eventual death.

Nine-week-old Becky Phillips and fifteen-month-old Claire Peck both died within weeks of each other in April. Becky Phillips and her twin sister Katie had been in and out of hospital several times since they were born. It wasn't until they were five weeks old that they were allowed home. The girls were premature but, to the delight of their parents, Sue and Peter, developed quickly. However, in the weeks following their arrival home they were sent back to the hospital on numerous occasions suffering from a stomach upset.

On one such occasion, Becky, Katie and her brother James were all in Ward Four with strange tummy ailments. They continued to be sent in and out of hospital, with Becky particularly affected. Doctors discovered she was allergic to the milk she was being fed. Once that was changed, her problems seemed to be over.

But it was not to be. Back home at 7.30 one evening, she started to have fits. Her eyes rolled in their sockets and she emitted a blood-curdling scream. At first her parents could not believe it was anything serious; after all, she had just come out of hospital. By 10.30 p.m., however, they decided to call the doctor. She had a third fit in as many hours. He reassured them when he said he thought it might he colic. And after his visit, Becky seemed better and settled down to sleep.

When the time came for the twins' night feed, however, she had another short fit. Sue and Peter took her into bed with them. It was Peter who first realized that she was no longer breathing. They rushed her to hospital in the car. But their race against time failed and she was pronounced dead. Her distraught parents were sent home by doctors, not knowing what had killed Becky. They said they feared meningitis had been the cause and they wanted Katie brought in straight away.

Within hours, she too was suffering fits. Sue and Peter kept a vigil by her hospital bed. It was during this time that the Phillips struck up a friendship with Beverley Allitt. The nurse had come back on shift on the morning of Becky's death and, as in all other cases, was told to look after Katie on a one-to-one basis. She stayed dutifully at her bedside for hours on end. It comforted Katie's parents to know she was always there. Beverley told them: 'Don't worry, I will be with her all the time.' The nightmarish irony was that those words of comfort committed the little girl to a journey that led her to the brink of death.

During one very bad fit, Katie was 'dead' for a full thirty-two minutes before she was brought back to life. And it was thanks in part to the tenacity of Sister Jean Saville, one of the most respected and experienced nurses at the hospital, that she was saved. Sister Saville spotted a tiny flicker of life long after all hope of saving the child had gone. The flying squad, with police escort, raced Katie to the Queen's Medical Centre in Nottingham.

Thanks to the careful attention she received, Katie began to show signs of recovery within two weeks. Her parents left her side only to attend Becky's funeral. Becky's cause of death had now been officially declared as 'Infant Death Syndrome'. But, like Liam's parents, Sue and Peter Phillips felt unease over the reason given for their child's tragic end.

Later, Jean Saville was herself to become a victim. During the subsequent police investigation the dark shadow of suspicion was cast over everyone in the children's ward. In a state of dreadful hopelessness, Jean took her own life, swallowing massive quantities of

Paracetamol. In a note, she begged everyone to believe she had nothing to do with the deaths of the children.

Jean Saville's death was a tragic waste. It came only days before Beverley Allitt was charged. These were days during which anguished parents and hospital staff still found it inconceivable that children could be murdered in a place which should have been the safest haven on earth. And, even more unbelievable, that a nurse, whose profession was affectionately known throughout the world as 'Angels', could be behind such vile deeds.

The next and final victim to die, Claire Peck, was not in any danger when she was taken into Ward Four by her parents on 22 April. Fifteen-month-old Claire suffered from bronchiolitis, a common childhood complaint, and arrived at Grantham and Kesteven from her home in Newark on the advice of the family doctor. Within half an hour on a ventilator, she had stopped wheezing and made a full recovery. But by 8.30 that night she was dead. Stunned and distraught, paediatrician Dr Nelson Porter, who had led the battle to save her, told Sue and David Peck that her death was a million-to-one chance, a freak event he could not explain.

It wasn't until Sue Peck's own parents overheard a chance remark made by a nurse that alarm bells began to ring. As her father Eric left the hospital, he overheard two nurses discussing the death. The phrase 'not another one . . .' stuck in his mind.

The following day, when he returned to the Grantham coroner's office to collect the death certificate, a woman at the reception desk made a similar remark. But for the fourth time the pathologist had decided that the cause of death was due to 'natural causes'. As with previous cases, no inquest was held.

While Claire Peck was fighting for her life, Sue and Peter Phillips had been keeping a bedside vigil for Katie, who had been transferred back to Ward Four for observation.

It was Nurse Allitt who told Sue about the death of Claire Peck, the fourth victim. Beverley rushed into Katie's room in floods of tears. It was natural for Sue to offer her comfort as by now they had become close. So friendly were they to become that not long after Katie was sent home, they asked Allitt to become her godmother.

Sue and Peter Phillips knew of three deaths in the ward: Liam Taylor, their own Becky and now Claire. They had also heard the rumours about viruses causing heart attacks among the young patients. And with Katie still being cared for, they wanted some answers – fast. Together, they challenged the hospital's general manager, Martin Gibson, who assured them that they had no reason for concern as the hospital had carried out tests and could find no evidence of any such disease.

But at last action was being taken. On 1 May 1991, the police moved into the ward. As operational head of Lincolnshire CID, Detective Superintendent Stuart Clifton led the initial twelve-man team of investigators. He immediately sought out the expert help and opinions of the chief paediatricians, Dr Nelson Porter and Dr Charith Sena Nanayakkara. But when he questioned them, he found they had differing ideas about events. Porter was convinced that something untoward was happening, while Nanayakkara had his doubts.

Dr Porter began to act on his suspicions. He had just returned from a medical conference where he had discussed the unusual spate of deaths and near deaths with fellow colleagues, and was reminded of the story of a woman who had tried to draw attention to herself by putting a pillow over her sick child's face, causing it to have fits, before screaming for help. Doctors mystified by the unexplained fits had secretly arranged to film the mother with her child. With that story ringing in his ears, Porter's first plan was to try to have video cameras installed in each cubicle on Ward Four. But before he could put the plan into action, Claire Peck died.

Porter then suggested his video plan to police, who arranged for a surveillance camera to be erected above the entrance to the ward in the hope that it would lead them to discover if a killer was sneaking in and out unnoticed.

It was to be a difficult and tedious investigation. The police had no real leads to go on: no suspect, no motive and no weapons. In the end it was good old-fashioned police work that put the evil Allitt behind bars.

Superintendent Clifton called in consultant paediatrician David Hull, to carry out a medical review on nineteen cases, which included children who had died at the hospital and those who had died within forty-eight hours of going home. He also had the parents interviewed by the Family Support Unit, a team of experienced police officers normally used in child-abuse cases.

After three weeks, thorough investigations had drawn a blank. Interviewed parents had nothing but praise for the way their children were looked after and Dr Hull reported that in his view only three of the nineteen cases he had been asked to look at were worth investigating thoroughly.

Despite all these disappointments, however, Superintendent Clifton refused to give up. He had a gut feeling that things did not add up, and returned to the case of five-month-old Paul Crampton, who had nearly died three times because his blood sugar levels had plunged so low.

When Paul had been transferred to the Queen's Medical Centre in Nottingham, tests on his blood had revealed that his insulin level was an alarming 148 milli-units per litre of blood. It should have been between four and six.

Even more frightening were the results that came back from experts at Cardiff University who carried out tests on the blood sample taken from little Paul on Ward Four before he was transferred. That reading went completely off the scale of their equipment. The laboratory could only say that Paul had an insulin reading in excess of 500.

Clifton immediately suspected that Paul had been deliberately given a massive overdose of insulin to kill him. But where was his proof? When he was told that pancreatic tumours could also cause high readings, he got in touch with Vincent Marks, professor of biochemistry at the University of Surrey and a renowned expert on insulin. The two men discussed the cases the police were investigating and Professor Marks agreed with Clifton that what had happened was highly suspicious. He, too, was sure that Paul had been injected with insulin.

More of Paul's blood was transferred to Guildford where Dr David Teal, a colleague of Professor Marks, tested it again. The results were mind-blowing. The level of insulin was now shown to be an amazing 43,000 milli-units per litre of blood – practically unheard of in the history of medicine. At last, Supt Clifton had his proof: Paul had been overdosed and was a very lucky child to have survived.

Police now faced the question that most needed answering: was this an accident, or did someone inject the child in order to kill him? Detectives questioned every nurse on the ward. At another meeting, the police had told them the reasons for their investigation and swore them under oath not to talk about it to the patients. The inquiry put a terrible strain on the staff. They ran a gamut of emotions from guilt to feeling that they were under suspicion of murder.

Armed with staff rotas, the inquiry team tried to establish if there were any nurses who were on duty regularly when the incidents happened. One by one, they were ticked off until in each case they found one name glaring back at them over and over again: Nurse Beverley Allitt.

On 2 June 1991, they arrested her and took her to Grantham police headquarters. For two days they questioned her about Paul, but she showed no emotion and never buckled under interrogation. Officers were astonished by her clinically cold approach to their questions as she continually proclaimed her innocence. Allitt was released on police bail on the evening of 4 June. The hospital took police advice and told her to stay at home on extended leave.

At first, Beverley Allitt did not tell anyone that she had been suspended, not even her new close friends, the Phillips. So close had they become that the Phillips had by now asked Beverley to be Katie's godmother. Allitt became a regular visitor to their home, accompanying Sue on shopping trips, and even took Katie and James out for trips on her own.

Sue Phillips, who remembered Paul and his mother Kath, still suspected nothing. It wasn't until 12 June that Beverley Allitt even mentioned the police investigation into Paul Crampton's near death. The nurse took James out that day with her friend Tracy Jobson and did not return until 7.30 p.m. It was then that Beverley confessed that the police had arrested her. She said that she wanted Sue to hear the news from her own lips and not by way of any gossip.

Sue was astonished when Beverley told her the police had accused her of trying to murder Paul and had even stripped her car and home looking for clues. She and husband Peter offered their new friend their wholehearted support. Peter helped to put Allitt's car interior back together again. Steadfast in the belief that she was innocent, Peter even hired a firm of private investigators to help her.

Meanwhile, Supt Clifton was approaching the investigation with renewed vigour, doubling his team to twenty-four men. Each child's case was meticulously examined by detectives working in pairs. The police chief knew that blood samples from all of the children held the key to the mystery of their deaths and near-misses. Detective Inspector Neil Jones began to track them down.

Becky Phillips's was the first sample police examined and tests revealed a shocking level of insulin recorded at 9,660, more than enough to kill. Next, Claire Peck's sample was checked. Horrifyingly, it showed her blood contained one of the most deadly poisons known to man: potassium chloride. Her bloodstream had more than twice the amount needed to kill her. Tests on Timothy Hardwick's samples also revealed a fatal potassium reading. All the post-mortems were proving to be wrong.

At this point, the police gathered together a panel of experts which included cot death specialist Professor John Emery, paediatric pathologist Dr David Fagin, Professor David Hull, paediatric consultant Dr Derek Johnston and Professor Marks and Dr David Teal. Chief Constable Alan Goldsmith and representatives of the Crown Prosecution Service also attended, along with Dr Porter, Dr Nanayakkara, representatives of the health authority and the hospital management.

On 2 July, after a meeting lasting more than five-and-a-half hours, they decided to prepare reports for the Director of Public Prosecutions, who would decide what action to take. Meanwhile, Allitt had her bail extended. She was by now seeing the Phillips family regularly and they felt very sorry for her. On one such visit Beverley took Katie for an outing. She was only gone five minutes when she burst through the door again with the awful news that the child was on the verge of another fit. It seemed the nightmare was starting all over again when their doctor immediately sent Katie back to Ward Four.

The Phillips were still unaware that Becky's death was part of the police investigation. So when two detectives called at their door on 17 June and invited them to the police station, that were completely unprepared for the news awaiting them. At the station, Superintendent Clifton told the dumbstruck parents about the high levels of insulin found in Becky's blood. They listened with growing amazement as he also told them that not only had they interviewed Allitt about Paul, but also about their two daughters and several other children. Their 'close friend' had never bothered to mention this to them.

They were only just beginning to digest the news by the time they arrived home. They could not believe their ears when Peter's sixteen-year-old daughter by his previous marriage, Emma, told them that Bev had called round and wanted to know if she could stay at their home for a while. This from the woman who was suspected of poisoning their little babies. Allitt had made the request because the press had at last got hold of the story and were on her trail. But the evil nurse now had nowhere to run.

On 20 November 1991, Beverley Allitt was charged on four counts of murder, eight counts of attempting to murder and eight of assault causing grievous bodily harm. Showing no emotion, she was taken to the police cells to stay overnight before her appearance in Grantham Magistrates' Court the next morning. The hearing lasted just four minutes and Allitt was remanded in custody to New Hall Women's Prison, near Wakefield, Yorkshire. Four months later, on 11 March, detectives visited her in prison where they read out six new charges.

As Allitt awaited trial, the police unearthed even more disturbing revelations. When the nurse had been turned away from the Phillips's home, her best friend and fellow nurse Tracy Jobson allowed her to stay with her mother Eileen and fifteen-year-old brother Jonathon in Orton Goldhay on the outskirts of Peterborough, south of Grantham. During her four months there, a series of strange events occurred. The bathroom curtains were found with scorch marks on them. Tracy's mother found a kitchen knife plunged in her pillow. Bleach was spilled on furniture and carpets. And things went missing, only to mysteriously reappear again elsewhere in the house. Even the family's dog was not untouched when one day it coughed up the remains of some tablets in the garden. But the most sinister event of all was when Jonathon suddenly collapsed while out shopping with Beverley and Mrs Jobson. Luckily he survived. Police later charged the nurse with attempting to murder Jonathon and causing grievous bodily harm by doctoring a drink with insulin-producing tablets.

They also charged her with attempting to murder 79-year-old Dorothy Lowe while moonlighting as a care assistant at an old people's home in the village of Waltham on the Wolds, only 10 miles from Grantham. Inquiries revealed that Allitt had been seen by another care assistant, Alice Stewart, giving the frail old lady an insulin injection which could have killed her.

A further charge involved Michael Davidson, just six when admitted to Grantham and Kesteven Hospital suffering from a gunshot pellet wound to his stomach. While recovering from the operation to remove it, Michael had suddenly suffered a cardiac arrest. At first police had discounted him from their inquiries, believing that he had hyperventilated as he was being given an injection of antibiotics by a doctor. But when the doctor revealed that Nurse Allitt had prepared and handed over the syringe, the police immediately began to suspect that it contained potassium chloride. They charged Allitt with Michael's attempted murder and causing grievous bodily harm.

The question still remained: What drove Allitt, a seemingly dedicated nurse, to kill and maim her young charges?

When the police had first arrived at the hospital, Dr Porter had spoken to Supt Clifton about Munchausen Syndrome. He explained that in some cases mothers had deliberately made their own children ill so that they needed hospital treatment, in order to draw attention to themselves. In some instances, nurses suffering from it turned on patients in their care. The syndrome was a personality disorder driving women to harm children. Those suffering from it would always make up fictitious medical complaints. Beverley Allitt was believed to be suffering from what was called 'Munchausen Syndrome by Proxy'. She made other people ill to gain attention.

Allitt had missed a total of 191 days through sickness during her two-year nurse's training course at Grantham. She spent hours in hospital accident and emergency wards with all manner of ailments, ranging from simple sprains to claims that she was suffering from ulcers or brain tumours. Often she would make repeat visits when her wounds became infected or stitches were ripped open.

In all she was treated twenty-nine times at hospitals in Grantham, Boston, Great Yarmouth and Peterborough. A hospital physiotherapist, knowing that Allitt was a nurse, once reported her to Grantham authorities, believing she was suffering from Munchausen Syndrome. But she was still allowed to continue nursing.

Even while she was awaiting trial, Beverley Allitt continued to inflict injuries upon herself. While on bail, she was fitted with a catheter for an apparent urinary problem. She also spent time in Peterborough hospital where staff suspected her of injecting water into her breasts so that her temperature rose at night, and she spent most of her time at Wakefield prison in the hospital ward suffering from a string of ailments.

Allitt began to lose weight until it became evident that she was suffering from anorexia nervosa. From a hefty 13 stone, she plummeted to a paltry 6 stone 13 1b. Worried officials transferred her to Rampton hospital, where doctors and nurses worked to stabilize her weight. She remained there until the start of her trial at Nottingham Crown Court on 15 February 1993.

Gaunt and pale-faced from the effects of the anorexia, she appeared in the dock, her blonde hair cut short, dressed in blue trousers and cardigan and a white shirt. She showed no emotion whatsoever in the dock.

The trial was in its fifth week when, during a three-day recess, Allitt collapsed in Rampton. Doctors at nearby Bassetlaw Hospital in Worksop, Nottinghamshire, struggled to keep her alive. The court was told she was now being fed by tube through the nose.

It was decided that the trial should go ahead even though Allitt was unfit to sit in the dock. When the case was reconvened, she sent the judge a letter explaining that she was fit enough to give instructions to her lawyers and that she wanted them to present her defence. She also added that she would not have wanted to give evidence herself in court, even if she could. Details about her Munchausen Syndrome were not presented at the trial, as it was feared these might prejudice the case.

The verdicts were returned over the course of a week. She was found: guilty of the murders of James Taylor, Becky Phillips, Claire Peck and Timothy Hardwick; guilty of attempting to murder Paul Crampton, Katie Phillips and Bradley Gibson; guilty of causing grievous bodily harm with intent to Kayley Desmond, Henry Chan, Patrick Elstone, Christopher King, Michael Davidson and Christopher Peasgood. But she was cleared of charges relating to Jonathon Jobson and Dorothy Lowe. The judge ordered that Allitt should be returned to Nottingham Crown Court to be sentenced to life imprisonment.

Although in some cases it was impossible to prove exactly how she killed or attempted to kill her victims, police discovered that Allitt used a variety of methods. These included deliberate massive insulin injections and deadly syringes of potassium chloride. But, more horribly still, in some cases Allitt literally took her victim's breath away by putting her hand over the child's mouth. She even crushed and broke five of Katie Phillips's ribs.

Today, some of those who managed to get away are still paying the price of crossing paths with Nurse Allitt. Surviving victims and their families have all suffered traumas. And the nightmare is not yet over for the Phillips family . . .

While Allitt was in prison awaiting her trial they were

dealt another devastating blow. Katie, by now a year old, was taken to the Nottingham's Queen's Medical Centre for a routine check-up. It was also suggested by the specialist that they carry out a brain scan. The tests took twice as long as normal and Sue and Peter were horrified with the results. Katie was severely brain-damaged.

It was discovered that the night Katie had died for thirty-two minutes in the Grantham and Kesteven Hospital, her brain had been deprived of oxygen. It was now only the size of a walnut. The damage was so extensive that the poor child was almost blind in one eye and would never walk or talk. She would never be able to do even the most basic things for herself.

Man As Monster

A simple peasant stands before a court in sixteenth-century France accused of being a werewolf. Like hundreds of other poor souls before him, he finds himself in the clutches of the country's most depraved inquisitor, a man whose actions make the butchery of the Revolution seem insipid by comparison. Perhaps he grovels or begs for mercy. He protests that he is the victim of misunderstanding or mischief. He pleads on his knees to be set free.

To Henry Boguet, Supreme Judge of the St Claude district in Burgundy and author of the French witch-hunters' bible *Discours des Sorciers*, the peasant's statement of innocence means nothing. The judge needs to obtain proof for himself and, with a dismissive nod to the torturers in his service, he signals that the horrors must begin.

Most often, the unfortunates would be strapped three or four at a time to a dread device known as The Wheel. This would then be slowly lowered close to the ground and turned – breaking bones and tearing sinews, yet never quite so efficiently as to kill. Perhaps in their suffering the victims might recall the chilling advice passed around by fellow werewolf suspects. That Boguet should be given a confession, however absurdly false it may be. At least it would lessen the excruciating pain, even if it meant the counting down of the hours until the burning at the stake.

There was one other tip for the accused: to cry! Boguet apparently believed werewolves were sorcerers and of course everyone knew sorcerers could shed no more than three tears from their right eye. But amid the screams and the fear and the pain, many terrified victims found their tear ducts stayed dry.

There can have been few more appalling sights in the annals of human misery than Henry Boguet and his measuring phials containing the tears of the tortured. He would inspect them at his leisure. Here was one barely damp with moisture – surely unequivocal proof of sorcery of the worst kind. And another almost one quarter full of tears . . . but weren't those tears shed from the wrong eye?

Boguet and his lieutenants did not rely only on The Wheel to obtain their evidence. There were many other sickening tools of his damnable trade: the rack, branding, whipping, crucifixion, or crudely tearing at the flesh with white-hot pincers – all had their place in his menu of torture techniques.

In his *Discours*, Boguet waxed lyrical about the tear theory, exhorting other judges to put it to the test when dealing with sorcery and werewolf trials. He wrote:

The doctors esteem it one of the strongest presumptions that exist as a test of the crime of sorcery. I wish to report what has come to my knowledge. All the sorcerers whom I have examined in quality of judge have never shed tears in my presence: or, indeed, if they have shed them it has been so parsimoniously that no notice was taken of them. I say this with regard to those who seemed to weep, but I doubt if their tears were not feigned. I am at least well assured that those tears were wrung from them with the greatest efforts. This was shown by the efforts which the accused made to weep, and by the small number of tears which they shed.

Yet if I spoke to them in private they shed tears and wept with all possible vehemence. The same happened when they confessed. They then showed themselves more lively and joyous than they had previously been, as if they had been delivered from a great burden. Besides it is probable that sorcerers do not shed tears, since tears serve principally to penitents to wash away and cleanse their sins.

Nevertheless, if you demand of sorcerers why they do not shed tears, they answer you that it is impossible for them to weep because they have the heart too much oppressed at seeing themselves disgraced by the imputation of a crime so detestable as that of sorcery.

Among the hundreds, if not thousands, who fell into Boguet's hands was one Clauda Gaillard, who, according to witnesses, was seen to assume the form of a tail-less wolf as she transformed herself behind a bush. The good judge regarded the case as a perfect example and recorded: 'Common report was against her. No one ever saw her shed a single tear, whatever effort might be made to cause her to shed tears.' We can only guess at the unspeakable tortures poor Clauda suffered before she was finally taken to be burned at the stake.

France at this time was a hotbed of werewolf activity, with an astonishing 30,000 cases reported in less than 100 years. Some of these can perhaps be attributed to rabies, a disease which turns its victims mad and produces some classic werewolf symptoms, such as loathing of water and uncontrolled fits of aggression. A proportion, too, can be explained away as people suffering from lycanthropia – a mental illness in which the patient believes he is turning into a wolf.

One of the worst lycanthropes of the time was the Werewolf of Chalons, otherwise known as the 'Demon Tailor'. He was arraigned in Paris on 14 December 1598 on murder charges which were so appalling that the court ordered all documents on the hearing to be destroyed. Even his real name has become lost in history.

The Chalons werewolf specialized in luring customers (the younger the better) into his tailor's shop where he would then subject them to his perversions before slitting their throats and dressing the flesh, almost as though he was a professional butcher. He would then eat them at his leisure.

This monster's other despicable habit took him to woods around the city where he would 'assume the form of a wolf' and prey on innocent walkers. The total number of his victims was never properly established but there is little doubt that it ran into dozens. When local government officials descended on his house they found barrels of human bones immersed in bleach hidden in the cellars, along with pieces of limbs and fragments of bone.

When he was sent to the stake the day after his trial, a huge crowd gathered to watch his final moments. And, unlike many another convicted werewolf who repented of his sins as the first flames licked around his legs, the Demon Tailor betrayed no hint of remorse. He could be heard cursing and blaspheming right to the very end.

Nine years earlier, Germany had hosted one of the most sensational werewolf trials of all time, that of Peter Stump.

Aided and abetted by his daughter and mistress, Stump had for years roamed the countryside, inflicting his atrocities upon the innocent. Whether he was truly a werewolf or not hardly matters. No servant of Satan could have contrived a more stomach-churning existence. The agonies that his torturers inflicted on Stump once he was brought to book are horrible to record. Yet they represent barely a tenth of the suffering he doled out to the unfortunates who crossed his path over a quarter of a century.

According to a German assessment of his foul deeds, published soon after his death, Stump sold his soul to the Devil for the ability to transform himself into a werewolf. Once he had tasted human flesh, the account goes, 'he took such pleasure and delight in the shedding of blood that he would night and day walk the fields and perform extreme cruelties'.

First among his targets were young girls, whom he would capture and rape while in human form before changing into a wolf to tear them apart. In five years, according to his German biographer, he killed thirteen women and children plus two pregnant women whose hearts he ate 'panting hot and raw'. Throughout this time he had a mistress, Katherine Trompin, and was committing regular incest with his daughter Beell who eventually bore him a son. Such was his depravity that he could not stop himself eating the child and was said to regard the brains as 'a most savoury and dainty delicious means' of satisfying his appetite for blood.

As his reign of bloodlust rolled on, the villagers of Bedburg became, not surprisingly, increasingly paranoid. Few roamed out alone at any hour unless they were properly armed or protected by others. Meanwhile, limbs of the dead were found scattered almost daily in the surrounding fields as stomach-churning proof of a werewolf on the loose.

At last Stump was caught – by a posse and a pack of dogs that believed they were on the trail of a real wolf. When hunted down, he is said to have made a desperate last attempt to resume his human shape as he hid behind a bush. But he was spotted, removing his 'Devil's girdle' and instantly marched back to Bedburg to face the music.

His fate matched that of his victims. A judge found him guilty and ordered that his body should be 'laid on a wheel and with red hot burning pincers in several places to have the flesh pulled off him from the bones; after that his legs and arms to be broken with a wooden hatchet, afterwards to have his head struck from his body; then to have his carcase burned to ashes.' The burning of the headless corpse was carried out alongside the stake executions of two other criminals: Stump's daughter and mistress, his accomplices.

Looking back, it may now seem to us as though the history of the werewolf dates only from the eighteenth and nineteenth centuries, amply fuelled since then by pulp fiction writers and some of Hollywood's horror specialists. In fact, folklore accounts of werewolfism predate the birth of Christ by almost a thousand years.

The cult of the werewolf has since spread across the globe, though there is surprisingly little variation of detail as to what the monster can and can't do. The change of skin and shape is put down mainly to a special witches' potion which, used together with the right rituals, is the pathway to becoming a wolf.

According to wilder claims it is even possible to turn into one by accident through astral projection. This is the phenomenon in which the soul is said to rise from the body and float freely across the earth at fantastic speed. Mystics claim they can do it at will; many others have described the experience as something they remember after recovering from near death.

Werewolf cultists say that whenever a soul is projected, the shell it leaves behind is in great danger of being taken over by a werewolf. This belief is probably linked to the old European custom of guarding a dead body from occupation by vampires whenever the deceased has passed on between Christmas and Epiphany – a time when the forces of evil are said to have much greater power on Earth.

Other supposed pathways to possession include sleeping outdoors in summer with the full moon shining straight on to your face, or conceiving a child on the night of a full moon (he or she may grow up a werewolf).

Symptoms of the afflicted are very precise and supposedly much easier to spot than, say, those of vampires in human form. A werewolf will have sunken, staring eyes, perhaps eyebrows which join up on the bridge of the nose, hair growing on the palms of the hands and the 'Devil's mark', a birthmark that's usually hidden from view. There may also be a long third finger, low-hung ears, fingernails shaped like almond nuts and a brownish tinge to all nails. In rural France, it is still often commented that a man sporting uncontrolled growth of a thumbnail is a wolf in human guise!

But where is the proof that these creatures actually exist? Unfortunately, it has never been produced to the satisfaction of scientists. That said, reports of werewolfism are not just the province of country simpletons or drunkards returning home at night from the ale house.

One highly publicized case transpired at the end of the

last century when an Oxford don, his wife and a friend took a summer let of a vacation house in remote Welsh woodland, close to a lake where they planned to fish. One day the professor chanced upon a massive skull which he suspected had once belonged to a large hound. He took it back to the holiday home and vowed to examine it much more closely later on. In fact, his chance had gone. That same night, as the Oxford man and his friend took the air, the wife heard a bizarre scratching sound coming from outside the cottage. Dashing to the door to lock it fast, she caught sight of a hideous part-man/part-beast staring balefully at her through a window. It was clear to her that the evil monster was trying to get in.

Details of this holiday nightmare are contained in a 1930s book called *The Werewolf*, by Montague Summers. In it he writes:

> The cruel, panting jaws were gaping wide and showed keen white teeth; the great furry paws clasped the sill like hands; the red eyes gleamed hideously. Half fainting with fear she ran through to the front door and shot the bolt.
>
> A moment after she heard heavy breathing from outside and the latch rattled menacingly. The minutes that followed were full of the acutest suspense and now and again a low snarl would be heard at the door or window and a sound as though the creature was endeavouring to force its entrance.
>
> At last the voices of her husband and his friend, come back from their ramble, sounded in the little garden and, as they knocked, finding the door locked, she was but able to open ere she fell into a swoon at their feet. When her sense returned to find herself laid

on the bed, and her husband anxiously bending over her, she told in halting accents what had happened.

That night, having made all secure and extinguished the lamps, the two men sat up quietly armed with stout sticks and a gun. The hours passed slowly until, when all was darkest and most lonely, the soft thud of cushioned paws was heard on the gravel outside and nails scratched at the kitchen window. To their horror in a stale phosphorescent light they saw the hideous mask of a wolf, with the eyes of a man, glaring through the glass, eyes that were red with hellish rage.

Snatching the gun they rushed to the front door but it had seen their movement and was away in a moment. As they issued from the house a shadowy undefined shape slipped through the open gate and in the stars they could just see a huge animal making towards the lake, into which it disappeared silently, nor did a ruffle cross the surface of the water.

Early the next morning the professor took the skull and, rowing a little way out from shore, flung it as far as he could into the deepest part of the water. The werewolf never returned to his hauntings again.

The implication, Summers concludes, is that the manifestation was a werewolf spirit, condemned to haunt the ground where his bones lay. Whether the sinking of the skull in the lake was enough to rest that spirit we shall never know. But in the county that was old Merionethshire, there are no reports of the monster ever returning.

Another, much more recent, werewolf report centred on a newly-built nurses' hostel in Singapore in 1957. Managers at the site gradually became aware of a series of werewolf-type attacks and as fear and confusion spread through the dormitories, young nurses began barring themselves in at night. For one young girl, though, precautions such as these were not enough. She later recalled: 'I woke to find a horrible face, with hair reaching down to the bridge of the nose, glaring down at me. The creature had two long, protruding red fangs. I saw him clearly because the room was bathed in moonlight. I tried to scream but could not. I staggered into the corner and collapsed.'

Local police were inclined to believe that the whole incident was a medical student's prank – until someone pointed out the neat puncture marks on the girl's wrists. They then switched their line of inquiry to tracking down an occultist who had undergone a wolfic ceremony with one of the island's numerous supernatural brotherhoods. The monster's fate remains a mystery to this day.

Even more recent was the tragic death of seventeen-year-old Andrew Prinold in the English Midlands in 1975. Andrew, of Eccleshall, Staffordshire, apparently stabbed himself through the heart at the nearest crossroads to his home in the absolute conviction that he was turning into a werewolf. The crossroads was chosen because it is regarded in folklore as a sure way to prevent the wolf spirit rising again to prowl the earth.

Andrew's was a classic case of lycanthropy. He had been attending seances in the months before his death in a bid to speak to his deceased father, but later confided to a friend that he suspected the Devil himself had taken control of his soul during one of the sessions. Another time, he convinced himself he was a black cat and was observed restlessly pawing the table.

As one of his school pals told the inquest: 'He told me his face and hands were changing colour and that he was changing into a werewolf. He would go quiet and then start growling. I told him to see his brother. He said he had a knife and was going to kill himself.'

Part of the torment for lycanthropes is that they tell themselves there is no earthly cure that will send them to rest, and so they set about finding unearthly ones. These include being shot with a bullet of inherited silver, being stabbed with a silver blade or undergoing an exorcism by a priest.

Simply to hear the medical advice was almost enough to kill your average werewolf of bygone years. Brandings on the forehead with a red hot iron, for example, was a favourite of the Arabs. Beatings with a thin rod (also the Roman way of curing nymphomania) was another. And if all else failed, the physician would bleed them – the favoured cure-all medicine for every malady.

One particularly bizarre ritual required three girls to equip themselves with slender ash twigs. They would then savagely whip the suspected wolfman, who was restrained in a seven-foot wide chalk circle. As the beating continued, the girls would chant, 'Grey wolf ugly, grey wolf old, do at once as you are told, leave this man and fly away, where t'is night and never day.' A variation of this was for the exorcism party to dip mugs into a boiling potion of tar and sulphur and pour it over the unfortunate werewolf. In between, there would be the usual whippings, pinchings and proddings. Today, this practice sounds rather more like the services offered by certain madams in red light districts. It has to be a distinct possibility that the 'wolf' at the centre of it all was simply a man disguised in animal furs who enjoyed sado-masochistic practices.

Our modern view of the werewolf is heavily influenced by Hollywood's image-makers. Very often – perhaps too often – werewolf movies also feature vampires in close proximity (and vice versa). As a result, horror culture has intertwined the behaviour patterns of both to the point where it is almost unthinkable for them to operate alone. Fang and fur now seem to go hand in hand, yet there is one major difference between them. There are scores of reports and stories of men and women becoming were-wolves out of choice (usually a bargain with the Devil). Vampiric volunteers, however, are hard to find.

Vampire culture is also far more recent. Its roots lie in stories told and retold by the paranoid, rural populations of central European states, such as Hungary and Poland. And from the moment *Dracula* hit the bookshelves in 1897 there was no looking back for this most feared of all supernatural night stalkers.

Vampires spread their evil legacy by biting mortals in their sleep. Once bitten, death may come quickly or slowly but the transformation almost always begins immediately. When he dies, the victim himself soon starts clawing his way from the coffin for a macabre night's rounds.

Suicides are also candidates for this ghoulish life. For years it was the custom in England to bury them at crossroads to save them from becoming vampires. Such makeshift burials became so common, however, and were so fraught with health hazards, that Parliament banned the practice in 1824.

The difficulty for vampire-hunters lay in identifying their quarry. Though these creatures were said to have no shadow in sunlight, and no reflection in a mirror or lake, it appeared a relatively simple task for them to avoid such tell-tale clues. Harder for them was to disguise the effects on them of a recent blood-gorging session. Their faces turned from ghostly white to healthy pink, their lips as crimson as their last meal.

The classic description of vampires comes from the eighteenth-century German theologian John Heinrich Zopfius. He writes: 'Vampires issue forth from their graves in the night, attack people sleeping quietly in their beds, suck out all the blood from their bodies and destroy them. They beset men, women and children alike, sparing neither age nor sex. Those who are under the fatal malignity of their influence complain of suffocation and a total deficiency of spirits, after which they soon expire.'

Methods of killing a vampire are, even today, known to most schoolchildren. A stake of aspen (the wood used for Jesus's cross) or whitethorn (his crown of thorns) is sharpened and plunged into the fiend's heart as he lies in his coffin. Garlic may also be spread about as an added defence.

According to Ennemoser's *History of Magic* (1854), villagers in the Yugoslavian community of Meduegna witnessed one of the most sensational vampire exorcisms on record. Their streets were being terrorized by a bloodsucking beast and the main suspect was one Arnold Paole, who had died in a fearful accident while working on a nearby farm some months earlier. Ennemoser tells of the scene when Paole's grave was at last prised open:

It was seen that the corpse had moved to one side, the jaws gaped wide open and the blue lips were moist with new blood which had trickled in a thin stream from a corner of the mouth. All unafraid, the old sexton caught the body and twisted it straight. 'So,' he cried, 'you have not wiped your mouth since last night's work.' The vampire ... looked indeed as

257

though he had not been dead a day. On handling the corpse the scarfskin came off and below that were new skin and new nails.

Today, such accounts seem wildly fictitious – the product of over-imagination coupled with the occasional heavy night in an alehouse. Yet, as with werewolves, a belief in vampires persists strongly in many corners of the globe. Tales of their foul deeds may not hit the headlines so often, and sceptics will continue to scoff and blame Hollywood for creating a modern myth. But the next time you walk past a graveyard alone on a cold, misty night don't be surprised if you feel your step quicken.

And keep your aspen sharp!

Michael Sams

Michael Sams smiled conspiratorially to himself as he bolted the door to his workshop. At last, the one-legged Mr Nobody was on his way to achieving his life's ambition: a place in the evil hall of fame alongside the Yorkshire Ripper, the Black Panther and Dennis Nilsen.

The frightened young woman who lay shackled inside a home-made 'coffin' was to be his passport to this other world. It had taken him fifteen obsessive years to perfect what he thought was the ultimate crime. Now he was playing a chilling game of 'catch-me-if-you-can' with the police, pitting what he thought was his extraordinary intelligence against them. And he was winning.

When train-spotter Michael Sams kidnapped estate agent Stephanie Slater, it was the culmination of years of meticulous planning, inspired by his meeting with murderer Donald 'Black Panther' Neilson while serving time in prison for a car crime. Sams had listened, enthralled, as Neilson told how he had abducted and murdered heiress Leslie Whittle. In his turn, Sams vowed to anyone who would listen that one day he too would be a master criminal and commit the 'perfect crime'.

'One day I will be as famous as the Black Panther,' he

had bragged. But, as with everything he touched, the pathetic Sams failed miserably in the end. In July 1993 he sat in the dock in the Old Bailey as the crowd – led by the very same, now-jubilant estate agent – erupted in cheers when the judge passed *four* life sentences on him. He had been convicted of the kidnapping and murder of teenager Julie Dart and the terror-kidnapping of Stephanie Slater.

Michael Benniman Sams was born in Keighley, West Yorkshire, on 11 August 1941. As a youngster he was like a character out of a *Boy's Own* comic. He seemed a perfectly balanced and normal child. Friends at St Mary's School in Riddlestone, Keighley, remembered nothing to indicate he could be capable of harming anyone. Excellent at sports, he was particularly good at running, football and cricket. He joined the Scouts and sang in the local choir. Sams was also railway-mad, a passion that stayed with him throughout his life, and played a central theme in his later criminal life.

His parents, both members of the Methodist Church, were very strict, making sure he was always polite and smartly turned-out. His father, Ernest Sams, a corporal in the Duke of Wellington Regiment, and his mother, Iris, a shop assistant, were especially proud of their son when he passed his 11-plus examination and went on to Keighley Grammar School. The intelligent little boy overcame his dyslexia and gained ten O-levels and three A-levels.

At home, Sams's father ruled with a rod of iron, bringing both his sons up in Army style, bellowing out their names, insisting they arrive home on the dot of the appointed hour and dishing out beatings if they disobeyed. Many years later, however, Sams would be shocked to discover that this man was not his real father.

While Sams was awaiting trial for the murder of Julie Dart and the kidnap of Stephanie Slater, psychologists began to unravel why he had turned into a Jekyll and Hyde character. The loner told them how he had three different 'fathers' during his childhood. After his mother had split from Ernest, she remarried Sidney Walker, taking Michael and his brother John with her. It was only in later years that Sams discovered that the man he thought was his dad was not his real father at all. During the war, his mother Iris had had a fling with a man called George Benniman, by whom she became pregnant. Ernest Sams, who had been away fighting the Nazis, forgave his wife and accepted the new baby, even allowing his name to be put on the birth certificate. Sams only met his biological father once, and even then his mother did not reveal his true identity, introducing him only as a friend. It was not until he was in his twenties that Sams made the connection between the man's surname and his own unusual middle name.

On the surface, Sams was an insignificant Mr Nobody. But in his disturbed mind he could be anything. As he played with his train set in his attic or stood in blustery weather following his beloved hobby of train-spotting, he fantasised about great plans and achievements.

In 1959 after he left school, he trained at Hull Nautical College for a year, then joined the Merchant Navy for a further year. He flitted from job to job after that, spending the years between 1962 and 1969 working as a lift service engineer before setting up his own business as a central heating installation engineer until 1977. In the same year, he divorced his first wife, Susan Little, whom he had married in July 1964. They had two sons, Charles and Robert.

During his early years with Susan, life seemed very rosy for Sams as he set up his successful firm, Axion Heating, employing six staff. Business was booming, and he and Susan moved into a huge five-bedroomed Victorian house, enjoying two foreign holidays every year. His obsession with railways grew and he added to his huge collection of toy trains.

However, the dark, sinister side of Sams was finally emerging. He turned to crime, becoming involved in a car-theft racket. He also began attacking Susan, beating her and dragging her across the floor by her long hair, often blackening her eyes or splitting her nose.

Susan recalls how Sams fantasized about committing the perfect crime. He became involved with petty criminals, committing tax fiddles and car insurance frauds, which eventually landed him in jail. In 1978 he served six months of a nine-month sentence in Armley Jail, Leeds, for being part of a car-ringing gang, even though he shopped his accomplices to the police. While he was in prison he developed a bitter hatred of police which was to obsess him for fifteen years. He blamed them for wrecking his life – and his warped determination to eke revenge on them eventually led to countless attempts at kidnap, blackmail and murder.

This deep loathing of the law intensified further when his wife told him she was leaving him for a policeman. Sams blamed the police in general for the break-up of his marriage, rather than his own terrible violence towards Susan. When she told him she was leaving, the vicious two-bit criminal beat her up. And in a prison letter he gloatingly recalled the event when he said, 'I probably beat her two or three hundred times.'

Sams blamed the police again when his home was fire-bombed while he was under their protection for informing on fellow crooks. As he leapt from a top-floor window, he severely damaged his right knee. During his prison term, he pleaded with doctors to open him up to discover what was causing him such intense pain. But it wasn't until he was six months into his sentence that they did so and discovered his leg was riddled with cancer. The disease was so bad that they had to amputate and fit him with an artificial tin limb. It was a shattering blow to a man who had always prided himself on his fitness. For years he ran up to 20 miles a day across the fells around Keighley, and was a champion runner with his local club, the Bingley Harriers.

Hell-bent on revenge, Sams was inspired by stories of the notorious Black Panther and came up with a 'perfect kidnapping', a crime that would never be solved by police and would make them look foolish at the same time. He tried to enlist his friend, jeweller Carl Metcalf, to help him. Like the Black Panther, Sams wanted to kidnap a millionaire's daughter, take her to the cellar in his house, where he had built a secret prison, and demand a huge ransom. Metcalf refused to get involved and Sams never carried out his plan.

During his months in prison, he advertised in the lonely-hearts section of a newspaper. The advert was answered by catering student Jane Marks, who visited him in jail and fell in love with him. She stood by him through his sentence and their romance blossomed. Just two weeks after he was released, they were married. Wedding photographs show dark-haired Sams propping himself up on crutches a month after his right leg had been amputated below the knee in October 1978.

On his release, Sams managed to get a job as a repairman with the tool company Black and Decker, working for them from 1980 to 1985. Jane dumped him after three years of marriage because of his obsession with trains – the final straw came when he fitted toy marshalling yards and main lines throughout their home. They were divorced in 1981. Once again, Sams' evil streak surfaced when he said he would shoot Jane if he had a gun.

Weirdo Sams was in fact so loco about trains that he was more upset about losing them than his wives. This Walter Mitty character once said: 'Take my wife away and I'll get over it and get another. Take my trains away and you take my whole life away.' The self-confessed 'mummy's boy' married for a third time, again finding his wife through a lonely-hearts column. Teena Cooper met him in 1983 in Birmingham and two years later they moved to Peterborough where he established Peterborough Power Tools. They eventually wed in 1989 after the tragic death from a brain haemorrhage of Teena's nineteen-year-old son from a previous marriage.

By then the couple were living in the village of Sutton on Trent, near Newark in Nottinghamshire, and Sams had set up on his own again, with T & M Tools. His workshop, only a few miles from their 300-year-old cottage, was to become the scene of terrible crimes, and eventually yielded the clues that were help put Sams away for life. It was there that he refined his years of planning the 'perfect crime', which climaxed in the vicious murder of Julie Dart and the terrifying kidnapping of Stephanie Slater.

Not long after he married Teena, Sams realized he had made a mistake and, like his other two marriages, it quickly disintegrated, leaving the evil and twisted man plenty of time to hatch elaborate plots, all of them meticulously recorded in fine detail on computer discs. During his trial, Sams was to claim that he had carried out the kidnapping because of pressure from Teena, who wanted to move back to Birmingham. He said he needed the ransom money to buy her a house there because he wanted to remain in Sutton on Trent.

Sams' kidnap 'campaign' started in earnest in 1991 and he made several failed attempts before seizing and holding Stephanie. At first he tried to snatch a prostitute in Chapeltown, Leeds, but the girl refused to get into his car. Then he decided his target would be an estate agent. On 26 June 1991, he arranged to meet Karen Langdon at a house in Crewe. Karen had a lucky escape when Sams left just as she turned up late for a meeting to view a property. A week later he tried to kidnap another estate agent but was foiled by a chatty builder. He had planned to capture 42-year-old Carol Jones in Crewe and hold her for a £175,000 ransom. Details of this kidnap attempt came to light when forensic scientists retrieved Sams' plan of action from a file in his home computer. It was when confronted with this evidence that he confessed everything to police.

On that near-fateful day, Carol had arranged to meet Sams at 71 Westminster Street, Crewe, to show him around the house that was for sale. Sams had disguised his face with stick-on warts. He had also altered his red Austin Metro by stencilling 'Blocked and Broken Drains' and a telephone number on the side. He waited outside the property clutching a red and white bag in which he held the tools of the planned kidnap: a rope, blindfolds and a gag. Hidden in a clipboard was a knife. Back at his workshop, he had prepared a macabre do-it-yourself 'coffin' – a wooden box made out of four sheets of 8 ft by 4 ft chipboard.

He told police that he planned to take the woman back to his workshop, chain her up in the box and demand £175,000 ransom. But a builder working on the house next door began talking to him, encouraging him to buy the house across the road. When Carol and a teenager on work experience turned up, Sams was forced to abandon his plan and left.

Just one week later, Sams was successful. He posed as a client to kidnap nineteen-year-old Julie Dart in the red-light Chapeltown district of Leeds where she had been soliciting. He tied her up, then blindfolded and gagged her before driving the terrified teenager back to his workshop. There he forced her into the wooden 'coffin' that had originally been built for Carol Jones. The following day he drove to Huntingdon, Cambridgeshire, where he posted two letters: one written by Julie to her boyfriend, the second written by himself to police in Leeds demanding a £140,000 ransom. In his letter, he said that if he did not receive the money, Julie would be killed and a city store fire-bombed.

In an attempt to throw the police off his trail, the sick pervert even invented a story of how he had sex with Julie and went on to describe it in lurid detail on one of his computer discs. He had intended to send a print-out of his imaginary sexual antics to the police in case anyone had seen him abducting Julie. In it, he never referred to Julie by her full name but detectives found it had been stored on a disc under a file called Julie D. He told how the girl had got into his car in the red-light district. 'The girl wanted £15 for sex behind a wall but £20 inside the car with the money up front,' Sams wrote. He folded down the rear seats and Julie removed her shoes. He added:

Before she could remove anything else I asked her if I could remove her clothes. She agreed for £5 extra . . . She undid the buttons on her jeans and I removed them. I undid the buttons on her blouse and undid that. For the record, Julie had on white briefs and a black lacy bra. We had penetrative sex with a condom provided by Julie. After sex I asked her to lay there for a while and talk. I said I would give her extra. I gave her a £20 note saying she had provided the best sex I had ever had and would be back. She wrote her name Julie D on one of my business cards.

But his carefully laid plan went wrong. Sams, alerted by the alarm system he had rigged up, found the teenager trying to escape. She was claustrophobic and could not stand being cooped up in such a small space. Sams knew that she could identify him. The evil killer coldly took a claw hammer and beat Julie senseless. Then he strangled her. Ten days after her kidnapping, Julie Dart's naked body was found in a farmer's field at Easton, Lincolnshire.

Despite his bungled attempts to extort money, Sams was determined to continue with what he called the 'campaign'. Once again he contacted police and threatened to kidnap another vice girl and bomb a city store. Three days after Julie's body was found, on 19 July 1991, he sent the first of a string of letters revealing how she had died. In one he had chillingly written: 'I can't get a bigger sentence for killing two prostitutes than one.'

Police finally agreed to hand over cash – to prevent a further death, and in an attempt to trap Sams. But the hand-over failed when an M1 service station phone jammed and a policewoman could not take instructions about the drop. Sams abandoned the plans and fled. He had intended to direct the officer to an isolated footbridge over a disused railway track where the £140,000 was to be put on a tray. He would wait overhead and pull it up by rope. He was then going to ride a motor scooter to nearby Dove Valley to evade pursuing police cars.

On 15 October that year, Sams tried to blackmail British Rail by threatening to derail a train unless they paid £200,000. He planned to cut the current as an express went through Millmeese, between Stafford and Crewe on the Euston-Carlisle line. Using a lump of sandstone and a cord over the gantry, Sams intended to knock off the pantograph through which the current passed. After being thwarted by stalling tactics carried out by police and British Rail, he eventually gave up.

After that Sams decided to lie low, and it was not until three months later that he resumed his sinister kidnap 'campaign'. On 7 January, Birmingham estate agents Shipways received a call from Sams calling himself Bob Southwall, with a request to view properties. He went into their office to pick up property details, disguising himself with glasses, latex to darken his complexion and dyed hair. He then wrote to Shipways asking to view a three-bedroomed house in Turnberry Road, Great Barr. It was ideal for his 'campaign' as it had an alleyway at the back. Later that month, on 22 January, Stephanie Slater left the Shipways office to travel to Great Barr for a 10.30 a.m. appointment with Sams, whom she believed was a genuine client. That day changed her life for ever.

As they wandered around the empty house, Sams lured her into the bathroom and threatened her with a knife and a chisel. The plucky 25-year-old tried to fight back, screaming – but quickly realized she was no match for him when he cut her hand and pushed her into the bath. He trussed her up, blindfolded her and when night fell dragged her with a rope to his car, which he had parked at the back of the house. She was bundled into the red Metro, which had its rear windows blacked out, and told to sit in the front seat which was reclined so that she lay almost flat. Then Sams covered her with a blanket and put a heavy box on her stomach to keep her down.

As they drove, Sams forced Stephanie to dictate a ransom message into a tape recorder. Then he telephoned Shipways to say there was a ransom note in the post. He drove Stephanie back to his workshop where she was forced into the same wooden coffin that had held Julie Dart six months previously.

During the eight days he held Stephanie captive, Sams kept a diary. Used during the trial as evidence, it gave a fascinating insight into his mind as he recorded every minute detail and the numerous conversations he had had with his victim. The sick Jekyll and Hyde character even said that those eight days with Stephanie were 'the happiest eight days in ten years', and that the girl had become 'like a daughter' to him. He also made macabre, detailed sketches of the box he kept her in and wrote down a description of it. He wrote in the diary:

The hide was a large plastic waste bin on its side, about 3 ft 6 inches square but only about 4 ft 6 inches tall, so a hole had been cut in the bottom and another box fitted on to allow Stephanie to lie straight. The smaller box on the bottom also provided the ideal shelf for the Kit Kat and milk she had with her, also a towel and small plastic bowl if she wanted the loo at night. I had also put a small 12-volt switch in her box. If she wanted me during the day she could switch it on, which illuminated a bulb attracting my attention. The box was large enough to sit up and turn in. Problem was it was very cold outside – minus 10 degrees centigrade most nights – which meant Stephanie needed a large thick duvet, plus a blanket for her feet, which then restricted movement.

Sams rigged up an alarm system which would detect movement inside the workshop. An infra-red detector was trained on the wheelie bin all the time. The sensor was wired to the re-dial button on a telephone in the workshop. If activated, it would ring the telephone at Sam's home and he would return immediately.

During her horrifying ordeal, Stephanie was blindfolded, handcuffed and gagged. She never once saw daylight or, indeed, Sams himself. He told her that there were boulders above her head which would crush her if she pulled on the bar to which she was shackled. He also said the wheelie bin she was in was connected to electrodes and that if she moved she would be electrocuted.

Sams later claimed in court that he had studied how other kidnappings had been carried out and he knew that he had to blindfold, gag and tie her up for the first day. Then the following day he would untie her and she would then trust him. Sams kept an account in his diary of her reactions to everything he did and said.

Sick Sams played a series of chilling mind games with Stephanie to test her trust in him, and also told her he had an accomplice. He used to terrorize her with a 12-inch knife and a bed of nails which was placed near the coffin-like box, telling the blindfolded woman that if she tried to escape she would be cut to ribbons by the nails. On one occasion, he sat her in a chair and told her to stay still and not to remove her blindfold. He told her he was going out for fifteen minutes, then pretended to go out but instead sat watching her. She never moved a muscle, even though only her hands were tied. Detectives believe that her obedience saved her life.

Stephanie had the great presence of mind to build up a rapport with her captor so that he would find it impossible to kill her. It worked – and the kidnap fiend began to fall in love with his helpless prey. He told her that a wheelie bin ready to receive her body should anything go wrong would now be removed because of the trust they had built up.

One-legged Sams was convinced that Stephanie shared his feelings. Detectives believe that his passion for her led to his downfall because he began to make mistakes. When he was eventually arrested, he broke down sobbing whenever her name was mentioned, even during his trial. He recalled in his diary how one night when the bound and blindfolded estate agent complained about the cold and a sore right foot, he had gently bathed her feet and massaged her toes in front of a heater. On the final night of Stephanie's captivity, Sams slept beside her on a separate mattress. He described that night in a prison letter while he was waiting trial. He lied when he wrote: 'It was dark but she was not tied, blindfolded or gagged or anything. She could have got up in the middle of the night, found a hammer or knife and done me in. But I could tell she was happy. We talked non-stop from 9 p.m. to 1 a.m. Then we slept like logs.'

The next morning, 29 January 1992, Sams put Stephanie back into the box before driving to collect the ransom. He telephoned Shipways manager Kevin Watt and instructed him to go to Glossop, Derbyshire, where messages left in a series of telephone boxes led him to a remote Pennine track in South Yorkshire. Sams also left other messages on traffic cones on a track near Barnsley, Yorks.

It was foggy by the time Kevin arrived at Dove Valley Trail, a disused railway track near Barnsley. A message there instructed him to place the money on a tray left on a wall. The wall was a parapet on a bridge that carried the disused railway. Sams, who was waiting underneath, tugged at a rope attached to the tray so that the £175,000 ransom money fell off the bridge and landed at his feet. He then scooped up the plastic-wrapped bundles of money and fled on his scooter.

Thick fog meant that visibility was down to 10 yards, thwarting a police helicopter waiting to follow him. Sams escaped – dropping £2,500 which was later picked up by a man out walking his dog. Hours later, he made his way back to the workshop, where Stephanie was by now hysterical. He had promised to return by 9 p.m., but was two hours late. When he freed her from the box, she collapsed, crying, the first time she had broken down in all the time she was held.

Later in court, 51-year-old Sams wept as extracts from his diary and letters recalling that night were read out. He said:

I informed her that everything was OK and she was going home. It was the first time I had seen her cry. She virtually collapsed into my arms with relief. Fortunately, she had her blindfold on and could not see my tears for her streaming down my face. I am ashamed, upset and thoroughly disgusted at my treatment of Stephanie and the suffering I must have caused to her parents. Stephanie will most likely insist she was well looked after, but during the time we talked, the sudden change of her smiling face to one taut and terrified was heartbreaking. I knew I was doing that to her. Even now my eyes are all filled up with tears. I wake up during the night actually crying. With a little luck Stephanie will get over it shortly. Myself? I don't think I ever will.

Sams adored Stephanie so much that he drove her to Birmingham where he released her only yards from her parents' home – a big mistake because an alert neighbour noticed his red car.

Cocky Sams thought that his kidnap plan had been foolproof. But modern-day forensic science and the tenacity of detectives working on the case unearthed many minute clues from his workshop that helped to convict him. Julie Dart's body was found wrapped in a sheet which was covered in clues, including hairs from Sams' dogs, Bonnie and Tara, and carpet and curtain fibres from his workshop. The fake bombs planted by Sams had been painted silver and the same paint was found in his attic where he used it to paint model trains. Envelopes found in the killer's home had a tiny printing flaw, as did those used to mail the ransom demands. Experts also retrieved information deleted from Sams' home computer discs which showed a link between the BR blackmail attempt, Julie Dart and Stephanie. Bloodstains found on the floor of his workshop came from Julie's rare blood group. Two of her hairs were also found in his workshop. Bricks found on a railway line during his bid to damage a train matched rare bricks found at the workshop. Handwriting experts saw through his disguised handwriting – he was an atrocious speller and experts concluded that both Stephanie's and Julie's ransom notes had been written by the same man, as they were riddled with the same spelling mistakes.

Sams' affection for Stephanie had caused him to let his guard down in one other way. It was the mistake which was to prove his downfall. He blundered when, upset by her distress, he phoned her office a day earlier than planned. Up to that point, he had always worn a peg over his nose and held a sweet in his mouth to disguise his voice. On this occasion he forgot to do so. He realized police had probably taped his voice – and from then on he didn't bother to try to disguise it.

Later, his taped ransom demand brought the break-through which directly resulted in his arrest. It was played on BBC's *Crimewatch* programme. His first wife, Susan, recognized his voice and called the police. The next day they went to his home in Sutton on Trent, where his wife Teena answered the door. She had also seen *Crimewatch* and when the photofit of Sams appeared on her screen had realized that it looked like him but had thought no more of it.

Police told Teena they were doing a routine check on red cars in the area and she told them Sams was at work. They drove the eight miles there to arrest him. Detectives were astonished when confronted with Sams. They had expected a strong, athletic man and were amazed when he shuffled towards them dragging his tin leg.

Within hours of his arrest, he had confessed to kidnapping Stephanie, but he denied all other charges, including a £200,000 plot to blackmail British Rail and the kidnap and murder of Julie Dart. A search of his workshop revealed £19,000 of the kidnap ransom but it wasn't until December 1992 that the bulk of it was discovered. Investigators recovered £140,000 buried under 4 inches of earth, not far from where Julie Dart's naked body was found. The cash was hidden in a 9 in by 18 in parcel wrapped in polythene and sodden newspapers.

Throughout his trial, Sams maintained he had nothing to do with Julie's kidnap and eventual murder. Even under oath in the dock he blamed an unnamed accomplice. He said that he had discussed his plan 'as a joke' with the mystery man, who then went on to commit the crimes himself. Because Julie was found ten days after her abduction, it was difficult to pinpoint the exact day she had died, and the callous killer's refusal to admit to her murder put her distraught mother through extra misery.

After the trial, police made a public appeal for Sams to end the Dart family's anguish and reveal what had happened to Julie. Four days later, in a dramatic about-turn, as Sams started four concurrent life sentences, he had a change of heart. He called detectives to his cell at Full Sutton Prison in York and told them what they already knew: that he had killed Julie.

Detectives listened as he recounted Julie's final hours. Sams said he killed her on the first day of her incarceration while she was suffering from claustrophobia and tried to flee. He told police: 'I wanted Julie's mother to know how and when her daughter died.'

University secretary Lynn Dart wept as she said: 'At least we now know when she died. It makes it a little easier. We did not know how long she had suffered.' She added, 'He knew all through the trial but he decided to deny it all. He is a completely evil man who should not be allowed to walk the earth. He is twisted, warped, a sadist.'

As Sams sat in solitary confinement watched closely by guards every fifteen minutes in case he tried to commit suicide – something common in people starting long life sentences – he may have silently congratulated himself on finally achieving what he set out to do. He may not have committed the perfect crime, but he certainly gained himself a place in the hall of evil . . . in the company of other sadists he idolized such as the Yorkshire Ripper and the Black Panther.

Voodoo Crazy

The night is darker than the grave, the plaintive whine of the wind drones round twisted rocks and stunted trees, swirling spectral columns of dust above a black and barren landscape. The glimmering of the moon makes eerie shapes of abandoned farm tools, casting here and there a wild, distorted shadow between pools of inky darkness. Otherwise there is not a sound. No night birds hunt in this wilderness, no nocturnal animal breaks the spell. It is as if nature has turned its back on this small, stagnant part of a godless world.

Suddenly a faint light, a candle perhaps, claws a hole in the gloom and a frightful chanting sends a shiver down the spine. The scene seems abandoned by God, but not by a small group of desperate and daring men. They gather in a circle in a rude nut, round an evil-smelling cauldron, and their blood-freezing chant is enough to stop the heart. Their leader, the high priest, bows before the cauldron and signals for silence. All eyes turn to what looks for all the world like a bundle of rags in a shadowy corner. Only now can it be seen that the bundle is jerking spasmodically and moaning piteously.

Two men, their faces hidden behind high-collared outfits, move to the corner and pull a fair-haired and cruelly

277

bound young man roughly to his feet. Screaming now with terror, the youth is dragged to the cauldron, where he is forced to bow his head to the evil brew inside.

Suddenly, in the dim light of the candle, there is a flash of steel as a machete slices through the youth's head, removing in one savage blow the top half of his skull. Bone, hair, blood and brains tumble into the cauldron. The boy was a human sacrifice to a savage and vengeful god.

Was this a scene from some ancient Aztec ritual? An act of religious frenzy from the darkest of Dark Ages in the tribal jungles of Africa? In fact, it took place just a few short miles south of the Texas border in August 1989. The sacrificial victim was a middle-class American student and the high priest was the wealthy leader of a voodoo-like cult that gained its power and its following through cruelty and violent death.

The callous inhumanity of Adolfo de Jesus Constanzo makes him, if not the king of the macabre killers, at least the equal of any of them. Constanzo's reign of terror was ended as a direct result of the human sacrifice described above. But it had begun a number of years previously.

Born in 1962 in Miami Beach to a fifteen-year-old mother of Cuban extraction, Adolfo de Jesus Constanzo grew up in Florida and Puerto Rico, nursing in his heart a dark secret: he believed that he was the chosen one of Palo Mayombe, a vicious and violent sect that once held sway in the Congo region of Africa.

His mother, like many of her expatriate peers, followed the Santeria, or Saint's Path, a quasi-Christian religion brought to the New World by African slaves hundreds of years ago and adapted to fit in with the ways of their Catholic masters. Palo Mayombe is the dark sister of the Santeria. If the Santeria, which involves sacrifice of animals, could be likened to 'white' magic, Palo Mayombe is definitely 'black'.

The religion accepts no after-life, so an adherent is free to do whatever he wants here on earth. The spirits of the dead exist in a kind of limbo, forced to wander the material plane. Newly dead spirits can be harnessed by a Palo Mayombe priest, if regularly appeased with fresh blood.

The religion centres round a *nganga* – a cauldron kept constantly filled with blood, a goat's head, a roasted turtle and, most importantly, a human skull, preferably that of a person who has died a violent and painful death. Non-believers, especially Christians, are considered to be animals and natural victims. The more painful and horrific their death, the more potent the spell that the High Priest can cast.

Constanzo, though never rich as a child, lived fairly well. His mother married a prosperous small businessman who took the family to Puerto Rico. But when his stepfather died in 1973, his mother remarried and moved back to Florida. This marriage was not a success, however, and after rows and quarrels it ended in divorce. At just twelve years of age, Adolfo found himself the man of the family.

Following the footsteps of so many of his fellows, he began shoplifting and trading in drugs. He became known to the police in 1975 when he was caught stealing, and at one stage the Miami drugs squad had him under observation. But so great is the volume of narcotics in that part of the United States and so small the staff of the agencies set up to deal with the problem that he had little trouble avoiding their attention.

At about this time, Constanzo discovered something else about himself: he was a bisexual with pronounced homosexual tendencies. He was later to sire two children, but during his teens, before he could slake his lust elsewhere, his principal sexual satisfaction came through frequenting gay bars.

It could be that things got too hot for the slim, dark and handsome youth with piercing eyes, or it could be simply that he saw his main chance south of the border. At any rate, at the tender age of twenty-one, Constanzo headed off to Mexico City, a smoky, sprawling urban mass peopled by everything from the very dregs of society to the fashionably bright young things, where grinding poverty held hands with undreamed-of opulence.

It was towards the wealth that Constanzo gravitated. Rich, bored businessmen and aristocrats were turned on by this youth and his exciting occult religion, and telling fortunes with apparently uncanny accuracy earned him his own fortune. His fame as a sorcerer spread and he soon became the darling of the wealthy and the powerful. But it was the drugs cartels that fêted him the most. At a time when the richest market for illegal drugs, the United States, was cracking down hardest on the trade, superstitious drugs family godfathers turned to him for advice and magical protection. In no time at all, Constanzo was earning $50,000 a time for spells to protect the smugglers.

It was subsequently discovered that much of his 'divination' came through corrupt Mexican police and customs officials. (Florentino Ventura, the head of Mexican Interpol, was later to shoot his wife before turning the gun on himself when investigations got too close.) However, the source of Constanzo's knowledge mattered not a whit to the drug barons. His word quickly became law. And all the time, dismembered and decapitated corpses were being regularly fished out of rivers and lakes.

By now Constanzo was calling himself the 'padrino' of his own Palo Mayombe group, selling his services to the highest bidders, who for a while happened to be a drugs family headed by Guillermo Calzada. Observing the wealth that was sticking to the fingers of the cartels, Constanzo went to Calzada and suggested that as his magic was the source of the family's success, he deserved half the proceeds. Calzada refused and Constanzo left in a rage. A few days later, he called Calzada to express regret for his demands and offered, as a sign of remorse, to perform a special ceremony that would give extra protection to the whole cartel.

On 30 April 1987, Calzada, his wife, his mother, his partner, his secretary, his maid and his bodyguard met Constanzo in an abandoned factory. All seven reappeared a few days later ... when their bodies were dragged from a river. All had been dreadfully mutilated before being killed. Their extremities – their fingers and toes and, in the case of the men, their genitals – had been sliced off. Significantly, their heads were missing; these had gone to feed the padrino's *nganga*.

Suddenly Constanzo had his own crime syndicate. He also began believing ever more implicitly in his own voodoo powers. Like the drug leaders he had wiped out, he was hooked on his own mumbo jumbo and even more felt the need to perform the ceremonies that would bring him protection. He decided to move his voodoo circle to the border town of Matamoros, where the drugs cartels were even richer.

Here he used an American ex-girlfriend, Sara Aldrete,

with whom he had had a torrid, though brief affair, as the tool to get himself into the family drugs empire of Elio Hernandez. Sara remained under Constanzo's spell, despite the fact that he lived in a weird ménage-à-trois with two homosexual lovers, Orea Ochoa, who played the 'wife', and Martin Quintera, who played the 'husband'. The American girl lured Elio Hernandez into the Palo Mayombe circle and, sure enough, his business picked up. But there could be no doubt who was running the gang: Adolfo de Jesus Constanzo.

The Hernandez gang was now totally under the spell of the Constanzo's voodoo group, and by 1988 the area round Matamoros was thick with dismembered corpses. Between May that year and March 1989, Constanzo tortured and ritually sacrificed at least thirteen people. All male, they were often rival dealers, but they also included innocent strangers picked up at random.

On one occasion, the victim was a police undercover agent who had infiltrated the gang but had been discovered, possibly through a tip-off from one of the police officers on Constanzo's payroll. On another, Hernandez himself was ordered to supply the coup de grâce to a struggling young victim at the bubbling *nganga*. Only after slicing off the youth's head did he recognize the green and white striped football shirt he was wearing. He had killed his own cousin.

Constanzo's normal method of sacrifice was to have the victim soundly beaten, then dragged into the shed containing the sacred cauldron. Here he would cut off the nose, ears, fingers, toes and genitals of the hapless wretch and partially flay him. Then the others would be ordered out while Constanzo sodomized him. Only then would there be a merciful release through death.

It was essential to the success of the ceremony that there should be as much pain as possible and the victim should die screaming. The spirit had to be confused and terrified as it left the body, thus making it easier to subjugate. And it was this particular evil that was to bring about Constanzo's downfall.

In March 1989 the selected victim was a small-time Mexican drugs dealer unknown to the gang. Every torture was applied to him, but the tough little man would not cry out, even when his upper body was skinned. He endured every torture, even castration, but died silently. Constanzo declared the ceremony a failure and sent his men out to kidnap a softer touch. He was easy to find. A group of American students were celebrating the end of term at their university by crossing the border for a night of cheap alcohol, perhaps a woman or two and possibly a session of pot smoking or cocaine sniffing. When one became separated from his colleagues, he was pushed into the back of a truck and driven to Constanzo's remote Santa Elena ranch.

His name was Mark Kilroy, a 21-year-old medical student and he must have screamed sufficiently to satisfy Constanzo before his brains were tipped into the *nganga*, for the padrino declared the ceremony a great success. The gang was now unstoppable. With an American spirit as well as any number of Mexican spirits to protect them, they wcrc not only safe but invisible to the law.

This time, however, the cultists had over-reached themselves. Kilroy's parents were devout and loving people who would not rest until they had found their son. They were aided by the boy's uncle, who happened to be a US Customs official. The manhunt that ensued stretched across both sides of the border.

Success came swiftly. Mexican police set up a road block near Matamoros. One of the Hernandez brothers, Serafin, was driving a truck when he came upon it. Should he stop? Was he not, according to his padrino, invisible? The stunned police, trigger-happy at the best of times, could not believe what they saw as the truck driver simply ignored them and drove right past the road block. They scrambled into their cars and followed at a discreet distance as Hernandez led them to Constanzo's ranch.

Here they found some evidence of drug trading – but of Constanzo himself there was no sign. Hernandez was arrested and taken to headquarters, where he was subjected to a Mexican interrogation. With the help of a little soda laced with tabasco squirted up his nostrils (an agonizing, though undetectable torture) he broke and revealed the horrors of his hellish ranch. Yet even now he believed himself to be beyond the power of the law, and on 10 April naively led police back to the Santa Elena and pointed out a number of shallow graves around the *nganga* shed. He also began to name names.

Detectives rounded up several of the cultists who, puzzled by the lack of promised protection and aided by ingenious police tortures, sang like birds. The disgusted police forced them to do the dirty work of digging up the bodies. One of the first they unearthed was that of the American student, Mark Kilroy. The grave was marked by a small piece of wire sticking out of the ground. Subsequent examination revealed that a strip of thin but strong wire had been pushed through the length of the boy's spine. Once the body had decomposed sufficiently, it had been Constanzo's intention to pull out the backbone and add it to the stomach-churning mix in his *nganga*.

Constanzo and his favoured inner circle had fled to

Mexico City, but suddenly they had few friends there. Influential support melted away; too many reputations were now at stake. After a brief stay in the capital, Constanzo fled south to the resort of Cuernavaca. The gang believed that there was not really much to worry about. Money buys anything in Mexico, and they had plenty of that. When the hue and cry died down, they would buy their passage across the border.

In fact, the group drifted back to Mexico City in May, where they lay low in one of Constanzo's many bolt-holes. However, he made one small error that led to his chance-in-a-million discovery. The apartment he was hiding in was in a poorer part of town – and he left his luxury limousine in the street nearby. Two beat cops saw it and strolled over to investigate, thinking it might have been stolen. When Constanzo saw them, he assumed the game was up. Suddenly the cops found themselves under fire from a nearby apartment building. They radioed for help, which soon arrived in the form of a heavily armed riot team.

Inside the apartment, panic reigned. As Constanzo's gunmen were exchanging fire with the police, the padrino himself was stuffing armfuls of cash into a furnace, or ripping it up and throwing it out of the windows.

As Sara Aldrete cowered with Ochoa under a bed, Constanzo and a hitman nicknamed 'El Dubi' emptied their guns into the street. At other windows more cultists were spraying the police with bullets. When they were almost out of ammunition, Constanzo suddenly became calm again. He called together El Dubi and his current lover, bodyguard Martin Rodriguez, whom he led into a walk-in wardrobe. Then he ordered El Dubi to shoot them both. When the gunman simply stared aghast, Constanzo smacked him hard across the face and ordered: 'Do it or I'll make things tough for you in hell. Don't worry, I'll be back.'

They were his last words. He and his lover died in a hail of lead.

The rest were taken alive, and their detailed confessions allowed the police to close their files on a number of mystery killings. There had been fifteen human sacrifices at the Matamoros ranch, two at another ranch nearby and several in Mexico City. Added to these were the killings of rival gang members and the savage murders of those of Constanzo's own followers who had been slaughtered to maintain discipline.

There is no death penalty in Mexico. The maximum sentence that could be handed down was fifty years for aggravated homicide. At the trial and in subsequent interviews, Aldrete proclaimed her innocence and complained bitterly about the tortures she said she had endured at the hands of the police. She found no sympathy. Nor was there sympathy for Constanzo's erstwhile lover Orea Ochoa, who, it was later discovered, was suffering from AIDS.

Back in Matamoros, the police had the *nganga* and the shed in which it was housed exorcised by a white witch and a priest. Then they doused the shed with petrol and burned it to the ground. Constanzo's body was claimed by his mother and taken back to Miami, where it was cremated. His mother, like many of her friends and neighbours, continued to follow the Santeria and to make sacrifices of small animals.

Is the sinister and sickening Palo Mayombe cult now dead? It seems not. The Miami river has been nicknamed the 'river of chickens' by the sanitation crews who work on it. In a three-day period, they dredged up the headless bodies of 200 chickens, 22 ducks and various other sacrificial creatures, including cats, dogs, snakes, iguanas and pelicans.

The Dingo Baby

It was a family camping holiday – and a bit of an adventure for the Chamberlains. There was Lindy, her Seventh Day Adventist preacher husband Michael, and their three children, Aidan, Reagan and baby Azaria. Together they had struck camp for the night near the mysterious Ayers Rock in the dead, empty, dramatically beautiful heart of Australia's Outback. It was 17 August 1980. The sun was going down. It was still warm as darkness began to sweep the desert.

The Chamberlains had just finished a picnic. They had only casually glanced at a sign – 'Dingoes Are Wild' – warning visitors not to encourage the dogs by putting down food. Michael lingered around the barbecue area while Lindy returned to the family tent to check on nine-week-old Azaria, who had been left contentedly in her cot.

What Lindy witnessed as she approached the tent was at first too frightening to take in. She saw a dingo coming out through the tent flaps, shaking its head from side to side. Lindy was too far away to see exactly what the creature was doing. But a terrible sickening feeling was hitting her in the stomach. She rushed to the tent.

Incredibly, little Reagan was sleeping peacefully. But

the baby had gone. At that moment Lindy knew the awful truth – but she still searched desperately, pulling up anything and everything that came to hand.

The words Lindy Chamberlain cried that moment were to go down in history: 'A dingo has got my baby . . . !'

That anguished cry heralded one of the most sensational murder trials ever. It was later to drive an innocent family to despair and poverty. It was immortalized in books and a poignant film. And it resulted in Lindy Chamberlain enduring worldwide outrage and horror when she was found guilty of murdering her own tiny baby.

Campers who heard Lindy Chamberlain's hysterical cries took part in a desperate search of the area around Ayers Rock, the sinister monolith sacred to the Aborigines. They were joined by 300 visitors and other volunteers but no evidence of the poor mite could be found. Lindy could not be comforted. Her new-born baby had gone, presumably dragged to a wild creature's lair and eaten.

'Our baby girl has been taken by a dingo and we are fully reconciled to the fact that we will never see her again,' Michael told a park ranger. 'The dingo would have killed her immediately, wouldn't it?'

The inquest was gruelling for the Chamberlains. Police and rangers had shot every dingo they could hunt down in the hope of making a gruesome but revealing find in one of the animals' stomachs, yet nothing had been discovered. Most of baby Azaria's clothing, found by another visitor soon after the child's disappearance, was carefully examined and analysed for clues. Without the evidence of a body, Alice Springs coroner Denis Barritt could only find that 'in the time they went to the campsite and the time Mr Chamberlain was at the barbecue area, the death was caused'.

Coming, as it did, four months after Azaria's disappearance, it was hardly a precise conclusion, and the uncertainty about the child's gory demise was a constant agony to the grieving parents. They had, however, been cleared of all blame. They were now left alone with their private anguish. The support of friends from Michael's church was a great help – but not enough to shield them from the terrible traumas of the months and years ahead. For what was to follow was not only to invade their grief but to lay it bare before an accusing world.

A year after the first inquest, the family had to relive the baby's disappearance all over again. Australia's Northern Territory police declared themselves dissatisfied with the original verdict and went about collecting evidence which would disprove it. That evidence was considered important enough to be presented before a second inquest in 1981.

Again, the Chamberlains found themselves at the coroner's court. This time there was a new police suggestion as to how their baby had been parted from its tiny clothing. The child had been decapitated, they said, and the proof was in a bloodstained hand-print found on the clothes.

What still had not been found was the white matinee jacket Lindy said her child had been wearing when she was snatched.

Neither had there been any sign of the body of poor Azaria, and that is what puzzled the inquest. Lindy yet again attempted to explain the discovery of the clothes minus the remains of her child. She said in a television interview: 'If you've ever seen dingoes eat, there's no difficulty for them to remove clothes. They never eat the skin. They use their feet and hands and pull back the skin as they go – just like peeling an orange. I knew my baby was dead. It was God's will.'

The police forensic department thought differently. They announced to the inquest their discovery of a hand-print, the size of a woman's, on the tiny all-in-one stretch garment. They alleged that the clothes had been touched by hands wet with blood. Not only that, but they believed Lindy had cut off her own baby's head with a pair of scissors!

Again, the Chamberlains' lawyers explained away this new piece of accusatory evidence by the fact that Lindy, hysterical at what had happened, had clutched the baby's suit after accidentally smearing her hand in the blood that spattered the tent. But yet more evidence was being compiled against her – and this time it was more difficult to explain away.

Police said they had found blood on the door handle of the Chamberlains' car, on the carpet, under hinges and under the dashboard. Expert witnesses were called to give evidence that these traces were of foetal blood: in other words, the blood of a newborn baby. Further examination of the personal items the Chamberlains had with them that terrible day also revealed blood spots and minute specks of baby hair in their camera bag.

The Northern Territory prosecutors at last felt they had enough proof that a murder had taken place. They accused 33-year-old Lindy Chamberlain of inventing the entire dingo snatch story in an attempt to get away with the cold-blooded slaughter of her own baby.

Lindy Chamberlain could barely comprehend the dread-ful allegations that were being made against her. Indeed, to most people following the case, journalists included, they seemed ludicrously far-fetched. Yet the unstoppable processes of the law ground on, even crossing the world.

A British forensic expert, Professor James Cameron, of London Hospital Medical College, was called in to give a second opinion. It was claimed that Lindy had slashed her baby's throat with a pair of scissors as she sat in the family car. The bloodied babe had then been held by human hands. The bloodstains, it was said, were not consistent with an animal's attack. Furthermore, no hint of animal saliva or fur could be found.

Coroner Des Sturgess caused a sensation by announcing that Azaria had been killed in the family car and that Lindy had revealed this awful truth to her husband. Mr Sturgess said there had been ample time to bury the still-dressed, bloody body of their child, dig it up again, remove the clothes and put them where they were later found at the base of Ayers Rock. With that damning statement, Lindy and her husband went from being a couple tragically deprived of their youngest child, to baby killers. Lindy was committed for trial on a murder charge and Michael was charged with being an accessory.

Sick T-shirts began to appear declaring, 'The Dingo Is Innocent', and malicious graffiti was daubed on walls throughout Australia. It became almost a cult joke. By the time Lindy and her husband went to court on 13 September 1982 to make their plea of not guilty, her case had fiercely divided the nation. The imagination of press and public had been fired. The Chamberlains were at the centre of the most intriguing murder story ever. There was talk of the couple's strange interest in sacred sites. Journalists couldn't believe their luck when they heard one of these sites was called Cut Throat Cave and that Azaria was supposedly an aboriginal word for 'sacrifice in the wilderness'.

It was obvious that Lindy and Michael stood no chance of a fair trial in Alice Springs, so it was decided they should go to Darwin. Their trial there gripped the world. It was also just a fragment of the legal machine so determined to find Lindy Chamberlain guilty that it would eventually cost Australian taxpayers £15 million.

Lindy was now heavily pregnant with her fourth child. She sat there while, before a jury of nine men and three women, she was accused of cutting Azaria's throat. Prosecutor Ian Marker said there was no doubt that the baby had been killed by her own mother. The dingo story was a 'fanciful lie', he told the court.

Recalled again to confirm his original evidence, Professor James Cameron did not waiver. Death had been caused by an incised wound to the child's neck. In other words, a cut throat. It had been slashed by a cutting instrument and the head had been held.

At times, Lindy's defence seemed to be going well. One Ayers Rock camper said that when Lindy had arrived with her family she had a 'new mum glow about her'. Another two witnesses gave evidence that the day before the baby went missing, two children at the campsite were confronted by a dingo. The animal, obviously used to humans that put out food for it, showed no fear. It grabbed the trousers of one of the children. Another witness to take the stand said a dingo had seized her own six-year-old son, causing bad bruising to his bottom. It had also left teeth marks and caused bleeding. When yet another witness said that a month before Azaria was taken, a dingo was shot as it went to snatch a three-year-old child from the seat of her parents' car, the outcome looked brighter still.

Then came the best news so far for the defence. A young man, Kyth Lenehan, took the oath and told quite simply how way back at that time at Ayers Rock, the caring Chamberlains had taken him to hospital in their car after he had been involved in an accident. He had been bleeding quite heavily from a head injury. That would explain traces of blood found in their car.

Melbourne consultant biochemist Finely Cornell said blood samples were less reliable when examined a year after the blood was shed, as had been the case with the second inquest evidence. He added that six samples of carpet taken from the Chamberlains' car had no traces of blood at all. (In fact, forensic scientists were later to be greatly embarrassed when the 'foetal blood' found under the car's dashboard turned out to be a bitumen substance used to dampen engine noise!)

The bloodstained clothing was shown to the court. So, too, were films of dingoes snatching dolls to show how they gripped the head. Two women jurors wept during the proceedings. So did Lindy. At one point, the entire court was flown to Ayers Rock to see the scene of death for themselves.

The trial lasted seven weeks. The prosecution called 45 witnesses, the defence 28. At the end of it all, the evidence filled 2,800 pages. The Chamberlains felt optimistic that they would at last be believed.

Lindy and Michael showed no emotion, however, when they were both found guilty. Supreme Court Judge Muirhead told Lindy: 'You have been found guilty of murder and there is only one sentence I can pass upon you with the law of this territory, and that is imprisonment with hard labour for life.' Michael was given an eighteen-month suspended sentence. He was also bound over in the sum of £300 to be of good behaviour for three years.

Lindy later said: 'I am convinced that Michael would

have killed himself if he had been sent to prison.'

Lindy gave birth to a baby girl, Kahlia, in prison. The child was taken away from her four hours later. Two days after the birth, Lindy was granted bail pending an appeal. Proving what a bizarre case it had become, this convicted murderer was now to be temporarily freed. Conditions were that she lived with her husband, two sons and her parents at a Seventh Day Adventist Church in northern New South Wales. Their church was to give more than spiritual support to the Chamberlains. Even when Lindy won her compensation years later, the couple still owed it a great proportion of the £700,000 loaned to help with legal costs.

Lindy's appeal was rejected on 30 April 1983, and she was taken back to Berrinah jail in Darwin to 'resume her sentence as soon as possible'. A second appeal the following year also failed. Lindy's future seemed to exist of nothing more than sweating in a prison laundry.

Then came a dramatic twist. But it had nothing to do with new evidence discovered by experts or submitted by lawyers. Lindy's freedom was to be won by virtue of a complete fluke . . .

In February 1986, climbers went out searching for British tourist David Brett, who had got lost climbing Ayers Rock. They discovered his body. He had obviously fallen from the rock, and his right arm, left hand and right foot were missing, apparently taken by dingoes. A search was made of the area and just a short distance away police found the remains of what looked like a baby's matinee jacket. The jacket was in such an inaccessible spot that no human without climbing skills could have placed it there. But any wild animal could have. It had to be Azaria Chamberlain's jacket.

Police could not question the identity of the jacket. Its description accurately matched that given by Lindy four years before. Furthermore, when forensic scientists were called in to examine what was delicately referred to as 'organic material' found near the jacket, they had to confess that it was human remains.

Lindy was released from jail. In a television poll, viewers were asked whether they thought she was innocent. A total of 52,250 said Yes, 48,242 said No.

A Royal Commission into the Azaria Chamberlain tragedy began in October 1986. Witnesses who had already told their story many times before were yet again called on to give evidence. Lindy, bowed but determined not to be beaten by the authorities she felt had treated her appallingly, announced: 'I don't like your form of law and I don't adhere to it. It's the reason for these courts in Australia being in such a mess.'

On 2 June 1987, after 92 days, 145 witnesses and court costs of £90,000 a week, Mr Justice Trevor Morling retired for his final adjudication. Although he felt there were discrepancies in Lindy's version of events, he came to the conclusion that there had simply never been enough evidence to convict.

The couple later received a pardon. This wasn't enough for Lindy, however. She said: 'There is no satisfaction in getting a pardon for something you didn't do in the first place. I want the conviction quashed and the authorities to admit I was wrongly accused.'

It was fifteen long months later, on 15 September 1988, that three judges in the Northern Territory Court of Criminal Appeal quashed the Chamberlains' convictions after only ten minutes of deliberation. Chief Justice Austin Asche told the packed court: 'We find the original trial is now attended with sufficient doubt to justify this court in quashing the convictions. Not to do so would be unfair and allow an unacceptable risk of perpetuating a miscarriage of justice.'

As the verdict was announced, Lindy stared intently ahead, but as the court rose her shoulders sagged and she almost fell back in her seat. Then she and Michael met the cheering Darwin crowd outside the court before going into hiding to pray. The couple's lawyer announced he would institute proceedings to win compensation for all the time they had lived under sentence of killing their own baby. And he pointed out that the true meaning of the baby's name, Azaria, was 'Blessed of God'.

Justice had been done. All Lindy and Michael had ever wanted was for an accusing world to know they were innocent.

While wrangles over compensation dragged on, the couple found it hard to adjust to being together again. Michael had looked after the two boys and baby Kahlia on his own. He had given up preaching, feeling it was wrong to continue after the convictions. He said: 'Lindy is quite new to me even though we lived together for thirteen years before all this happened.'

But Lindy said: 'I always knew sometime it could come right; I just didn't know when. If you let your self-esteem go, if you lose your self-respect, you lose your grip on everything else. I didn't. I'd fight first.'

Meanwhile, the astonishing tale and trials of Lindy Chamberlain had been followed closely thousands of miles away in London by film producer Verity Lambert. Determined to tell the tragic and bizarre story, she travelled to Australia to meet the couple at the heart of it all. The film Verity Lambert eventually made was a £10 million production called *Cry In The Dark*.

'I had to make it,' said Verity. 'Lindy was tried and convicted by religious prejudice and Australian television and press. Nobody really knew what Seventh Day Adventists were about so they made up rumours about ritual human sacrifices.'

To prepare for the leading role, actress Meryl Streep arranged a meeting with Lindy and also visited the jail where she had been. Said Meryl: 'It is a bleak place. I thought about her giving birth there and immediately having to give up her baby. I would have died. There is no question about that.' Having read all she could about the case, Meryl said that neither was there any question that Lindy was innocent. 'When I met her I knew that and I was very moved,' she said. (The film would win Meryl Streep the Best Actress Award at the 1989 Cannes Film Festival.)

It was not just the critics who saw previews of *Cry In The Dark*. Lindy Chamberlain herself was curious to see how her 'missing' years were portrayed for cinema audiences. Her verdict was: 'Meryl Streep's accent was not quite right but she was pretty good. It was a lot harder to act me than anyone thought. They reckon I am a complicated character. Sam Neill, the actor who played Michael, was brilliant. He *was* Michael. The film broke down a lot of hostility. People started writing to me saying they were once convinced I was guilty but now admit they were wrong.'

Lindy was later to write her own personal, poignant story in *Through My Eyes*. Neither the film nor Lindy's book, however, brought enough financial reward to cover the legal bills that had been run up to prove the Chamberlains' innocence. The couple's troubles were still not over. They asked for £690,000 to cover legal fees, and wanted

£2 million compensation. The Northern Territory Government refused to pay anything at all, stating that the Chamberlains had failed to declare exactly how much they had received from selling their story. But Lindy and Michael were heavily in debt to their Seventh Day Adventist Church. It was that church, too, that continued to help the couple, providing Michael with work cutting up firewood. Lindy said she and her husband were now so poor that they could not even afford shoes for their children.

'Please believe us,' she begged. 'We have made nothing out of any of it.'

All they had left, she said, was their 1970 car, the one in which she was accused of murdering her own child. Eventually handed back by the police, its gearbox and engine removed, it stood useless outside the modest bungalow in Cooranbong, northern New South Wales, to which Lindy and Michael had moved.

Friends of the Chamberlains believed the government's reluctance to settle up was because it didn't want to be seen to admit there had been a ghastly error in its legal system. Lindy felt this, too, saying publicly that the voice of authority that had condemned her was now silent in offering official admission of her innocence. Lindy also insisted she and her husband had been victims of Australian authorities desperate to deny any danger of dingoes which might threaten its newly promoted tourist industry at Ayers Rock. Michael added that it was simply the government having a 'last swipe' because it could no longer get at them any other way.

The couple battled on. Then, in June 1991, the Northern Territory government agreed the paltry figure of £195,000 to cover legal bills. Shortly afterwards they were awarded compensation: just £210,000 for wrongful imprisonment. It ended eleven years of bitter fighting to see justice done, but it was much less than Lindy felt she deserved. Three years of her life had been lost while she languished in jail for a crime she did not commit.

Today there is still talk about the Dingo Baby Case. Some refuse to believe it was as straightforward as both the Chamberlains and finally the courts insisted. 'Some people will die believing we are guilty,' says Lindy. 'We just have to live with that.'

Lindy now wants to forget 1980 and the dreadful years that followed. She and Michael have managed to stay together despite the pressures on them, although they both admit they have changed their outlook on life. The campsite where the Chamberlains stayed that fateful night has changed too; it is now an aboriginal reserve. But Outback campers are still plagued by dingoes sniffing around tents . . .

Herman Mudgett

In the early 1890s, the inhabitants of Chicago began to believe they were living in a truly great city. It had won the right to stage the coveted World Fair in 1893 and the years leading up to that momentous event saw new trade, commerce and wealth pour in. Prosperity, however, brought with it an army of thieves, swindlers, hoodlums and rum-runners. Entire neighbourhoods were colonized by racketeers, establishing a tradition of crime which Chicago has to this day had cause to regret. In all its bloodstained history, though, there is one man whose sheer evil secures him one of the highest positions in not only Chicago's but the world's black gallery of infamy. He is listed in the *Guinness Book of Records* as 'the most prolific murderer known in recent criminal history'.

To his neighbours, he was known as Dr H.H. Holmes, a respectable, hard-working young man with a keen business sense and a responsible position as prescription clerk in a drug store on the corner of Sixty-third and South Wallace streets in the city's Englewood district. In fact, he was Herman Webster Mudgett, a master of deceit and a nineteenth-century Bluebeard who tortured, butchered and murdered as many as 150 victims, most of them young women, within the dark, eerie corridors of his three-storey 'castle'.

He had arrived in Chicago around 1886, aged twenty-six, claiming to be a graduate of the Ann Arbor Medical School, Michigan, and quickly secured his job in the pharmacy owned by a widow named Mrs E.S. Holton. The dapper, moustachioed Holmes soon established a winning rapport with customers – especially the female ones – and business boomed. Within months, Mrs Holton and her young daughter vanished, Holmes telling customers they had moved to California after selling the shop to him. They were never seen again.

As the 'good doctor's' drug store flourished, so did his desire to expand his empire. He bought a double plot of land across the road, at 701 and 703 Sixty-third Street, and began to build a huge two-storeyed bride house, quickly dubbed 'Holmes Castle' because of the battlements on the street front of the building.

To finance this enormous venture, Holmes concocted a series of outrageous schemes, some of which actually paid off. He marketed a 'sure-fire' cure for alcoholism which he sold for $50 a bottle; he sold ordinary tap water as an all-purpose 'miracle' elixir for five cents a glass and, in one of his most audacious swindles, he 'invented' a device that turned water into domestic gas. (A gas company inspector actually offered him $25,000 for the process before realizing it was a con!)

Holmes Castle itself, the brand new centre of his fly-by-night operations, was paid for by a series of elaborate frauds. So many bogus deeds were drawn up that when completed, the huge mansion contained some 100 rooms of varying sizes, false partitions, staircases which led nowhere, long, dark corridors, trapdoors and secret passageways.

Charmed by the dark-haired 'good doctor', young girls flocked to it to work on his various operations. He once boasted how he liked 'a nice, green, young girl fresh from a business college'. As Dr Holmes, Mudgett travelled across the United States carrying out swindle after swindle. The dapper womanizer married three different girls in three different cities, two of his 'brides' returning with him to the mansion in hometown Chicago, never to be seen again.

As the mysterious Holmes Castle began to arouse deep public and police suspicion, Mudgett dreamed up perhaps his most elaborate scheme of all. With an occasional partner in crime, a small-time thief named Benjamin Pitezel, he plotted to earn a fortune from the Fidelity Mutual Life Insurance Company. The conspirators aimed to defraud Mutual Life by faking Pitezel's death and cashing in a huge policy taken out on his life. To achieve that, they needed a corpse – a victim bearing as close a resemblance as possible to Pitezel himself. They also needed a crooked lawyer, and found one through a train robber called Marion Hedgepath, who was promised $500 for the introduction.

On Monday, 3 September 1894, police entered a back room above a shop at 1316 Callowhill Street, Philadelphia. They had been alerted by a customer, who was worried by a terrible stench. The ghastly sight that greeted them confirmed the worst: a corpse so bathed in sunshine that was streaming through a window that it had begun to putrefy, making some of its features unidentifiable. This was not, however, the body of an innocent victim unfortunate enough to look like Benjamin Pitezel. It was Pitezel himself, murdered by the double-crossing Mudgett. And, incredibly, Mudgett almost got away with it.

The Mutual Life Company had already issued a cheque

for $9,715 to the 'widow' of Benjamin Pitezel when Mudgett came unstuck. He had also double-crossed Marion Hedgepath by failing to deliver the promised $500 for finding a bent lawyer. The duplicitous Hedgepath squealed to the police.

Mudgett was arrested by Philadelphia detectives, who cabled the already suspicious Chicago police. After years of dark rumour, a warrant was obtained to search the notorious 'Holmes Castle' on Sixty-third Street. Detective Sergeants Fitzpatrick and Norton, accompanied by Pinkerton Detective Agency operative Frank Wind, led the search. What they found gave them nightmares for the rest of their lives.

A labyrinth of blind hallways, concealed rooms, trapdoors and sealed passages awaited them. A graphic account of the time says:

> The second floor contained 35 rooms. Half a dozen were fitted up as ordinary sleeping chambers and there were indications that they had been occupied by various women who worked for the monster, or to whom he had made love while awaiting an opportunity to kill them.
>
> Several of the other rooms were without windows and could be made airtight by closing the doors. One was completely filled by a huge safe, almost large enough for a bank vault, into which a gas pipe had been introduced. Another was lined with sheet iron covered by asbestos and showed traces of fire. Some had been sound-proofed while others had extremely low ceilings and trapdoors in the floors from which ladders led to smaller rooms beneath.
>
> In all of the rooms were gas pipes with cut-off

valves. But the valves were fakes. The flow of gas was actually controlled by a series of cut-offs concealed in the closet of Holmes' bedroom. Apparently, one of his favourite methods of murder was to lock a victim in one of the rooms and then turn on the gas. Police believed that in the asbestos-lined chamber he had devised a means of introducing fire, so that the gas pipe became a terrible blow-torch from which there was no escape.

In the monstrous doctor's bedroom was an electric bell which rang whenever a door was opened anywhere on the labyrinthian second floor. In his office stood a huge, six foot high stove. Part of a bone was found in the ash pan and a human rib lay in the grate. A badly scorched woman's slipper and a piece of dress were also found in the ashes. Clinging to brickwork behind the stove was a bunch of human hair. In one of the second floor bedrooms, police found bloodstained overalls and a blood-spattered undershirt. More stains, all of which proved to be human blood, were discovered in an adjoining bathroom in which there was a concealed trapdoor that led down secret stairs to the basement.

It was the basement which contained the grizzliest evidence of maniacal murder. Scattered or buried everywhere were human bones, among them the ribs and pelvis of a child no more than fourteen years old. A barrel with extra-heavy hoops was found to contain acid, and in a corner of the basement stood a dissecting table with a box of surgical knives. Under the table were several women's skeletons – one theory being that Mudgett sometimes separated the flesh of his victims from their bones and sold the skeletons to medical schools. A storeroom nearby revealed a bloody noose, beneath which were two brick vaults filled with quicklime. Also in the basement was a medieval-style torture rack on which, it was claimed, Mudgett tested his macabre theory that the human body could be stretched as much as twice its normal length.

The explosion of headlines across America about the foul deeds of Herman Webster Mudgett came at the same time as, by cruel coincidence, England recoiled in horror at the slayings of Jack the Ripper. The Ripper was never caught, but society did eke its revenge on Mudgett the Monster.

At 8.40 p.m. on Saturday, 2 November 1895, a twelve-man jury returned from their deliberations at the Court of Oyer and Terminer, Philadelphia. The courtroom fell silent. Then the clerk rose and said: 'Jurors, look upon the prisoner; prisoner, look upon the jurors. How say you, gentlemen of the jury? Do you find the prisoner at the bar, Herman W. Mudgett, alias H.H. Holmes, guilty or not guilty?'

The condemning words came quickly from the jury foreman: 'Guilty of murder in the first degree.' Mudgett, tried and convicted in the city where he had killed his one-time accomplice Benjamin Pitezel, had protested his innocence throughout the sensational six-day trial.

Even after the guilty verdict, it was not until 9 April 1896 that Mudgett signed his name to a lengthy, prison-cell confession to twenty-seven further murders and six attempted murders in Chicago, Indianapolis and Toronto. A wheeler-dealer to the end, he signed a $10,000 contract with newspaper tycoon William Randolph Hearst granting him the right to syndicate his confession to the world's press. It was money that Mudgett had no hope of getting his hands on. The sentence of death by hanging was due to be carried out a month later. Before his date with the hangman, Mudgett refused to confess to further crimes – although police believed his toll of murders stood close to 150.

On the morning of 7 May 1896, Mudgett was led from his cell in Philadelphia County Prison to the gallows. 'Ready?' asked the hangman. 'Yes, don't bungle,' replied Mudgett. He took fifteen minutes to die, carrying his dark secrets to the grave for ever.

Pol Pot

In its heyday, Cambodia was a colourful land of fertile plains, ancient temples and smiling, friendly people. Its capital, Phnom Penh, throbbed with the sounds of jazz music from bars and to the cries of ice cream vendors. Wafting through the tree-lined streets was the mystical aroma of spices being blended for a feast. It was a land of plenty.

Yet this same country was, a few short years later, brought to its knees. Gone were the happy sounds and genial faces. The mouthwatering smells of cooking were replaced with the stench of fear and death. Now the only fertile lands were those fed with the mouldering bodies of slaughtered men, women and children. The remainder of its people were hollow-eyed, disease-ridden and starving, mute in terror of a regime as harsh as that of the Nazis and even more sadistic.

Behind this appalling destruction was leader Pol Pot. He was a man who longed to see communism in action. And in his view, the only way for this dream to become a reality was to turn the clock back and return Cambodia to a medieval peasant economy where all were equal. There was no longer any need for the educated classes: in fact, thinkers who questioned the wisdom of the crackpot communist theories were a veritable threat. So Pol Pot got rid of doctors, teachers, clerks and many more, in brutal and systematic executions. To have once been a student was crime enough to attract the death penalty.

An estimated two million Cambodians died – about one quarter of the country's population – during the four years Pol Pot held power, either killed at the hands of his enthusiastic henchmen or victims of the terrible deprivations he imposed on his people.

All contact with the outside world was broken off, except for a healthy relationship with Pol Pot's sponsor, China. But there was mounting international concern over the massacres. In March 1978, Britain reported Pol Pot and his cronies to the United Nations Commission on Human Rights. In response, the communist Khmer Rouge embassy in Peking issued a rambling denial which said: 'The British imperialists have no right to speak of the rights of man. The world knows well their barbarous and abject nature. Britain's leaders are living in opulence on top of a pile of rotting corpses while the proletariat have only the right to be unemployed, to steal and to become prostitutes.'

It was a curious flight of fancy by the Khmers. Even as the official mouthed the words, more of his people were dying, sacrificed on the altar of Pol Pot's hard-nosed communism. The full extent of the tragedy wasn't realized until long after Pol Pot was ousted by an invading Vietnamese army. For most, the story wasn't revealed until the making, years later, of two films: *Year Zero*, a shocking documentary by Australian journalist John Pilger, and *The Killing Fields*, a hard-hitting movie which detailed one man's fight for survival during those dark years. Cinemagoers across the world were left wondering: how could this depraved and demented ruler have ever got to power?

* * *

Cambodia had always been in turmoil with internal squabbles and wars until the French moved in to establish a colony there in 1864. The shackles of colonial rule were not thrown off until 1953 when Prince Norodom Sihanouk took power. Although he had plenty of shortcomings as a ruler, Prince Sihanouk managed to maintain peace in his country when war waged all around, with the Vietnam conflict in full swing. There was some covert support for the North Vietnamese forces, however, which perhaps cost Sihanouk his throne. The Americans devoted much effort to obliterating these supply lines. 'Neutral' Cambodia was secretly bombed by US pilots and air crews who later falsified their log books to hide their illegal forays. As the people suffered, they looked towards a new leader who would protect them from the rain of American firepower.

In 1970, Prince Sihanouk was overthrown by General Lon Nol, but still the carnage continued. In August 1973, a B-52 bombed a Mekong river town in error, killing more than 100 villagers and wounding many more. The US Ambassador to Cambodia, Emory Swank, visited the village soon after and handed out 100-dollar bills to each grieving family by way of compensation.

But resentment of the Cambodians festered, and the countryside which had received the worst of the bombing became a recruiting ground for the swelling communist forces, known as the Khmer Rouge. Soon their forces were strong enough to overwhelm the entire country. In command were Pol Pot and fellow Marxist thinker, Khieu Samphan.

Pol Pot was born on 19 May 1925 into a peasant family.

Details of his early life are vague. His own accounts are possibly the product of his warped imagination. It seems he was educated in a Buddhist monastery and even became a monk for two years. Then he moved on to Phnom Penh to study carpentry at a technical school. In 1946, he joined the freedom fighters aiming to oust the occupying French under the leadership of Ho Chi Minh. Ironically, three years later he found himself in Paris itself, nominally studying electronics but in fact spending most of his time learning revolutionary theories.

On returning to his homeland, Pol Pot spent nine years teaching in a private school, only leaving when his communist sympathies were suspected by the police. He joined forces with fellow left-winger Khieu Samphan and together they ran the new Cambodian Communist Party.

Early in the morning of 17 April 1975, the Khmer Rouge took Phnom Penh. Armed soldiers clad in black pyjama suits, most of them only teenagers, strode down the streets, watched guardedly by the two million or more inhabitants. Were the communists really to be feared and loathed? Or would the new order bring prosperity and peace to the region at last?

As early as 1 p.m. on the same day, the question was answered. The city was to be evacuated immediately, the triumphant forces announced. The people were told to start walking out towards the countryside that instant, leaving belongings and, if necessary, sick or elderly members of their families. The wounded were dragged from hospital beds and forced on the march. Surgeons had to leave patients in mid-operation. More than forty orphaned babies were abandoned in their hospital cribs to die.

Cars and trucks were left shunted together in traffic jams as walking was deemed the only ideologically correct method of transport. Money was also abolished. In their contempt for this capitalist symbol, Khmer Rouge forces blew up the banks and paper money fluttered aimlessly down the street, its only use now as fuel for camp fires.

This was the shocking welcome for Cambodia's city-dwellers to Year Zero, the birth of the Republic of Democratic Kampuchea. The sole option for the population now was to work in the fields, and children as young as seven were expected to do their share. Every town and village was emptied to boost the numbers preparing paddy fields or building new irrigation schemes, most of which were ill-conceived and never used.

For the workers, conditions were horrendous. They were woken as early as four in the morning and forced to work until eight or ten at night, sometimes even later during harvesting. Food rations consisted of tiny amounts of rice, a sloppy porridge and an occasional slice of dried fish. Hungry and tired workers were installed in flimsy shelters which once would have been thought inadequate even for cattle. These shacks offered little protection against the elements or invading insects and there was no sanitary system whatsoever. It was only a matter of time before disease became rife among every commune's weary dwellers. Malaria, dysentery and smallpox were just a few of the hazards this new breed of peasant had to face.

Family relationships meant nothing to the Khmers, who saw kinship as a major hindrance to their master plan. Under the guidance of Pol Pot, the aggressive young soldiers saw to it that husbands and wives, mothers and children and brothers and sisters were split up. They were housed in separate communes and allowed to meet only periodically, if at all.

The only form of education was indoctrination, which

315

came daily in the form of speeches by commune leaders and stirring revolutionary songs broadcast over the paddy fields. They had, the Khmer Rouge troops insisted, known terrible hardship while fighting from jungle bases to free Cambodia. Their sacrifices had been enormous, their commitment to equality beyond question.

Religion was banned among the mainly Buddhist people. Beautiful and historic temples were dismantled, brick by brick, icons and statues destroyed. Revered carvings of the wise and compassionate Buddha lay in fragments on the ground, the religious sites left to the mercy of the weeds and weather. A modified language was instituted in which the words 'thank you' and 'sorry' were abolished. Anyone found carrying books and money came instantly under suspicion: they were stripped of those meagre goods which, along with treasured photographs, were burnt.

Worse was to come, as the excesses of the controlling forces spiralled out of control. At first, those who fell sick while working in the fields were left where they dropped, deprived of food because they were no longer productive. Then teams of phony 'doctors' moved in to the communes to practise what the inhabitants imagined were medical skills. The unwitting patients were completely at their mercy.

Untrained soldiers would brew up concoctions from roots and herbs and dispense them either as tablets, known among the workers as 'rabbit droppings', or as a serum injected through filthy syringes. This itself was frequently enough to kill. Then the 'doctors' moved on to operations, cutting open their victims with dirty instruments and without anaesthetic. Afterwards, witnesses told how internal organs were often removed and examined on the grassy bank beside the stricken body. The patient screamed in agony as the fake medics coolly probed. The reward for carrying out macabre activities like this was food – valuable extra rations which were now the only currency of value.

The exterminations continued unabated. The Khmer Rouge leaders were determined to wreak a perverse revenge on anyone with an education. Even those with the most mediocre qualifications were executed. Not surprisingly, therefore, the terrified citizens kept quiet about their backgrounds. Under questioning, all claimed to be farmers or field hands, the only acceptable occupation in Kampuchea. The troops were always suspicious, always on the lookout for intellectuals who may have slipped through the net.

Soldiers organized underhand tests to flush out former government workers. They would broadcast an appeal for administrators to help the new government in Phnom Penh. Anyone with the relevant experience was desperately needed and would find favour with Pol Pot's forces, they said. Tired of labouring in the fields, many came forward to snap up the offer. Volunteers were driven away from their communes looking joyful and relieved. Nobody saw them again. But workmates would soon see their clothing on someone else's back, their familiar shoes on someone else's feet. Comrades were left to guess at what tortures their former colleagues had suffered before dying.

Anyone who could read was easily tricked by a simple trap. A Khmer guard clutching a rarely seen bottle of American medicine would plead for someone to read the instructions to save an ailing colleague. To step forward out of humanity was as good as signing your own death warrant.

Spies were everywhere, listening in to conversations during the day in the paddy fields and at night in the camps. With the incentive of extra food, children began reporting their parents for 'crimes' against the Khmer Rouge. One-time friends in the former Cambodia would inform on each other, careful not to incriminate themselves.

Reconnaissance teams comprising the most senior Khmer Rouge forces were all-powerful and widely feared. If they pointed a finger, someone was surely doomed. The most hard-hearted of all were those aged between twelve and fifteen, who often killed some or all of their families to reach lauded positions in the Khmer Rouge. Brought up in the ranks, they had known nothing but discipline and barbarity. They would kill a baby without a second thought.

Swift justice was meted out for other misdemeanours, too. Sex was strictly forbidden except between married couples who had official permission, which was rarely given. Any couple discovered illicitly copulating were arbitrarily shot. Even a smile out of place between a boy and girl would result in a beating or even death. A broken tool, a damaged crop or a wrong word could be fatal. Anyone found wandering 'out of bounds' was dragged off and murdered. There were also allegations made by the Khmer Rouge about peasants spying for the CIA or the KGB – ridiculous when the so-called spy was no more than a bag of bones whose main concern was not international espionage but where the next bowl of rice was coming from.

Each commune had its own 'killing field'. A few kilometres from the living quarters and paddy fields was a hastily dug pit, a dumping ground for corpses. The barbaric killers often did not bother burying those they had slaughtered. The bodies piled up one on top of another and began to decompose. Workers guessed where the pits were by the appalling smell which drifted from them. Barred from roaming from the commune, few witnessed the terrible scene until a few moments before their own demise. Anyone who did stumble on the killing field by accident would first be alerted by the shocking stench as they sank knee-deep into the mound of acrid flesh and bones.

The weapons of death were spades, clubs, pickaxes, bayonets, mortar shells, knives or daggers. Those considered to have committed the worst crimes were disembowelled before having their throats slit. Their entrails would be paraded around the commune for all to see. Others were buried up to their necks in the ground and left to die. Then their heads were lopped off and stuck on stakes as a warning to others. Dith Pran, the interpreter and journalist who survived the brutal regime and on whose story *The Killing Fields* is based, was told his brother and family had been fed to crocodiles.

The working peasants grew ever more weak and desperate for food. The famine spread countrywide, through ignorance and mismanagement of the once lush soil, although the hunger was worse in some regions than others. Starving people would eat anything that came their way, including snails, snakes, insects, rats, frogs, scorpions, tree bark and flower blossoms. In the worst-hit areas, people dug up the corpses of newly executed victims and feasted on them in desperation. There was grave robbing, too, in the cemeteries of hospitals. The saga of hunger and illness seemed endless, and the misery caused widespread depression among a demoralized and frightened population. Children as young as ten were hanging themselves rather than face another day of toil and starvation.

In 1977, a new rations system was introduced. One day in

ten the paltry rice allowance was forgotten and everyone was allowed to eat as much as they liked. By now workers had stick-thin limbs, distended stomachs and thought constantly about food. Their eyes bulged in anticipation as they were given the freedom to help themselves from the rice barrels, the only rule being that they had to eat as much as they took.

It sounded too good to be true. Peasants weakened from two years of deprivation and hard labour staggered to their shelters with huge mounds of rice. They gorged themselves on it without chewing, throwing down each mouthful as if it was their last. On the first day most people were sick – their neglected bellies were unable to tolerate the rice mountain that was forced inside. In one small commune alone, five people died after the food orgy. The special rations system was abandoned after just one month.

All the while, the Khmer Rouge forces, who lived in decent, sanitary houses, tucked in to the plumpest fish and the cleanest rice. They even had enough left to barter with the peasants, stripping them of their last possessions such as wedding rings, wristwatches and gems. Behind closed doors, the plump-faced Khmer girls would parade in their new-found finery, sometimes in front of illicitly owned mirrors. Their vanity, abhorred by the regime, went unnoticed and unpunished.

Untutored except in the art of killing, Khmer Rouge families revelled in the power they wielded. But when the work-force of peasants was purged, ardent revolutionaries began investigating their own men. Ambitious underlings looked with envy at the perks and privileges of high position. It was simple enough to lure the uneducated commune leaders into an incriminating conversation about lusting after women or coveting edible tit-bits. The information would be taken to a higher authority and the tricked commune leader soon disappeared.

Finally, there was a backlash against the harsh Khmer Rouge from within its own ranks. The conflict was savage when, once again, Cambodian was pitted against Cambodian in a ruthless do-or-die struggle.

The threat of a visit to a 're-education centre' was always there. Little education went on, only degrading and agonizing torture. Prisoners were kept like animals in huts with no windows. Chained together in the fields, they were forced to pull ploughs and were whipped as they toiled by guards flexing thorny canes. Close by was another open grave dug by the victims themselves, slowly but surely being filled.

When journalist John Pilger entered Cambodia in 1979 after the fall of the Pol Pot government, he found just such an establishment being run in a former primary school. In his book, *Heroes*, he told how he entered the centre called Tuol Sleng and toured classrooms, labelled 'interrogation unit' and 'torture and massacre unit'. . .

People were mutilated on iron beds and we found their blood and tufts of their hair still on the floor. Between December 1975 and June 1978 at least 12,000 people died slow deaths here: a fact not difficult to confirm because the killers, like the Nazis, were pedantic in their sadism. They photographed their victims before and after they tortured and killed them and horrific images now looked at us from walls; some had tried to smile for the photographer, as if he might take pity on them and save them. Names and ages, even height and weight, were recorded. We found, as at Auschwitz (the infamous Nazi death camp), one room filled to the ceiling with victims' clothes and shoes, including those of many children.

Pilger learned that the punishment for knocking over a box of excrement was to lick the floor clean, or torture or death – or all three. Prisoners were filled with water and given electric shocks or had their hands crushed in vices. He was struck by the silence in the streets, the official vandalism of institutions like hospitals and the skeletal bodies of scavenging orphans. Their eyes held a vacant stare. Four years of indoctrination and deprivation had taken their toll. Through an interpreter, Pilger asked one boy his age.

BOY: I remember, I am twelve years old.
PILGER: What is your name?
BOY: I forget.
PILGER: Where are your parents?
BOY: I forget . . . I think they died.

The regime was finally toppled by an invasion by neighbouring Vietnam. Flanked by both China and Kampuchea, Vietnam was suffering a series of skirmishes on two fronts and finally decided to take action against one. The Khmer Rouge soldiers, so tough when they were up against unarmed, ill-fed peasants, fell away in terror when confronted by the might of a well-disciplined army.

Vietnamese soldiers were shocked by what they saw. Vietnam's Foreign Minister, Nguyen Co Thach, said after the invasion: 'I would like to be clear. We did not go into Cambodia to save them. We went there to save ourselves. But what we found shocked even us who have seen so much war. Go and ask any soldier there.'

It was not an end to the atrocities, however. Pol Pot led some faithful troops into the border area adjoining Thailand and mounted a guerilla campaign. Those he left behind found themselves among vengeful survivors. Desperately seeking anonymity among the hordes of people searching for relatives, former friends and homes, the murderers were sought out and killed on the spot.

Someth May was a survivor who recorded his dreadful experiences in the book *Cambodian Witness*. He recalled how he saw angry mobs mete out justice to a former commune leader: 'He was sitting quietly on a rice sack, staring at the ground, apparently miles away. Three men came up behind him and, before he had even time to turn, his head came clean off his body and rolled at his feet, so that just for a split second it looked as if he was sitting there contemplating his own head.'

The four-year communist experiment had left Cambodia scarred. Starvation was widespread among the remnants of the population. This man-made disaster left few women fit enough to bear children and provide another generation. With liberator Vietnam internationally portrayed as an arch-villain, following the war with the USA, the rest of the world was slow to respond with aid. Butcher Pol Pot continued to be recognized as the rightful leader of Cambodia, even though he had exterminated several million of his people. When international help finally was sent, it was jetted in to the border area with Thailand and distributed among the Khmer Rouge troops, the very men who had grown fat off the backs of the people they had abused for so long.

In 1980 Khieu Samphan told foreign journalists his regime had made mistakes – mainly in their implementation of policy. Yes, he admitted, over-zealous commune leaders had often forgotten to give workers their one day off in ten. Foreign Minister Ieng Sary went further. The orders from Pol Pot had been 'misunderstood', he said. The massacres had been 'a mistake'.

The Waco Siege

With his engaging dimples, velvet eyes and soft wavy hair, Vernon Howell had the cute looks of a rock hero. Guitar-strumming Howell thought his wholesome charm and musical talents would take him to the dizzy heights of fame. But when his chart-topping ambitions crumbled, he changed his name and turned into a sinister cultist who led scores of his followers to a fiery death. While Vernon Howell failed to set the world on fire, his alter ego David Koresh lit a deadly fuse with devastating results.

Koresh achieved notoriety worldwide as the man who holed himself up with his devout disciples following a bloody shoot-out with law enforcement officers. Then, with his dream of heaven on earth in tatters, his followers finally died in a white-hot hell hole of terror and pain. As smoke poured from the Texan citadel which was home to the crazy sect, the horror of Koresh and his mind-bending ways was laid bare.

Far from being an earthly saviour, he had sexually abused girls as young as twelve, sadistically tortured children and babies, and gathered a powerful arsenal of weapons around him. No one knows why he had this astonishing collection of firepower. Was his ultimate aim to extend his empire with a blistering attack on the nearby town of Waco? Or did his dangerous paranoia induce him to fear attack at all times? It is perhaps more likely that he craved a showdown with the authorities, revelling in the power he wielded and taking a bizarre delight in the blood-letting. In short, he yearned for a massacre to satisfy his inner lust for killing.

Vernon Wayne Howell was born in 1959 in Houston, Texas. His mother was Bonnie Clark, a nursing home assistant who was aged just fifteen. For two years Bonnie stayed with his carpenter father, twenty-year-old Bobby Howell. But after they split, she met and married Roy Haldeman, moving to a suburb of Dallas. Clashing with his stepfather, Vernon found solace in the Bible. It was an early indicator of his obsessive nature that he had learned the New Testament by heart at the age of twelve.

Although fervent in his studies, he dropped out of high school before he was eighteen, determined to make his name as a musician. Like so many young men and women, however, he soon realized that his chances of cutting a hit record and being elevated to the realms of rock legend were remote, so he returned to his first love: religion. It was to the peace-loving Seventh Day Adventist Church that he turned, enchanted by its philosophy of a second coming of Christ. However, his interpretation of the scriptures which he knew so well caused anxiety among church elders. They considered him a bad influence and expelled him within two years.

Still bristling with ambition, confidence and dubious ideals, 23-year-old Howell turned to the Branch Davidians. Bulgarian immigrant Victor Houteff, similarly ejected from the Seventh Day Adventists, had founded the move-ment in 1942 after he led a small following to Texas to begin a community at the Mount Carmel centre near Waco. He seized on a theme in the Book of Revelations in which all but the most faithful were slaughtered by a vengeful God before the Second Coming.

The expected Apocalypse hadn't occurred before Houteff's death in 1955. His wife Florence took the reigns of power but lost her credibility when she predicted a doomsday – on 22 April 1959 – which never happened. The group fell into disarray until the arrival of Benjamin Roden, a charismatic preacher who strengthened the membership with his persuasive sermons. He died in 1978, leaving his wife Lois at the helm. Most believed their son George would eventually take command. And he might have done, too, had it not been for the arrival of the hungry Howell.

Vernon Howell quickly impressed the movement with his detailed knowledge of the Testaments, easily able to outwit anyone who dared question his wisdom. From this unassailable position of power, he employed clever editing of the word of God to convince people that he was indeed the Chosen One. George B. Roden was not so sure. He had already quarrelled with his mother about the direction of the movement, claiming in court he was the Messiah. Now he harboured a jealous loathing of his quick-witted rival.

Howell had been smart enough to share a confession which he rightly guessed would win him friends. Soon after he joined the sect, he told with touching humility how he could not stop masturbating. Lois Roden was so moved by his raw honesty that she took him to her bed. Despite the difference in age of around forty years, they wanted a child. She reportedly suffered several miscarriages.

Certainly, their pillow talk must have centred on son George, with crafty Howell urging the ageing woman to kick him out once and for all. Branch Davidians, concerned at George Roden's outlandish behaviour, lent their support to Howell, who further consolidated his position by marrying the fourteen-year-old daughter of a cult elder.

George armed himself, marking a departure in the sect from the long-held principle of pacifism. When his mother died in 1986, there was an inevitable clash between the two would-be Messiahs. Roden laid down a challenge. He ordered the coffin of Anna Hughes, a cult member who had died twenty years earlier, aged eighty-five, to be exhumed. The casket was laid on an altar and covered with a flag featuring the emblem of the Star of David. Whichever man could resurrect the long-dead corpse was the true Messiah, Roden claimed.

Howell was careful enough not to get involved in such macabre antics and instead of taking part in a hocus-pocus ceremony, he contacted the local sheriff's office with news of the grave robbery. When the authorities refused to act until they were convinced a body lay in the coffin, Howell and his cronies decided to take a photograph of the body as evidence.

Under cover of darkness, Howell led seven heavily armed men, all wearing camouflaged clothes, into Mount Carmel. They kept their cover until schoolchildren and other workers left the compound before launching an attack, all guns blazing. Even though the shoot-out lasted twenty minutes, the injuries were astonishingly light. Howell, however, failed to get close to the coffin before the lawmen arrived.

Howell and his men were taken to the sheriff's office and ultimately charged with attempted murder. Roden, however, was unhappy with the actions of the court and foolishly filed a volley of abusive motions. While his attackers were on bail, he was charged with contempt of court and jailed for six months. Howell wasted no time in establishing himself back at Mount Carmel.

When Howell finally appeared in court, he was neatly dressed and softly spoken. He claimed he and his comrades had fired into the air trying to scare Roden into surrender. When Roden took the stand, any sympathy he may have had was lost when the disgraceful body-snatching episode was exposed. Finally, the 'foot soldiers' were acquitted, while a mistrial was declared in the case of Howell. The charges were eventually dropped.

Howell now looked for new recruits, organizing membership drives as far afield as Britain, Australia, Jamaica and Hawaii. Anyone who made the mistake of attending one of his prayer meetings was trapped for hours and bamboozled by rambling preachings. His aim was to lure them to Texas to see for themselves the religion in action at Mount Carmel. Once inside the Branch Davidian fortress, it was difficult to find an escape. Those who accepted the teaching of the self-styled Messiah were praised, flattered and given a new sense of worth. Those who voiced opposition were reviled and threatened.

In 1990, Vernon Howell became David Koresh through a legal name change. Koresh was the surname of God, he informed his followers, while David was picked for its Biblical connotations.

The tough regime inside the walls of Mount Carmel diminished the will of those who desired freedom. They were up early to carry out mundane chores. Their meals were paltry and unappetizing, and treats like beer, chips or ice cream were strictly forbidden. Then there were evening preaching sessions to hear the gospel according to Koresh, which would last until the early hours.

Koresh himself would rise around midday or even

later, full of energy for the forthcoming fire-and-brimstone monologue, during which he would often slurp a bottle of booze or would snack on a delicacy denied to his congregation. His quarters were equipped with TV, radio, stereo, heating and air-conditioning – none of which were afforded to his followers in their bleak accommodation. He alone was allowed to wear his hair long. Worse, he demanded that his disciples turn over their weekly wages or social security payments to the cause. This meant those who wanted to leave had nothing to go with. The presence of the 'Mighty Men', armed guards whose duty it was to protect Koresh and the compound, was another deterrent for desperate escapees.

The fate of the children was miserable, too. Koresh not only beat children, including his own son, Cyrus, at the slightest provocation, but withheld food, sometimes for days. Before he was five, Cyrus was punished for some minor felony by being made to sleep on a bare bench in a garage – after Howell lectured him on the presence of large, hungry rats. His ability to inflict psychological torture like this on his own flesh and blood was astonishing.

Koresh was such a 'control' freak that he even sought power over babes in arms. Two parents witnessed him beat their eight-month-old girl with either a wooden paddle or spoon until he was satiated with the sight of blood pouring from the wounds he inflicted on her bottom. Following the beatings, he hugged the child closely.

He further strengthened his position by splitting up couples and families. It was his right, he broadcast, to sleep with all the women in the compound, child or adult, married or single. He bragged about the sex exploits of his harem and fathered ever more children. The men were denied sex, even with their wives. They could look forward to their reward in heaven, Koresh promised, where they would have the perfect wife fashioned from their own rib. This latest, outrageous proclamation sparked a tremor of defectors, much to the fury of the master. One woman – a long-term mistress of Koresh and mother to one of his sons – left the cult when she realized her own mother had joined the ranks of his bed partners.

Meanwhile, his teachings became increasingly frenzied and violent in subject and tone. He became obsessed with a forthcoming showdown with the authorities. It was a topic which frequently featured in the evening preachings. Once Koresh even prophesied that he would appear on television in 1993 and then die by fire. So pessimistic was the mood at Mount Carmel that many of the followers referred to their home as Ranch Apocalypse in recognition of its no-hope future.

No one could guess at the truth of the grim vision expounded by Koresh until March of that year when the peaceful everyday existence of Mount Carmel was shattered for ever . . .

It was the weekend that a local newspaper was running revelations about Koresh 'The Sinful Messiah', based mainly on the stories of disaffected followers. Everyone was up and about early, even Koresh. Wary of the tense atmosphere, many took up arms. One 42-year-old Harvard-educated attorney cut a ludicrous figure as he strung grenades around his neck. Soon the news which both alarmed and excited Koresh arrived, first by telephone and then by messenger. Agents from the Bureau of Alcohol, Tobacco and Firearms (ATF) were on their way to raid the ranch.

They had search and arrest warrants on the grounds that

weapon laws were being violated at Mount Carmel. Intelligence gathered during the previous year had indicated that guns and grenades were being stockpiled by the secretive sect. The ranks of bureau men were heavily armed with a range of Smith & Wesson guns, pump action shotguns, semi-automatic rifles and even machine guns. It was only a fraction of the armoury held by their target, as they discovered to their cost.

As the ATF brigade drew up outside the compound on the morning of 28 February 1993, they were confronted by Koresh himself, momentarily peering through the door. Government helicopters whirred overhead and the engines of the vehicles transporting the mini-army roared. Above the din, the federal agents warned they had warrants. In reply, Koresh slammed the doors shut and a hail of gunfire rained down.

Agents were felled in the ferocious blast of fire. Through the blue haze of gunsmoke, they hardly had a chance to glimpse their ambushers who were clad in black pyjama suits and hoods, reminiscent of garb worn by Vietcong troops during the Vietnam War. In the Mount Carmel armoury there were numerous automatic and semi-automatic weapons, including a 50 mm Howitzer capable of bringing down a helicopter. In addition, there were more than one million rounds of ammunition.

Seeing their comrades either dead or moaning in agony from gruesome injuries caused by high velocity bullets, the ATF men dived for cover. Along with pressmen, they took refuge where they could, pinned down by the continuing clatter of firearms. Their carefully drawn-up tactics shot to pieces, they soon pulled back to safer positions, picking off the cultists where they could.

Inside, there was terror among women and children,

who cowered under beds and behind furniture. Choking fumes from stun grenades tossed in by the retreating ATF forces hung in the air like clouds on a simmering volcano. But the brewing storm had well and truly erupted. Bullets whizzed close, ricocheting from walls and doors, and the screams of those taking shelter in the dormitories were drowned by the perpetual blasts of awesome firepower.

The battle continued for two hours before a cease-fire was negotiated, giving both sides time to retrieve their dead and injured. An estimated 10,000 rounds of ammunition had been spent. Four ATF men died and an unknown number of cultists were killed or wounded.

After the gunfight, Koresh proved himself such a pathological liar during negotiations that his first claim of two deaths was later judged to have no credibility. His inability to speak the truth would be a source of endless confusion during talks aimed at breaking the deadlock. Koresh would make a promise, then break it without a second thought. (It was only later that weary negotiators realized that he preached that it was perfectly fine to deceive someone who was not a Branch Davidian.) In his warped mind, Koresh could hardly determine fact from fiction any more. Both sides settled down to a stand-off.

Koresh played fanciful games with the government and the FBI, both searching for a peaceable end to the siege. Koresh demanded concessions in return for the lives of his followers. Several times he promised to surrender. Always, he failed to keep his word. He threatened suicide but never found the courage to carry it through.

Lawyers acting on Koresh's behalf brought back encouraging news after meeting with the zealot. They pledged a date for the end of the siege – but he made them look fools.

In return for the release of several children, he won the right to broadcast on local radio, and his barely coherent burblings lasted into the small hours. The numbers leaving the surrounded compound were always a trickle, never a flood as the government had hoped. Those who had emerged were labelled 'zombies' by social workers, so brainwashed were they by the man they all knew as their father. They were hardly able to communicate. While there was no chance of escape, the Branch Davidians, or Koreshians as some preferred to be known, had enough food to endure a year-long siege. It seemed little would move the self-styled Messiah to surrender, and his manner with negotiators became ever more deranged.

Certain that he was unlikely to commit suicide, Attorney General Janet Reno finally won the approval of President Bill Clinton to make a move and break the deadlock. After all, these were murderers who had to be brought to justice. There was also a real fear that the twenty-five children thought to be left inside the compound were at risk from assaults by Koresh and disease from human waste and even dead bodies, lingering unburied from the battle. High-tech bugs giving negotiators an insight into the private thoughts of Koresh revealed that he wasn't about to give up.

As dawn broke on Monday, 19 April, a government negotiator warned Steve Schneider, loyal henchman to Koresh, that a plan to crash through the walls of the compound with armoured cars firing tear gas was going into operation that day. Schneider ripped out the telephone he was using and tossed it out of the window. In the following frenzied few minutes, the cultists donned gas masks. Children fought a tide of panic as their faces were covered in the unpleasant rubber masks, while men and women grabbed guns and took up positions, awaiting the onslaught.

Soon a fleet of armoured vehicles trundled into view and began barging their way in, letting off generous amounts of CS gas which permeated the rooms and corridors. Koreshians fired back furiously but this time the law men were taking no risks. They were safely behind several inches of armour and the bullets made no impression. The invaders did not need to fire a shot. Inside, some cultists tried to blot out the battle by resuming their normal lives, performing everyday chores to keep their minds off the horror to come. Did they know what was in the mind of the Living Prophet?

As tanks rumbled on towards his inner sanctuary, Koresh realized his battle was hopeless. He gave the doomsday order. Just after noon, black-clad cultists were spotted by FBI men lighting fires on both sides of the compound. A hovering helicopter filmed the simultaneous outbreak of flames. The gusty wind fanned the flickering flames to an inferno within minutes. As flames roared through the compound, they sparked ammunition and a volley of fireballs rocked the hell hole.

TV cameras captured it all. America watched as Mount Carmel was dramatically reduced to ashes. Friends and relatives of those inside were tortured with the thought of what the inmates were going through. One woman emerged from the building, her clothes and body alight. An FBI man tackled her and tried to beat out the flames. But she broke away and returned to her blazing home.

Only nine of those inside survived, four of them critically injured with charred skin and smashed bones. Some eighty-five people perished. As the ruins smouldered, there was the sporadic echo of ammunition exploding in the heat.

It took investigators days to discover who the victims were. Their task was a grisly one. They had to identify bodies where arms and legs had been completely burned off. Flesh had turned to ash. The bodies of young children could have been eaten up altogether by the ferocious heat. Many of the victims were found in or near bunkers specially built around the site. They probably cowered there in the vain hope that they would be protected from the inferno. Most died from smoke inhalation, as pathologists later established, but there were several bodies bearing gunshot wounds. It seemed that those who finally took flight in a bid to escape certain death were felled by cultists, determined that no one should escape the fate ordered by the leader.

It was a flashpoint for the government too, however. There were serious misgivings about both operations carried out against Koresh. The high death toll was blamed on tactical blunders. Survivors added to the debate by insisting the fire had not been lit by followers. They claimed that Koresh had not wanted to lead a mass suicide and had even planned a day to surrender. One law enforcement official thought differently. 'Koresh's desire was to have as many people killed in that compound as possible,' he said. 'That is why it was named the Ranch Apocalypse.'

Burke And Hare

By day, Surgeons' Square in Edinburgh appeared the perfect model of respectability. A place where the frontiers of medicine were daily pushed back. Where young men of intelligence were schooled by the world's best doctors. Where exploration of the human body was advancing at an inexorable rate. Yet to further these altruistic aims there was a darker side. In the early eighteenth century, it was practically unheard of for anyone to donate their body to science. How were the surgeons of the future to learn their craft if not through first-hand experience at the dissecting table? There was only one answer. A supply of corpses had to be provided . . . the fresher the better.

Word had long since spread around the city that doctors at the college would pay good money for a 'corp'. So it was on a night shortly before Christmas 1827 that two furtive strangers presented themselves to the duty staff at No. 10, Surgeons' Square, the establishment of the brilliant anatomist Dr Robert Knox, to enquire whether he could spare them a few moments.

The doorman was unsure what to make of these nervy characters, their faces shadowed in the flickering gaslight. But he knew enough of the kind of tradesmen with whom his master did business to button his lip.

The gentlemen were asked to wait awhile. Shortly afterwards they were confronted by three juniors – Doctors William Fergusson, Thomas Wharton Jones and Alexander Miller.

Initially, the conversation was bizarre in the extreme. The two strangers had never been seen at No. 10 before and the medical men chose their words carefully in the knowledge that dissecting bodies was prohibited by law. The visitors clearly had something to sell but seemed unsure exactly how to sell it. Finally, they found their voices. They had a corpse to offer, still quite fresh, and delivery could be guaranteed that night. Would Dr Knox be interested?

The men were told to return with their merchandise and a meeting was arranged close to midnight. They arrived with the goods in a sack which Dr Knox himself inspected and pronounced acceptable. The price was struck at £7 10s and all sides left well satisfied with the macabre night's work. Dr Knox had more flesh to slice for the benefit of his students; Burke and Hare had just sold their first cadaver. It was easy money. The pair were sent on their way with the words of the doctors ringing in their ears: 'We'll be glad to see you again, gentlemen, when you have another to dispose of.' The meeting was to prove the opening chapter in the case of Scotland's most celebrated and gruesome serial murderers.

William Burke was born at Orrey, County Tyrone, Ireland, in 1792. His parents were hard-working cottars and were proud when their son began a respectable career with the Donegal Militia. On leaving the army, however, William went astray. First he fell out with his father-in-law over the rights to a piece of land. Then he deserted his wife and young family, emigrating to begin a new life in Scotland.

Burke managed to find work as a labourer, helping construct the Union Canal between Glasgow and Edinburgh. At nights he returned to lodgings in the village of Maddiston and began a passionate relationship with one Helen M'Dougal, a woman of dubious morals. She already had two children by another man but had abandoned them and run off to Peebles with her new lover. The couple eventually found themselves in Edinburgh in 1827, where they took a threepence-a-night room at one of the city's 'tramp hostels' in Tanner's Close, West Port. The Irish-born landlords were William Hare and his wife, Margaret.

William Hare, like Burke, was of low-born class yet had managed to claw himself a little way up the social ladder by getting Margaret to fall for him. Her first husband, a tradesman whom Hare had known and detested, died in 1826 and the new man in her life wasted no time moving into Tanner's Close to comfort her. Scotland's benign laws of wedlock at that time meant the couple could call themselves married on the grounds of 'habit and repute'. To the vagabond Hare, it was a dream come true. He had an income, an agreeable status and the advantage of not having to work for a living.

The couple were greedy landlords, however, and took grave exception to their tenants falling behind with their rent. So when an elderly army pensioner known as 'Old Donald' finally succumbed to a long illness, Hare was sorely grieved. The man owed him £4. There seemed no chance of recovering the debt.

Then Hare hit upon a plan. Why not sell the corpse to the doctors at Surgeons' Square? All he needed was an accomplice, and his countryman and fellow whisky-lover Burke fitted the bill perfectly. The pair talked and plotted over large quantities of drink and decided to swap the body that lay in a coffin in their backyard for a bag of tanner's bark. The undertaker left with a casket suitably weighted while Old Donald's cadaver, now showing signs of rigor mortis, was tumbled into a bed and covered with a sheet. That same night Burke and Hare made their fateful visit to Dr Knox.

In the following days it struck this unholy alliance that selling bodies was the perfect business partnership. The only problem lay in maintaining a steady supply. Hare's lodging-house might have been an unhealthy, stinking cesspit but dead tenants were still a rarity. They could raid graveyards, of course, but these were now well guarded at night because of previous raids by grave robbers, and many tombs even had iron bars around them. The only solution was to 'make' corpses to sell to their distinguished customer at No. 10.

Their first victim was an old man called Joe the Mumper. He fell ill of a high fever, an event that worried Hare considerably 'in case it should keep away lodgers'. Poor Joe was far too weak to offer resistance as Burke and Hare laid a pillow over his face and held him down until he suffocated. A porter was hired to lug the body round to Surgeons' Square. As the evil killers walked away with their blood money, Burke was to hear for the first time his partner's triumphant squawk of glee on completion of a sale: 'Sold to Dr Knox for £10.'

The second of sixteen victims was despatched in what became the hallmark of Burke and Hare's murder technique. This English lodger's misfortune was to be confined to his bed with a nasty attack of jaundice. He was helped on

340

his way by his landlord who, together with Burke, climbed above the bed while the man was asleep and held his mouth and nose until there was no sign of breathing. Neither of them even knew the poor soul's name – and neither cared to find out.

Third to die was an old woman tramp, Abigail Simpson, who had arrived at the lodging-house on 11 February 1828. She was lured there by Mr and Mrs Hare after consuming a large number of drams with them in a city bar. As the drink flowed, Abigail's tongue loosened and she boasted of her beautiful daughter who was in need of a husband. Hare told her he was a bachelor and would be happy to marry the wench, insisting that the woman stayed the night so the matter could be discussed further.

The landlord's evil designs were temporarily thwarted, however, when he was rendered incapable of murder by falling into a drunken stupor. But the following morning's hangover proved no such obstacle. Hare clamped his hand over Abigail's mouth and nose while his partner laid himself across her to prevent her struggling. The corpse was stripped, tipped unceremoniously into a tea chest and the partners headed for Surgeons' Square to close the deal. One of Dr Knox's keen young students met them and arranged for the body to be delivered to a porter at the back of Edinburgh Castle that same night. In the later trial, one witness told how Knox 'approved of its being so fresh, but did not ask any questions'.

Already, the sale of victims had made a big difference to the odious gang's lifestyle. Burke and Hare began patronizing the best tailors, while their women toured shops in search of ever more outrageous finery. By night, the Tanner's Close house seemed to be the venue for a never-ending party, with enormous quantities of drink flowing until the early hours. By way of cover, the women let slip to neighbours that Mr Hare had been fortunate enough to receive a sizeable legacy. The word in surrounding streets, however, was that Burke and Hare were professional bodysnatchers who worked graveyards throughout Scotland in search of corpses to sell.

By now the gang had also drawn up a tariff for distribution of Dr Knox's regular tenner. Burke and Hare would take £5 apiece, with Burke paying Mrs Hare a £1 'royalty' in recognition of her support and provision of his lodgings.

In the spring of 1828, the killers saw off two more lodgers, both destitute women. On these occasions each man carried out the deed alone, though in both cases the work was considered 'firm's business' and the profits split accordingly. Then, on 9 April that year, came the murder of a prostitute, Mary Paterson, a voluptuous girl on whom both Burke and Hare may have had designs. Whether they succeeded was never made clear. What is known is that Burke was discovered by his wife lying on a bed with the drunken and semi-conscious Mary at his side and another prostitute, Janet Brown, sitting next to him.

Unsurprisingly, Helen M'Dougal flew into a jealous rage which culminated in Burke throwing a whisky glass at her, cutting her badly above the eye. He hustled her out of the house, no doubt reassuring her that the girls were there for killing, not for sex. His wife was unimpressed. She didn't mind her man's murderous habits but she took exception to him sleeping with the goods first.

Burke returned to the bedroom and tried to persuade Janet to lie down on the bed with Mary. Meanwhile, Helen pounded on the door outside screaming such awful curses as to make poor Janet beside herself with fear. Seeing he was not to get two victims without an enormous struggle, Burke allowed Janet to leave, marching her past his astonished wife and out into the street.

Minutes later, Hare returned from a meeting with Dr Knox and was quickly appraised of the situation. It was agreed that Burke should stay out of sight in case Janet should come back to find her friend. The girl did indeed return, accompanied by a friend, but accepted the explanation that Burke and Mary had gone off by themselves. Unbeknown to her, the pitiful girl had already been suffocated, and her still-warm body lay on a bed, covered by a sheet, only a couple of feet away.

Mary was sold for the usual £10 and the sight of her naked body, barely six hours into death, aroused great excitement among the medical students. One lad claimed he recognized her and Knox's doorkeeper, a David Paterson, decided to make inquiries of how Burke came by her. He was assured the corpse had been sold by Mary's own relatives.

Mary's shapely figure and good looks raised huge press interest, even inspiring a story in one of the London 'penny dreadful' magazines. Dr Knox gladly milked the publicity. Rather than take the body straight on to the dissecting table, he had it placed in whisky for three months, permitting it to become something of a tourist attraction. His junior assistant, a Dr Lonsdale, later wrote: 'The body of the girl Paterson could not fail to attract attention by its voluptuous form and beauty; students crowded around the table on which she lay and artists came to study a model worthy of the best Greek painters. Here was publicity beyond the professional walk.'

Burke and Hare, meanwhile, were already back at their business. An elderly female cinder gatherer called Effie was strangled after being rendered insensible with drink.

Soon afterwards, Burke was taking his customary morning stroll in search of likely prey when he came across a drunken woman being escorted along the street by a policeman. He intervened, feigning a humane interest, and audaciously convinced the officer that he was a Good Samaritan. The hapless wretch was released into Burke's care, where, later that evening, she duly breathed her last and was heaved on to the cart bound for Surgeons' Square.

In June 1828, the partners committed what was later acknowledged to be the vilest act of their appalling careers. Burke had been out as usual looking for innocents and had persuaded a frail-looking drunk to accompany him home for free whisky and lodgings. On the way, however, Burke was grabbed by an Irishwoman leading a young boy by the hand. She had come, she said, all the way from Glasgow in search of a family in Edinburgh who would take her in. Would the gentlemen help her find them? The courteous and smiling Burke professed it was an astonishing coincidence; he knew the very people personally. Of course he would help her and of course she would spend the night with him. He would not hear of her tramping the streets.

The drunk was given a swift elbow in his ribs and told to get on his way. He wailed and moaned at the loss of the promised whisky, yet had he known how close he had come to death he would, no doubt, have gladly gone on the wagon for good.

The replacement victim was murdered in the usual way later that night. But Burke and Hare were unsure what to do with her grandson, who was dumb. They thought at first that he could be 'wandered' (turned out on to the street) in view of the fact that he could tell no tales. Eventually they decided not to take chances. While Hare went to look for some boxes in which the bodies could be stowed, Burke took the boy over his knee and, as he put it later to police, 'broke his back' while the terrified youngster stared piteously into his face. The two victims were then stuffed into an old herring barrel, the usual tea chest being far too small for them both, and sold for £16 the pair.

It was shortly after this piece of butchery that some uneasy tensions among the body-traders began to surface. Burke took his wife on holiday, to stay with her relatives in Falkirk. Before they left, Hare's wife tried to persuade him to convert Helen Burke into 'merchandise' – on the grounds that, as a Scotswoman, she could not be trusted. He seems to have resisted the idea and apparently put forward the name of one of her cousins, Ann M'Dougal, as an alternative target.

When Mr and Mrs Burke returned from their holiday, such matters were quickly forgotten, as a new, more serious, quarrel broke out – after Burke discovered from a source at Surgeons' Square that Hare had been trading on his own account, selling the body of a woman for £8. The pair fought bitterly but their joint vow to dissolve the partnership and never work together again was soon forgotten. Within months they were back in business, with poor cousin Ann, down on holiday from Falkirk, the chosen victim following the usual all-day session with a whisky bottle.

Next to be stifled was a charwoman, Mrs Hostler, whose body Burke hid in the coal cellar pending removal to the doctors' quarters. She was quickly followed by the prostitute Mary Haldane (easily identifiable to her clients by virtue of the single, large tooth that became visible when she smiled) and her daughter Peggy.

Throughout the whole, inhuman business, Dr Knox never once questioned where these fresh bodies were coming from. By the time of the fifteenth murder – a hapless idiot well known to the folk of Edinburgh as Daft Jamie – Knox must surely have had the gravest suspicion of what was going on. Yet if he felt a twinge of remorse he did not show it. And his students, taking their lead from the great anatomist who was almost a hero figure to them, also kept their mouths shut.

In the end Burke and Hare were trapped by the enemies of all serial murderers: over-confidence and carelessness.

On the morning of Friday, 31 October 1828, Burke was enjoying his morning 'heart-starter' in Rymer's bar when an old Irish beggarwoman entered. Her name was Docherty. She needed money to sustain her while she searched for her son. Could the gentleman help? Burke replied that not only could he help, his own mother's maiden name was Docherty. They must surely be long-lost cousins. He insisted the crone should at least stop the night with him to enjoy a proper rest.

By now Burke and his wife were living in their own quarters, conveniently situated near the Hares at Tanner's Close. After handing his latest target over to Helen, Burke went in search of Hare to reveal the news that he had 'a good shot in the house for the doctor'. ('Shot' was the term the loathsome pair used to describe any saleable human corpse.) It was agreed that on this occasion the murder should be carried out at Burke's place. His lodgers, James Gray, his wife and child, would be offered a bed at Hare's house on the pretext that Mrs Docherty wanted to be with her relative.

Everything went according to plan and later that night

the Hares, Burke and M'Dougal ensured that their guest put away more drams than she had drunk in years. Later, neighbours would talk of a wild party, drunken mirth, a violent quarrel, even the sound of a woman banging on the inside of Burke's door screaming 'Murder'. The passer-by who heard that cry did go to look for a policeman but couldn't find one. When he returned, everything was quiet and he continued on his way home.

The following morning, the Grays returned for breakfast. Burke explained that his relative had gone because she had become 'ow'r friendly' in drink and M'Dougal had kicked her out. But his behaviour struck the Grays as odd. He began throwing whisky around the room for the ridiculous reason that he wanted to see the bottle empty. And twice he ordered Mrs Gray not to go near her mattress.

Her suspicions aroused, Mrs Gray waited until she was alone and then dashed to the bed. As she delicately lifted the straw cover, her husband could not mistake the gasp of horror. Before them lay the body of a naked crone, her face horribly bloodstained. The Grays packed their few pieces of luggage and prepared to leave, but not before they had confronted Helen Burke with what they had seen. She begged them to stay silent, promising it would be worth £10 per week to them, but they refused her offer and headed straight for the police station.

Had the Grays been more easily corruptible, God alone knows how many more unspeakable crimes Burke and Hare would have inflicted on the poor unfortunates of Edinburgh. As it was, they were arrested, together with Mrs Hare and Helen, and questioned intensively for weeks. But because all of them denied murder, and because medical evidence was insubstantial, Scotland's

Lord Advocate, Sir William Rae, found himself in a quandary. He could not risk a trial on less-than-sound evidence – juries were all too likely to acquit in capital punishment cases. Equally, he was sure he had the guilty men.

There was only one solution and it was provided by William Hare. Given an opportunity to turn King's Evidence (and therefore obtain immunity from trial) he grabbed it with both hands. Burke and his wife were denounced by his business partner. Mrs Hare, on the other hand, escaped his damning account because under British law a man cannot be compelled to give evidence against his spouse.

The trial began early in the morning of Christmas Eve, 1828, and continued without pause until the last guilty verdict was returned against Burke at 9.20 a.m. on Christmas morning. Incredibly, the jury found the charges against M'Dougal not proven and her husband, standing alongside her in the dock, was first to congratulate her. 'Nellie,' he ventured, 'you are out of the scrape.' Not so Burke. The chief judge, Lord Meadowbank, informed him that the court's only unresolved question was whether or not his body should be hung in chains after he was executed. In the end, the court's decision was a piece of poetic justice. Burke would publicly hang and his body would be used for medical science ... to be publicly dissected by the anatomists.

As he waited for the execution date, Burke seemed to be attempting a religious conversion. Yet he still showed little sign of remorse. On one occasion, speaking to a welfare visitor, he insisted: 'I think I am entitled, and ought to get, that £5 from Dr Knox which is still unpaid on the body of the woman Docherty.'

'Why?' replied his visitor. 'Dr Knox lost by the trans-action as the body was taken from him.'

'That was none of my business,' said Burke acidly. 'I delivered the subject and he ought to have kept it. I have got a tolerable pair of trousers and since I am to appear before the public I should like to be respectable. I have not got a coat and waistcoat that I can appear in and if I got the £5 I could buy them.'

At 8.15 a.m. on Wednesday, 28 January 1829, William Burke breathed his last on the gallows in High Street, Edinburgh. A crowd of around 25,000 – the largest then seen in the city – gathered to watch, with all the most fashionable Edinburgh figures occupying prime positions in the surrounding houses. Some seats had been rented out long ago for anything up to £1 and one of the best views was enjoyed by the poet Sir Walter Scott.

When the corpse was cut down, the mob dived forward, fighting in the pouring rain to grab fragments of the rope as ghoulish souvenirs. Then it was round to the medical rooms of Professor Alexander Monro, chair of the Anatomical School, to watch a few dozen invited guests arriving for the dissection. The day quickly degenerated into farce when hundreds of students, who also wanted a look, fought pitched battles outside with police. Eventually, Monro calmed the situation by allowing them entry in batches of fifty at a time to see the body.

The following day, the general public was admitted and filed past Burke's remains at the phenomenal rate of one every second (30,000 in total). After the last curious visitor left, the murderer was further dissected, salted and put into barrels for use in future discussions.

So what of the other players in the macabre blood-money world of Burke and Hare? Hare, of course, was freed, but lived out his life in misery – taunted everywhere he went by mobs spitting hate. He eventually died a poverty-stricken blind beggar in London. Helen Burke was another victim of the mob, though she later found anonymity in the West Country. Mrs Hare fled to Belfast, where her fate is unknown. And Dr Knox found himself locked in a career which spiralled ever-downwards as others of his profession sought to distance themselves. He died in disgrace, of apoplexy, on 20 December 1862. Perhaps in his last moments he would have recalled the taunting rhyme that in the mid-nineteenth century was known the length of Britain:

> Burke's the murderer, Hare's the thief.
> And Knox the boy who buys the beef.

Although the names of Knox, Burke and Hare are synonymous with body-snatching, they were by no means the only culprits. There was a big market for corpses among the Edinburgh anatomists well before Burke and Hare were even born.

The law at that time said that doctors could only wield their scalpels upon convicts who died in jail, children who died between weaning and working (or going to school), babies dead at birth, bodies with no known relatives to claim them and executed felons. It might be thought that such legislation would have ensured no shortage; in fact the opposite was true. Such was the unending demand in Surgeons' Square that a new breed of 'tradesmen' sprang up – the ironically named 'Resurrectionists'.

These gruesome opportunists were originally medical students who watched graveyards for signs of a fresh corpse being buried. They would then wait until the mourners had gone before returning at dead of night to conduct unofficial exhumations. It was a risky business because the Scots took the literal view of the Bible and believed the whole body was resurrected in heaven after death. If the medics cut bits off, it hardly bode well for loved ones on the other side! Thus any ambitious young student risked a severe beating, or even death, at the hands of a deceased's family if his name was linked to a stolen corpse.

The students were giving Edinburgh's College of Surgeons such a bad name that in 1721 the senior doctors agreed to include a clause in the indentures of their apprentices forbidding the violation of graveyards. This was clearly nothing more than a blatant public relations gimmick, for the grave-robbing went on much as before and the surgeons continued to ask no questions. In 1725, things got so bad that a furious mob descended on the rooms of Professor Monro and almost demolished them.

Such outpourings of public anger did little to dissuade the Resurrectionists, however. Neither did the penalties for their crimes, which ranged from fines and imprisonment to transportation. By now a lucrative trade had sprung up, even extending to London and Ireland. The Leith smack sometimes carried as many as twelve bodies at a time from the capital to the Edinburgh surgeons and the only law being observed was the economic one of supply and demand.

In March 1742 anger at grave-plundering suddenly welled over into mob justice. On 9 March the body of a man who had been buried in West Kirkyard was found at the home of surgeon Dr Martin Eccles. Eccles' house was wrecked and others nearby, also belonging to surgeons, were attacked. The doctor was charged but never convicted. There was not enough evidence against him.

Four days later the mob attacked the house of West Kirk's beadle – they dubbed it Resurrection Hall – and burnt it to the ground. On the 18th, a gardener called Richardson, of Inveresk, said to spend a little too much of his time tending graveyards, found his home in flames. And on the 26th, two Edinburgh worthies were banished from the city after being caught at Nether Bow port in possession of a dead body seated in a chair.

In 1752, the first major case of 'murder for medical research' surfaced and a female duo, Helen Torrence and Jean Waldie, were sent to the gallows for killing a child. The loathsome hags had been asked by a surgeon to supply the body of a dead adolescent but, being unable to find one, they kidnapped and killed instead. They sold their goods for 2s 6d, the price of a few drams.

By the turn of the century, the Resurrectionist trade was at its height. The most eminent anatomical lecturers were now in unofficial competition to obtain a steady supply of corpses for their classes. More corpses meant more research and the chance to test new theories, thereby enhancing a surgeon's medical reputation. Students, each loyal to their respective teachers, entered into the spirit of this macabre contest by spending much of their spare time in the cemeteries.

The most popular burial ground of all was the one adjoining Surgeons' Square itself. It was used to bury the unclaimed bodies of dead patients – but as far as the students were concerned, it was fair game for corpse-hunting. Rival groups would post lookouts to watch for interments, and as soon as dark fell the students would be out with their spades.

On one occasion the remains of an old folk singer called Sandy McNab were spotted by surgeon Professor Barclay's students. They dug Sandy up, tipped him into box and carried him to a place below the upstairs window of their classroom. The idea was to draw the corpse up by ropes; but after the bodysnatchers had gone inside to start pulling, rival students from Professor Monro's camp discovered the box and body and started to make off with it. They were stopped in the nick of time by Barclay's boys and a fight ensued which woke the entire neighbourhood. Barclay's side won the day and the Monro gang fled into the night before the law arrived.

One of the best known body-hunters was Dr Robert Liston. In his student days he would travel far and wide for the right 'material', and often had no choice but to leave Edinburgh. By now the wealthier families were employing night watchmen to guard the graves of their loved ones while the poor took turns to guard a fresh corpse. So, when Liston heard of an unusual death in Fife, he decided he had to have the body to carry out his own inspection. He and an accomplice disguised themselves as sailors, rowed into the town at dead of night, dug up the body and left it in a sack under a hedge while they went for a celebratory drink.

Unfortunately, their dumping of the sack was witnessed by a real sailor who had been dozing half-drunk under a hedge. Believing the package was stolen goods, and an adherent of the finders-keepers philosophy, the man heaved it on his back and stormed into the inn with the words: 'There, and if it ain't something good, rot them chaps there that stole it.' The sailor slit open the mouth of the sack only to see a dead man's head loll out. The pub emptied in seconds and Liston wasted no time in getting the body back on to the boat and away into the night.

Liston was the brains behind many another callous grave robbery. He once grabbed the fresh corpse of a drowned seaman at Rosyth after waiting patiently for the man's distraught lover to finish casting flowers on the beachside grave. She wandered back to find her sweetheart's body gone. Her piteous cries didn't stop Liston from making good his escape in a rowing boat.

It was generally believed that after a few weeks a body in a coffin would have decomposed sufficiently to have lost its value to the snatch teams. However, in the case of a particularly rare or unusual fatality, this was not so. Liston and an accomplice, a Londoner named Crouch, waited for weeks to get their hands on the body of a young boy who had died of hydrocephalus in Fife. They were desperate to conduct post-mortem examinations on the poor lad and kept watch on his grave until the guard was discontinued. Then, dressed like gentlemen, they calmly turned up in a dog cart at a local inn and announced that they were awaiting a delivery. Their package duly arrived in a bag, and it was only later that a grim discovery was made at the dead boy's grave.

Often a grave robbery would go badly wrong, especially when the bodysnatchers had little experience. One report tells how three of Professor Monro's students exhumed the body of a farmer's wife from a burial ground near Gilmerton. They had forgotten to bring a sack so it was agreed that the strongest of them should carry her on his back, still wrapped in a shroud. As he staggered along beneath his ghoulish burden, the woman's feet popped through the bottom of the shroud and every so often touched the ground causing a leaping movement. The would-be thief got the wrong idea.

'By God she's alive,' he cried to his fellow novices – and the three of them fled as fast as they could. When the farmer found his spouse's remains in the lane the next day, he at first feared she had been buried alive. Only later was he told the truth.

The best known firm of Edinburgh Resurrectionists was a foursome headed by a medical student called Andrew Lees. He was known as 'Merry Andrew' among his fellow students on account of his idiot grin when he pulled off a sale. Dr Lonsdale described him as follows:

> Of gigantic height, he was thin and gaunt, even to ridiculousness, with a long, pale face and the jaws of an ogre. His shabby clothes, no doubt made for some tall person of proportionate girth, hung upon his sharp joints more as if they had been placed there to dry than to clothe and keep him warm. No less grotesque were the motions and gestures of this strange being. It seemed as if he went upon springs, and even the muscles of his face, as they passed from the grin of idiot pleasure to the scowl of anger, seemed to obey a similar power.

His three assistants were a deaf-mute nicknamed 'Spune', a man dubbed 'Moudiewarp' (a dialect word for mole) because of his speedy burrowing ability, and a creature called 'Praying Howard', who posed as a minister so that he could conduct pauper funerals and mark down suitable graves to raid. This appalling team would spend their spare time trying to find dying people who had no friends. When the time came for such bodies to be claimed, there would be Merry Andrew or Praying Howard to assert that they were the beloved's next of kin and that they were arranging the funeral.

Sometimes, Merry Andrew would fall victim to a student prank. On one occasion a young medic spotted him hanging around in the darkness by the house of a dying woman, a Mrs Wilson, where he had an 'arrangement' with the nurse. Andrew was waiting for news of the patient's decline and was delighted when the passing student whispered in his ear, 'She's dead.'

Instantly, Lees bounded into the house and cheerfully greeted the nurse by saying: 'It's a' ower I hear, so when'll we come for the corp?'

The old hag hissed back: 'Wheesht ye mongrel, she's still lively as a cricket.' Unfortunately, the terrified patient clearly heard every word of the conversation. Its effect was predictable. She died the next day.

Andrew duly arrived within hours of the death, only to discover that the nurse was having second thoughts about the deal. 'A light has come down on me frae haven,' she cried 'and I canna.' The Resurrectionists produced whisky and pound notes but to no avail. Then, in the middle of the negotiations, a man turned up claiming to be Mrs Wilson's nephew and asking for the body. Lees and Co. slunk away, but the nephew pursued them to their lodgings demanding to know what business they had lurking around the dead body. The stranger never went back for his 'aunt' – which is unsurprising considering he hadn't a clue who she was. He was the same medical student who had given Andrew that earlier tip!

It was said in Surgeons' Square that Lees, Spune, Howard and Moudiewarp would sell their own sisters' corpses if they had the chance. Indeed, Andrew Lees actually managed such a transaction – and did it in competition with the rest of the gang. When his sibling died at Penicuik, Lees traipsed off to pick up her body. But Spune and Moudiewarp, angry over a debt they claimed he owed, got there ahead of him in a donkey cart with the aim of recovering their loss by selling Andrew's own kin.

As they retrieved her body, a blood-curdling scream echoed around the misty graveyard and a tall apparition in white emerged flapping from behind a headstone. Spune and Moudiewarp fled before they could hear Lees' chuckles. He had got wind of their plan, turned the tables and lost little time in collecting his customary tenner from Surgeons' Square.

Leonard Lake

It was just another day ... just another shoplifter. The California sun, a great golden globe in an azure sky, dripped lethargy on an already drowsy Sunday city. The only cloud in sight was rising over the eerie island fortress of Alcatraz, then gently settling to engulf the old prison like a wispy shroud. Two tired cops in their battered squad car were planning where to go for a meal break when the call came in. A Chinese man had been seen walking out of a south San Francisco hardware store with a vice he had not paid for.

'More paperwork,' groaned one. 'And the court will just let him off with a caution,' sighed the other. The eternal grumbles of police everywhere.

They could not have known that the shoplifter, a Chinese man called Charles Ng, was shortly to become America's most wanted man, nor that as a result of this simple, bungled theft attempt they would stumble on the most macabre case of mass murder in the annals of violent California crime.

But all this was in the future as they drove into the store car park where a bearded man in a car was arguing with shop staff. The Chinese man they were expecting to find had been apprehended as he tried to put the vice in the car boot, but in the ensuing confusion he had made good his escape. The cops had then turned their attention to the bearded man who had been with him.

At first he swore that the runaway Chinese man thought he had paid for the vice, then offered to pay the $75 himself. But the stolen vice quickly paled into insignificance when the officers looked into a holdall that was lying in the boot. They found a handgun with a silencer.

The cops immediately drew their own weapons and the bearded man was shackled and shaken down. His driving licence gave his name as Robin Scott Stapley. It was an alias. When a check call was made to the station, the computer revealed that Stapley was a 26-year-old who had disappeared without trace some months previously. The name was on record because shortly after his disappearance, his truck had been involved in a slight accident. It was being driven by a young Chinese man . . .

A further computer check on the car in the hardware store car park revealed it was registered to one Paul Cosner, another missing person, who had last been seen by his girlfriend some weeks previously. He had told her he was on his way to sell the car to a 'weird-looking' man who was prepared to pay cash.

It was enough for the cops. The bearded man was taken to headquarters. Yet to unfold were the grisly, stomach-churning details of a series of crimes so cold-blooded that case-hardened detectives would grow pale and retch.

At the station, the man was calm. He asked for a glass of water and a pencil and paper to write out a statement. But when he was alone, he calmly took the cyanide pill that he always carried with him, washed it down with the glass of water and scribbled a note to his ex-wife, a dubious character called Cricket Balazs. It read, 'I love you. Please forgive me. I forgive you. Tell Mama, Fern and Patty I'm sorry.'

Then he called the detectives back, revealed that his real name was Leonard Lake – and fell forward unconscious. He never came round and died four days later.

In Lake's pockets were bills made out to a man called Charles Gunnar, with an address at Wisleyville, in Calaveras County, about 150 miles north of San Francisco. The local sheriff, Claude Ballard, confirmed that Gunnar owned a small ranch in the area which he shared with a young oriental. He also confirmed that the man he knew as Gunnar was, in fact, Lake.

Sheriff Ballard had been taking an interest in the ranch because Lake advertised furniture and TV sets for sale on a regular basis. He had thought some of the articles might be stolen property. Ballard recalled that what had first drawn his attention to the ranch was the sale of furniture of a couple called Lonny Bond and Brenda O'Connor. Lonny and Brenda had been neighbours of Lake, but they had suddenly disappeared without trace, as had their six-month-old baby, Lonny Junior. Lake had claimed they had left him their furniture to settle a debt.

In the light of the new information Ballard received from San Francisco, he recalled another mystery disappearance from a local camp site, when a couple vanished leaving their tent and equipment – and even a pot of coffee boiling on the stove.

Hackles rising, officers prepared to raid Lake's home in Blue Mountain Road in rural, wooded Wisleyville. The two bedroom cabin was set in three acres. From outside it seemed idyllic. But they were sickened by what they found.

In the master bedroom they saw hooks in the ceiling and walls and in a box they found shackles. They had stumbled upon a torture chamber. Inside a wardrobe they found women's underwear and flimsy nightgowns. In the yard they found charred bones that looked human.

Dug securely into the hillside near the cabin was a bombproof and well-concealed bunker. Lake, a former Marine who had been drummed out of the service on psychiatric grounds, believed that World War Three was about to break out, and in his warped mind he saw himself as the kind of man who should survive. The bunker was provided with all amenities and stocked with food to see him through the coming holocaust.

In the meantime it served to fulfil his other fantasy: domination over women. It was also, it transpired, the centre of a perverted business empire based on his cruel, warped fantasies. As well as sleeping, living and toilet facilities, there were other rooms that looked for all the world like prison cells, complete with shackles and leg-irons. There were also pictures of naked and semi-clad women adorning the walls. Some of the pictures appeared to be of newly dead corpses, their faces twisted in pain.

With the principal character now dead and his accomplice on the run, the police took the place apart in an effort to uncover the grim truth. They already feared the worst – but even so, they were not prepared for what they were to find. In a cabinet were full records of Lake's twisted career, on film, in pictures and in two 500-page journals written in his own hand . . .

Leonard Lake was born into a poor family on 20 July 1946 in San Francisco, where he died by his own hand on 6 June 1985. In the 38 years and 11 months of his perverted life, he had been a trader, teacher, fireman, Marine and circus showman.

He had also been a drugs dealer and the director and co-star in his own 'snuff' videos: pornographic home movies in which the victim – almost invariably a woman or a child – is subjected to sadistic sexual practices or ritual torture and, as a climax, is killed while the camera lingers over the gruesome, graphic detail. Lake had not just satisfied his blood lust, he had made a lucrative income from it.

At last, all was revealed in Lake's own video library. Shocked police who viewed the films took it in turns to leave the room as one after the other became sickened by what he saw. One film, labelled only 'M Ladies Kathy/Brenda' opens with a young woman, hands cuffed behind her back, sitting on a chair in the cabin. A voice off-camera tells her: 'Mike owes us and he can't pay. We're going to give you a choice, Kathy.'

The menacing, disembodied voice continues: 'You can co-operate and in approximately thirty days we'll either drug you or blindfold you and let you go somewhere in the city. If you don't co-operate, we'll put a bullet in your head and bury you some place. No witnesses. While you're here, you'll wash for us, you'll clean for us, you'll fuck for us. That's your choice. It's not much of a choice unless you have a death wish.'

Lake, heavy-set, bearded and balding, then comes into view to put leg irons on Kathy. 'My name you don't know,' he tells her, then adds: 'His is Charlie.'

As he says these words, another man enters the frame. It is Ng – the Chinese man who inadvertently set the investigation in motion with his bungled attempt to steal a $75 vice. Lake removes the handcuffs and orders Kathy to strip. The woman, later identified as missing person Kathy

363

Allen, removes her outer clothes and her bra, but is reluctant to take off her panties until Ng points to the gun on the table. Finally, shaking and crying, she strips naked and is sent to take a shower with Ng.

A later scene in the video has Kathy strapped, still naked, to a bed. It is four days later and Lake is threatening her as he takes pornographic photographs. He tells her that Mike (her boyfriend) is now dead, and soon it will be her turn.

The scene shifts back to the cabin, where a young woman called Brenda sits shackled in a chair as Kathy did before her. Beside Brenda, holding a vicious-looking knife, stands Ng. As Lake gives Brenda the same instructions he gave Kathy, Ng uses the knife to cut away Brenda's blouse. This time, though, the threats carry more menace. Lake tells Brenda that her baby has been given to a family in Fresno. She becomes hysterical and begs for the return of the child. Lake and Ng laugh.

'Why do you guys do this?' she asks plaintively.

'We don't like you,' says Lake.

As Ng removes the shreds of her blouse she pleads: 'Don't cut my bra off.'

'Nothing is yours now,' says Lake.

'Give me back my baby. I'll do anything you want.'

'You'll do anything we want anyway.'

Ng slowly cuts away the woman's bra. At last the sickening tape comes to an end.

It was the last that was ever seen of Kathy Allen and Brenda O'Connor. Their remains were subsequently found with those of nineteen others in shallow trenches near the cabin. Also found were the teeth of Lonny Junior – the child Brenda had pleaded so desperately for.

It was not the only film police had to sweat through as

their rage and frustration mounted. There was a collection of films depicting all manner of ritual tortures, rapes and degrading sex acts. And many of them culminated in the horror of real on-screen murder. These, along with a lucrative drug-trafficking sideline, were the basis of Lake's income. There were also pictures of naked women in chains, and pictures of dead bodies, their faces frozen in the agony of death. And there were bags of human bones which had been boiled down to a soup.

In Lake's journal, investigators read: 'The perfect woman is totally controlled, a woman who does exactly what she is told and nothing else. There is no sexual problem with a submissive woman. There are no frustrations, only pleasure and contentment.'

What could explain Leonard Lake's macabre fixation with wanton murder and the subjugation and degradation of women?

Lake's family had a history of mental disorders and alcoholism. At the age of six, poverty forced his parents to send him to live with his grandparents, where he received a tough, militaristic upbringing. Meanwhile his younger brother Donald, an epileptic, remained at home, becoming something of a mother's boy. But despite the attention he received from her, he developed a cruel streak that he exercised on animals – and on his sisters. He started setting fires and had he not himself been murdered, as we shall see, he might also have become a serial killer.

Donald tried to rape his sisters on numerous occasions. Lake was asked by them for protection and in turn demanded – and received – sexual favours. His interest in the nude female body began in late childhood and, incredibly, his mother encouraged him to take photographs of naked girls, including his sisters and cousins.

365

As a youngster, he was obsessive. He studied and experimented with pet mice, tracing genetic features through numerous generations. Through such single-mindedness, he became a self-taught geneticist. He also had a compulsion for cleanliness, washing and showering many times a day. In his torture videos, the victim was always made to shower before the degrading and bloody action began in earnest.

Leonard Lake lived in a world of fantasy, dreaming of Vikings, Valhalla and stirring adventure. He boasted of his deeds in Vietnam – but in reality had never seen combat. Thrown out of the Marines, he found work as a grade school teacher and circus showman. He was one of a team that created a 'unicorn', grafting a single horn on to the head of a goat. Later he was the barker for the attraction at a sideshow belonging to Barnum and Bailey. However, another employee recalled later walking into his motel room and seeing a large pot boiling on the stove. When he lifted the lid, he found the head of a single-horned goat boiling into soup.

A fingerprint check showed that Lake (under yet another name) was wanted in Humboldt County for jumping bail on charges of burglary. Following up, local sheriffs discovered that he had started to build another survivalist bolt-hole, and found maps with marks pointing to 'hidden treasure'. These, too, turned out to be the graves of his victims.

One of these was none other than his own brother, Donald. He had visited Lake to try to get some money – but his elder brother had coolly murdered him. Another grave belonged to the one man who had befriended Lake in the Marines: Charles Gunnar, whose identity Lake later assumed.

Among the bodies that were dug up were those of two blacks. Ng had been seen driving two black men to the ranch, even though he was known to hate blacks and Hispanics. One further mystery seemed to have been solved: that of a San Francisco couple, Harvey and Deborah Dubs, who had disappeared along with their baby. A policeman recalled seeing a Chinese moving furniture from their home. By coincidence, the same policeman was now working on the Lake–Ng case.

Attention now focused on the escaped Ng, and police delved into his background, which was almost totally the reverse of Lake's. The son of wealthy Hong Kong parents, he was born in 1961. He was sent to an English boarding school in Yorkshire, but was expelled for stealing. For a time, he lived in Preston, Lancashire, until he was sent to San Francisco to complete his education.

At eighteen, he was involved in a hit-and-run traffic accident and joined the Marines to escape arrest. Although never in his life short of money, he was a kleptomaniac, and was soon arrested at Kaneoke Air Force base in Oahu, Hawaii. The charge was stealing weapons worth $11,000. He managed to escape and returned to San Francisco, where he met Lake. When they were both picked up on a burglary charge in Humboldt County, he was identified as a deserter and served time at Fort Leavenworth, Kansas. Paroled, he returned to Lake and the two set up their evil business.

Now Ng had become the FBI's most wanted man. The first lead to his whereabouts came a few days after the raid on the cabin, when a San Francisco gun dealer rang the police to say that Ng had phoned him about a gun he was repairing. He had asked the dealer to post it to Chicago and when it was explained to him that it was against the law to mail guns across state lines, Ng had cursed and rung off.

On Saturday, 6 July 1985, five weeks after Lake was seized, Ng was seen stealing from a store in Calgary, Canada. When challenged, he pulled a gun and shot a security man in the hand. As more guards arrived on the scene, Ng showed he was adept at martial arts but eventually he was overpowered.

When FBI agents interviewed Ng in Canada, he told them he knew of the murders, but played no part in them. He was, however, able to describe the murders of Paul Cosner (whose car had been found in Lake's possession) and two removal men, one of whom was burned to death.

A Canadian court sentenced Ng to four-and-a-half years for armed robbery. After serving part of his sentence, he was extradited to California where he was found guilty of murder and sent to death row, there to pursue a string of appeals.

As American serial killers go, Leonard Lake was not a record breaker. The toll of his victims numbered probably between thirty and forty, but at no time did he hold a community in the grip of terror as did Albert DeSalvo, the Boston Strangler; Carlton Gary, the Stocking Strangler; or Wayne B Williams, convicted (many believe wrongly) of the Atlanta child slayings.

Neither did he earn an exotic sobriquet of the kind handed out by the press and police to other mass killers. Lake never found fame such as The Sunset Strangler, he will never be remembered as the Skid Row Slasher (just two of the nicknames earned by relatively minor American serial killers). No such fame could be his – his murders were never so much as suspected until after his death.

What makes Leonard Lake unique in the annals of serial killer crime is the way he turned the blood lust that drove him to kill neighbours, friends – even his own brother – into an efficient and well-organized business. Adverts offering to buy or sell various goods were the lure to get people to the cabin. They never left alive. Film of their torture and appalling deaths, however, fed the fantasies of perverts across the state.

And all the time, the outside world saw him as a thoroughly nice guy who helped impoverished old folk and under-privileged youngsters.

Relatives were reluctant to talk, though his ex-wife Cricket Balazs was a little more forthcoming. She was not surprised to hear of her ex-husband's snuff video operation. He had been making porno videos while they were married – and she had been the star. Her role had been to act out various sadomasochistic roles, as she mouthed the name of the client. She had wondered at the time whether he was making other, weirder films on the side.

Even after the damning evidence was laid bare, Lake's mother, a nurse who worked in a mental hospital, could not believe her son was capable of violence. His sister Fern, also a nurse, had always looked the other way, while his grandmother would hear no ill of her darling Leonard, insisting he was a good child who had been led astray. After all, Lake was a volunteer firefighter and he gave his time to a charitable organization that provided free equipment for old folks' homes. His cover was perfect.

It was left to a man who had lived with Lake in a commune a few years before his death to sum up the pornographer and mass-murderer behind the mask of a neighbourly charity volunteer. Lake was, he said, 'the pleasantest unpleasant guy you could ever meet'.

THE
JACK THE RIPPER
A TO Z

**FOREWORD BY
DONALD
RUMBELOW**

PAUL BEGG, MARTIN FIDO AND KEITH SKINNER

THE JACK THE RIPPER A TO Z

– the most comprehensive book ever written on the
enduring mystery of Jack the Ripper.

Compiled in encyclopedic format by three of the
world's leading experts on the subject, **THE JACK
THE RIPPER A TO Z** provides completely up-to-
date, fresh and unbiased accounts of the many
theories as to his identity. It also describes all the
main suspects (including the hitherto unidentified
police suspect, Michael Ostrog), giving details of the
policemen, politicians and innocent bystanders
caught up in the case. It provides a wealth of
topographical detail and social background which
put the crimes into their proper historical context –
thereby helping to explain why they created such a
sensation at the time and why they continue to exert
such a fascination over a century later.

'This book has to be the anchor of future Jack the
Ripper studies' – Donald Rumbelow, author of *The
Complete Jack the Ripper*

TRUE CRIME/REFERENCE   0 7472 3676 3

More True Crime from Headline:

THE

SCOTLAND YARD

FILES

150 YEARS OF THE C.I.D.
1842-1992

PAUL BEGG
AND KEITH SKINNER

150 YEARS OF CRIME
AND DETECTION

150 years ago, amid considerable public suspicion, a tiny squad of eight plain-clothes detectives was set up at Scotland Yard. From this grew the formidable Criminal Investigation Department, renowned throughout the world for its unparalleled skill and experience in catching criminals.

The Scotland Yard Files **scans the fascinating history of the C.I.D: from the first Great Train Robbery in 1855 to Jack the Ripper; Crippen to the Kray Twins; the Siege of Sidney Street to the Iranian Embassy Siege. It also chronicles the scandals which have periodically rocked the force and profiles the great characters who ensured its survival.**

NEW INSIGHTS INTO
LANDMARK CRIMES

NON-FICTION/TRUE CRIME   0 7472 3963 0

A selection of non-fiction
from Headline